The Politics of the Canoe

The Politics of the Canoe

EDITED BY

BRUCE ERICKSON AND

SARAH WYLIE KROTZ

UNIVERSITY OF MANITOBA PRESS

The Politics of the Canoe

25 24 23 22 21 2 3 4 5

University of Manitoba Press
Winnipeg, Manitoba, Canada
Treaty 1 Territory
uofmpress.ca

Cataloguing data available from Library and Archives Canada
ISBN 978-0-88755-909-9 (PAPER)
ISBN 978-0-88755-911-2 (PDF)
ISBN 978-0-88755-910-5 (EPUB)
ISBN 978-0-88755-912-9 (BOUND)

Cover image by Jonathan Goldner
Cover and interior design by Jess Koroscil

Printed in Canada

The University of Manitoba Press acknowledges the financial support for its publication program provided by the Government of Canada through the Canada Book Fund, the Canada Council for the Arts, the Manitoba Department of Sport, Culture, and Heritage, the Manitoba Arts Council, and the Manitoba Book Publishing Tax Credit.

Funded by the Government of Canada | Canada

To those who float, especially
those going upstream.

CONTENTS

Preface
The Politics of the Canoe

BRUCE ERICKSON AND SARAH WYLIE KROTZ

Before embarking on our careers as academics, we were canoe tripping guides at the same summer camp. There, we had the privilege of spending our summers paddling and portaging with groups of teenage kids through some of the most beautiful parts of northern Ontario and Saskatchewan. Maps and route logs from past trips helped us find our way through the intricate lake and river systems, lily-filled marshes and bogs, and rugged portage trails.

For this book, we had no such map. When we first envisioned it, we were not certain what exactly it might become. What we did know was that we wanted to expand and vary our conversations around a cherished national icon (that had once been our lives and livelihoods) by bringing together a range of voices and perspectives on the canoe's diverse political meanings. We also wanted to bring these conversations to a wider audience of canoeists and readers, beyond the academic realms we both now inhabit. (As one of Bruce's favourite paddling partners had recently put it: "when are you going to write something that *I* can read?") The result is this collaboration with a diverse group of authors, and we are quite pleased with what it has become. The voices in this book come not just from academia, but also from the worlds of canoe builders, paddlers, and Indigenous community leaders, elders, and knowledge keepers. These contributors bring a broad range of skills, disciplines, experiences, and histories to bear on the question of the canoe's political significance, ensuring a multifaceted examination of a vessel that, while structurally simple, is remarkably complex in its meanings.

The aims of this essay collection were collaborative, so our process was too. The first glimpse we had at the depth and range of these chapters was at a workshop we hosted in Winnipeg in June, 2018. We gathered at FortWhyte Alive, an outdoor education centre and marsh on the edge of the city, where contributors read and responded to each other's work, learning from one another's stories and approaches. This workshop generated great questions and conversations, the fruits of which are contained in these chapters, as well as ongoing friendships and collaborations. We are grateful to those who made the workshop happen: the Clayton H. Riddell Faculty of Environment, Earth and Resources and the University of Manitoba Conference Sponsorship Program for funding; FortWhyte Alive and the Mere Hotel for space; Liam Kennedy-Slaney and Corey Pletsch for logistical support, driving, and camaraderie; and of course the generosity of the contributors who came together to share their inspiring stories and research and turn them into the essays you have before you.

The workshop in Winnipeg opened with a public viewing of two films about canoes. First was *United by Water* (dir. Derrick LaMere), which documents the first canoe journey of the five tribes of the Upper Columbia River on their traditional waters after the flooding caused by the Grand Coulee dam seventy-five years ago. The second film, *Glwa: The Resurgence of the Ocean-Going Canoe* (dirs. Hillary Beattie and Vina Brown), follows members of the Heiltsuk Nation on their Tribal Canoe Journey on the Pacific coast (see Chapter 1). To bring some of our most pressing conversations to the public, the weekend concluded with a panel discussion held at the Canadian Museum for Human Rights, about the role canoes can play in creating progressive Indigenous-settler relationships. There, Larry McDermott, Chuck Commanda, John B. Zoe, and Rachel Cushman spoke powerfully about canoes as important sources of Indigenous healing, decolonization, community building, reconciliation, governance, and sovereignty. Bringing together perspectives from both sides of the Canada-US border, the discussion made it abundantly clear that the canoe is not merely a symbol of Indigenous heritage—it is a living agent of resurgence across many parts of this continent. We are grateful to the presenters for sharing their experiences and deep knowledge, and to the staff at the Museum for hosting us, especially Chandra Erlendson, Angeliki Bogiatji, and Lindsay Affleck. The films were presented as part of the Decolonizing Lens film series, which is supported by the National Centre for Truth and Reconciliation, the Women's and Gender Studies program at the University of Manitoba, the Margaret Laurence Endowment Fund, and the University of Manitoba Indigenous Initiatives Fund. Both of these events drew a diverse audience into a critical set of conversations that are continued in this book.

The move from the workshop to the book you have in your hand would not have been possible without the fantastic work of the staff at the University of Manitoba Press. Jill McConkey and David Carr were on board from the start, and Glenn Bergen and David Larsen saw it through the final steps. Katarina Djordjevic helped format the chapters for submission and Maureen Epp did a wonderfully thorough copy edit of each of the chapters.

We are grateful to all those who have paddled with us, whether physically or metaphorically, while this book was taking shape. You know who you are, and you float our boats.

Introduction

BRUCE ERICKSON AND SARAH WYLIE KROTZ

How to Steal a Canoe, a short film dramatizing Anishinaabe writer and filmmaker Leanne Betasamosake Simpson's poem of the same title, opens with a woman walking through a birch forest at night. Her world is not the real world but that of a museum diorama, populated by models created by Amanda Strong and brought to life by stop-motion animation. The scenes of this film are haunting in the way that museum dioramas are haunting, their figures caught in a three-dimensional half reality. The film unfolds in a dream-like sequence as "kwe" (a name derived from the Anishinaabe-mowin word for woman) enters a warehouse of birchbark canoes hanging in grey darkness from the ceiling. Carrying us through this space amid strains of softly moaning cello, the narrator reads the searing words of Simpson's poem: these are, we learn, "stolen canoes"; with "bruised bodies / dry skin / hurt ribs / dehydrated rage"; they hang in "canoe jail" as part of a white man's 'collection of ndns' that threatens to turn these living vessels into "dehydrated" artifacts, relics, static and dead.[1]

There is, however, life in them yet. Kwe moves, singing, among them, "pray[s] to the old ones by dipping her fingers / into a plastic bottle of water / & rubbing the drops on the spine of each canoe," and then responds to one canoe's whispered plea to "take the young one and run." By the end of the film, she has freed the young canoe, set "Her" afloat in the water among the birch trees before she "sinks Her with seven stones / just enough to / suspend Her in wet." This sinking, however, is not a drowning but a freeing and ceremonial

FIGURE 0.1. AND 0.2. Stills from *How to Steal a Canoe*, Leanne Simpson and Amanda Strong. Courtesy of Spotted Fawn Productions Inc.

return to life, use, and interconnectedness; as the poem concludes, "kwe sings the song / & She sings back."[2]

Simpson's film does more than tell a compelling story that turns on the ironic reversal of theft and rescue. It invites us to recognize that these canoes are political in deep and manifold ways. For Anishinaabeg, canoes are much more than the inert objects that museums put on display: they are living beings and intimate participants in spirituality, ceremony, and identity. In this light, the stolen canoes in Simpson's film are at once victims of colonial theft and powerful—indeed, animate—agents of Indigenous resurgence. To hang them in a warehouse is to wrest them from their relationship with the land, expressed through the knowledge and values embodied in the processes of canoe building and paddling, and through their role in Anishinaabe practices such as the harvesting of *manoomin* (wild rice). The poem also evokes the larger story of colonialism. "Canoe jail" captures the contradictions of Canadian settler colonialism, which celebrates Indigenous peoples at the same time as it marginalizes them (all too often in actual prisons). Similar concerns reverberate across Indigenous canoeing cultures: in his poem "relics," for example, the Stl'atl'imx poet and scholar Peter Cole describes a museum display of his grandfather's cedar canoe as similarly imprisoning. The canoe, he writes, is "trapped" in "imported time" and "white space."[3] In the face of such entrapment, "how to steal a canoe" is about reclamation and reconnection, about bringing the canoe back to life and to its fullest significance.

The warehouse collection of stolen canoes in Simpson's film prompts reflection on how these boats have been (mis)appropriated elsewhere. Birchbark canoes hang in museums and personal collections across Canada and the United States. The Canadian Canoe Museum (CCM) in Peterborough—a museum Simpson knows well—is the largest of these collections. Developed out of the private collection of Kirk Wipper, the CCM holds over 600 canoes and other watercraft, many of which are Indigenous boats. Like many museums, the CCM is having to address the complicated history of its collection and how best to recognize and respect the Indigenous canoes it exhibits. Given that canoes aren't just cultural objects but are fundamental to many communities' relations—as family members, as embodied heritage and sovereignty, as living parts of the land—the implications of placing them on display differ depending on the traditions from which the canoes came. In other words, context matters.

To address these issues, the CCM has used its collection as a vehicle to build relationships between Indigenous and non-Indigenous people. Early partnerships with First Nations and Métis in the Peterborough area established a design committee with Indigenous members. Indigenous canoe builders have held residencies at the museum, and the museum board includes First Nations representation. In 2006, the CCM exhibited Alex McKay's *Treaty Canoe*, a canoe constructed with cloth covered in the texts from various Canadian treaties. *Treaty Canoe* places Aboriginal Title at the centre of our understanding of the canoe, reminding Canadians that their enjoyment of the canoe depends upon these negotiated treaties, many of which have not been fully honoured.[4] In Canada, the Truth and Reconciliation Commission (TRC), which concluded its nationwide proceedings in 2015, has had a lasting impact on how settler institutions like the CCM address the legacies of colonialism. The TRC began a national process of grappling with, and hopefully healing from, the traumas caused by residential schools; in the process it has also helped to foreground the intertwined histories of dispossession, theft, and cultural genocide that continue to haunt Indigenous and settler communities. In the years following the TRC, the museum has engaged in a number of events aimed at opening a dialogue on colonialism through the canoe. In 2017, it held a canoe trip from Peterborough to Ottawa called "Connected by Canoe," which acted as a floating conversation on the future of Canada in the context of reconciliation. While these events grapple with colonial history, some still argue there is more that could be done. Literary scholar Misao Dean points out that while the museum mourns the fact that some traditional building skills have been lost, it fails to address colonialism's role in this loss of knowledge. "There is," she writes, "no gallery of cultural genocide."[5]

Canoes, as most history books will tell you, were an integral part of life on Turtle Island before and long after the arrival of European settlers. Nations across the continent had developed different varieties of these boats to suit the landscape and their socio-economic needs. Canoes were, and are still, integrated into the fabric of those nations and their relationship with nature and other nations around them. Europeans arriving in Canada recognized the utility of canoes for traversing the land, adopting them for their own purposes independent of their role in Indigenous social and economic life. Samuel de Champlain saw the logistical value of canoes on his way up the St. Lawrence, at the rapids that came to be known as Lachine, where his larger boats proved too big and clumsy for either carrying or lining. From this developed a long relationship between Indigenous paddlers and builders and European explorers moving through the continent: up the St. Lawrence and Ottawa Rivers to Lake Huron; through Lakes Ontario and Erie, across the divide into the Mississippi watershed; to the head of Lake Superior and through the boreal forest to the prairie ocean of Lake Winnipeg; through Hudson Bay and up the Churchill, Nelson, Severn, and Winisk Rivers; across the prairies on the Saskatchewan and Missouri to the edge of the Rocky Mountains; north again to the Mackenzie and Peace Rivers; through mountain passes and down rough waters to the Pacific coast. These journeys were motivated by both the drive for profit and the desire to acquire new lands, where companies, governments (both European and Indigenous), and the people who paddled the boats (who were mostly Indigenous) negotiated the terms of habitation and trade in a relatively new world of cooperation and conflict.

As the settler landscape became more entrenched, the balance of power shifted and new technologies pushed the canoe aside. While they were still relied upon as an economic and social vehicle in many parts of the continent, in the urban and settled rural landscapes of the East (Ontario, Quebec, New York, New England, and the Maritime provinces especially) canoes moved into the leisure sphere. Used as individual crafts of enjoyment rather than travel, canoes soon became part of regional organizations, with canoe clubs developing that brought paddlers together in what the *New York Times* called "The Canoe Boom."[6] The largest of these, the American Canoe Association, held two-week regattas starting in 1880 that brought paddlers together for socializing, skill development, exploring, and racing.[7] It was in the leisure sphere that the symbolic dimensions of the canoe—its mythic legacy as a national vehicle—took hold. From the late 1800s on, canoeing became a privileged method to explore the North American wilderness, which paddlers in Canada connected to the country's developing nationalism. From the hiring of famous canoeist (and infamous Indian surrogate) Grey Owl by the National Parks in the 1930s to the prominent role of the canoe in the centennial celebrations of 1967, the recreational canoe became synonymous with Canada and Canadian wilderness.

Leanne Simpson, along with scholars such as Peter Cole, Misao Dean, and Bruce Erickson, pushes many of us to reflect on our beloved canoes and their histories in unfamiliar, even unsettling, ways. As attached as paddlers are to their boats, canoes tend to occasion less contemplation than do the places to which they carry us. Indeed, for many recreational canoeists, paddling is appealing because it frees us from the burdens of thought, its meditative rhythm interrupted only by the occasional speculation about what we might see around the next bend in the river; the animals and vegetation along the route; or the location of the next portage, set of rapids, or campsite. Many relish and even romanticize the canoe's lingering associations with explorers, voyageurs, and Indigenous guides, but few of us devote much time to thinking about the canoe's multifaceted and multinational histories. Indeed, by offering "escape from civilization" the canoe risks erasing its own politics. And yet, the complicated histories and meanings that these stories (among the many others in this book) illustrate present opportunities to think differently, not just about these vessels but about modern life.

The Political Canoe

The canoe, in other words, is not merely a simple object of wilderness enjoyment, a neutral vessel in which paddlers invest their own personal meanings. It has deep and varied historical, cultural, and political significance—significance that changes in different contexts. Colonialism certainly looms large over the history of the canoe, but canoes are also intertwined in histories of masculinity, wilderness, consumption, and industrialization, among others. The birchbark canoe that kwe rescues from imprisonment in a warehouse in Simpson's poem is the same canoe that has become an icon of Canadian wilderness culture, "preserved" in museums as a relic of Indigenous craft and fur trade history, marketed through numerous retail brands (Beaver Canoe being the most prominent, but you might be surprised at how many beer cans sport the iconic boat), and adopted by Pierre Trudeau to assure all Canadians that anyone could be a "child of Nature." Each of these contexts has a politics behind it: of Anishinaabe sovereignty, of erasure, of primitive-chic consumption, of Canadian unity and wilderness preservation.

This book contributes an array of perspectives to an ongoing conversation about the canoe as a political object. As scholars of canoeing culture have shown, canoes are embedded in power relations and shaped by the beliefs, ideologies, and institutions by which we govern ourselves or are governed. They contribute to the stories we tell ourselves about how we fit and conduct ourselves in the world. Thus, they are intimately and inextricably linked to negotiations of territory, nation, history, environmental issues, class, gender, race, ethnicity, and culture. The Canadian story has been filled out most recently by two books, Misao Dean's *Inheriting a Canoe Paddle* and Bruce Erickson's *Canoe Nation*. These books show how the canoe has been drafted to launder a history of colonialism by becoming simply a boat of leisure. As Dean and Erickson look deeper into the history of canoe, from early fur trade practices and the rise of a recreational canoe industry to the Bill Mason films and the birth of the Canadian Canoe Museum, they illuminate a myriad of political dimensions. For example, the development of a canoe-based recreational fishing industry actively pushed out Indigenous subsistence fishers from many of the lakes and rivers of Ontario.[8] As Dean underscores, the politics of Aboriginal Title in Canada unsettle nationalist celebrations that perpetuate the myth of the canoe as a unifying symbol of the state. Recognition of Aboriginal Title reminds us that unity is itself a myth. Thinking about the politics of the canoe brings out these disjunctures and conflicts that shaped the continent. As we hope this volume will show, doing so also opens up space for more multifaceted meanings and stories, bringing the canoe to life in diverse contexts, not just specifically Canadian ones.

The North American colonial story is one among many layers of the canoe's political significance. On Turtle Island, the canoe has a long and varied Indigenous history. It not only ensured mobility and access to food but also shaped relationships between nations as they negotiated alliances and territories. These political relationships were forged through the canoe long before European settlers arrived in North America, and they continue today in a variety of forms and venues. As Simpson so powerfully conveys, and several chapters in this volume explore in more detail, for many Indigenous nations, canoe building and paddling involve protocols that reinforce ties to land, governance, diplomacy, and sovereignty. Tribal Journeys along the Pacific Northwest coast and Whaèhdǫǫ̀ Etǫ K'è in the Northwest Territories (described in Chapters 1, 2, and 3) are just a few examples of activities that emphasize the canoe's role in maintaining strong communities with deep knowledge of and attachment to the land and waterways. With long histories that predate colonization, the contemporary resurgence of Indigenous canoe journeys turns attention away from the founding myths of Canada and the United States to emphasize the canoe's ongoing significance as an agent of Indigenous sovereignty.

Canoes were also instrumental in forging the relationships upon which both Canada and the United States were built. As Europeans moved across the continent, canoes shaped the alliances and conflicts between Indigenous and European peoples that historian Richard White, in his study of the Great Lakes, has famously described as "the Middle Ground." White reminds us that European jurisdiction in North America was not easily established. From the seventeenth until the late eighteenth century, French and English authority in areas beyond the Eastern Seaboard was secured only with the help of Indigenous alliances, and these depended upon the canoe, which facilitated communication between posts and cities built through river networks. The terms and features of the middle ground changed dramatically as power shifted to colonial governments, but in many ways its legacy can still be discerned in canoeing culture today. In Canada after Confederation, the canoe emerged as a significant feature of Canadian governance. Government employees used canoes to police landscapes, negotiate treaties, establish territorial boundaries, collect taxes, and communicate with distant outposts. Canoes carried Canadian soldiers to Red River to quell Louis Riel and the Métis resistance, and have transported Indigenous children to residential schools.

As the settler nation got older, these practical and tactical uses of canoes gave way to more theatrical and symbolic events celebrating the nation's canoeing and colonial history. The 1967 Canoe Pageant, a canoe race between provincial teams from Rocky Mountain House in Alberta to the site of the World's Expo in Montreal, used the centennial anniversary to elevate the mythology of the voyageur in the national imaginary. Pierre Elliott Trudeau's connection to the Canadian nation was often illustrated through the canoe, from his trips on the Nahanni to the birchbark canoe (built by Patrick Maranda from Barriere Lake) that he paddled on Meech Lake. More recently, Bill Reid's celebrated sculpture, *The Spirit of Haida Gwaii*, sits outside the Canadian Embassy in Washington, DC, and its image adorns the back of many Canadian twenty-dollar bills.

Both within and beyond Canada, the canoe has also played a significant role in environmental activism. In 2015, to protest Royal Dutch Shell's plan to send the Polar Pioneer drilling rig to drill in arctic waters, self-proclaimed "kayaktivists" in Seattle organized a flotilla of kayaks, canoes, paddleboards,

FIGURE 0.3. Drilling Kayaktivists vs. Shell Polar Pioneer. Photo by Daniella Beccaria.

and other boats to show their opposition. Dubbed the "Paddle in Seattle," the protest drew hundreds of boats that surrounded the drilling rig as it was docked in the harbour. Talking about the protest, one of the organizers stated that it is a "Perfect on-water tactic . . . It makes people happy. When they see a big swarm of kayaks, it gets people excited."[9]

Similar protests have happened in Vancouver in opposition to the Trans Mountain pipeline expansion. On the Peace River, in northern British Columbia, environmental groups, farmers, ranchers, and Indigenous communities have shown their opposition to the Site C hydroelectric dam in a yearly Paddle for the Peace. Starting in 2005, the Paddle for the Peace is an impressive multi-stakeholder movement that draws attention to the loss of both wildlife and human livelihoods that will come with the dam. Setting a powerful precedent for these episodes of canoe activism, in 1990 Cree and Inuit paddlers journeyed in a custom-built boat from James Bay to New York City to protest a major hydroelectric development similar in scope to Site C Dam. The Great Whale Project threatened to flood the communities and traditional hunting territories of the Cree and Inuit living at the mouth of the Great Whale River. The Odeyak, a hybrid of a canoe and kayak, ended its journey in New York City, in the state that had contracted to buy much of the electricity that would have been produced from the new dam. The publicity garnered by the 2,200-kilometre voyage proved successful: New York pulled out of the agreement and the Great Whale Project was shelved. Cameron Baldassara's account of similar protests on the Petawawa River in Ontario (Chapter 9) reveals how canoe-based activism can spark new recreational canoeing cultures as well as block development.

The recreational sphere, of course, has its own political dimensions as the canoe's agency extends from collective activism to individual freedom of movement and opportunity. As Albert Braz shows in his discussion of Don Starkell's monumental journey from Winnipeg to the Amazon (Chapter 8), this freedom meant a great deal to a working-class foster kid. The implications of canoe trips reverberate across gender, sexuality, and race as well as class lines. Nineteenth-century Canadian literature is full of stories of women enjoying the independence that canoes afforded. Writers such as the British-born Susanna Moodie and Anna Jameson and, later, the part-Mohawk, part-English E. Pauline Johnson (Tekahionwake) describe exhilarating pleasures that would have been unfamiliar to their British female forebears. Moodie prided herself on learning to paddle her own canoe. For Johnson, the canoe became a symbol not only of autonomy and mobility, but of sexual freedom. Her most popular canoeing poem, "The Song My Paddle Sings," is charged with thinly veiled sexual imagery as the solo female paddler shoots a set of rapids. Whether the lover is nature or a man (as it is in her poem "The Idlers"), for Johnson the canoe became, at least in her poetry, the conduit of intense erotic pleasure.

Johnson's erotic visions anticipated the canoe's role in a politics of sexual expression and policing that escalated for decades afterwards. The freedom that canoes afforded courting couples in the nineteenth and early twentieth centuries ranged from the socially acceptable to the scandalous. By the early decades of the twentieth century, canoe manufacturers such as Old Town capitalized on what has come to be known as "canoedling" by designing boats wide enough to accommodate reclining seats, cushions, and gramophones for the explicit purpose of having "a hot time in the Old Town tonight." Indeed, "the make-out potential" of canoeing led to restrictive laws in several states,

FIGURE 0.4. Emily Pauline Johnson in a canoe, c. 1890s. Photo: Brant Historical Society.

FIGURE 0.5. Postcard from the early 1900s. Source: Benson Gray.

including lake curfews and fines for kissing; at least one journalist worried in the *Minneapolis Tribune* that "misconduct in canoes has become so grave and flagrant that it threatens to throw a shadow upon the lakes . . . and to bring shame upon the city."[10]

While sexual liberation has moved out of canoes to other (perhaps softer) venues, canoes remain important agents in the creation of alternative spaces where people can free themselves of traditional roles and restrictive social norms. The philosophy behind all-women trips such as those organized by Wild Women Expeditions, among many others, recalls the pleasure, confidence, and independence that canoes offered women such as Moodie in the nineteenth century. These expeditions promise women and girls both adventure and skills, developed outside the bounds of patriarchal and heteronormative society. Similarly, canoe trips have been organized to provide safe space for lesbian, gay, bisexual, and trans paddlers. With an even more explicit social-justice mission, Outward Bound runs trips for women who have experienced sexual violence and abuse, veterans, Indigenous youth, and youth at risk, emphasizing the strength- and character-building benefits of canoe trips that afford relief from—while at the same time helping to address—social landscapes of violence, racism, and poverty. Such trips extend the long-held idea that recreational canoeing has an important restorative dimension that reaches beyond the more obvious escape from the pressures of city life—a quality that holds, implicitly if not explicitly, great potential for social critique. For all of their liberatory potential, however, canoe trips can also reinscribe stereotypical gender roles. Anyone who has portaged on a summer camp canoe trip knows how much stock is placed in being strong and agile enough to solo carry a boat. Given the masculine heroics associated with such feats, it might not be a stretch to say, as Liz Newbery does, that "when we carry a boat, we are also carrying the weight of liberal humanism, dis/ability, gender, class, and race; we carry the weight of Western culture."[11]

This cursory outline of canoes and politics—sketchy and incomplete as it is—is meant to suggest not a coherent history but rather the wide variety of ways in which the canoe can be understood as more than just a vessel that carries us on our expeditions; more, that is, than a mere means of travel, aesthetically pleasing and physically engaging but otherwise devoid of political meaning. The essays in this book open up this idea in a range of contexts to show still further how the canoe has been and continues to be a political agent: an actor that shapes our multifarious relationships with one another and with the land. In so doing, they also complicate—and even unsettle—the canoe as a Canadian national icon. Canoes, after all, can draw us into many divergent stories. As the chapters in this book underscore, "the canoe" refers not just to one kind of object but to numerous boats with just as numerous places of origin, designs, construction materials, and cultural histories. The name "canoe" comes from the Arawak word *canoa*, but we could also call it by many other names: *chimàn* (Anishnaabemowin), *kanim* (Chinook), *elà* (Tłı̨chǫ), *glwa* (Hailhzaqvl), *wa'a* (Hawaiian), *gwitn* (Mi'kmaq), *ona:ke* (Kanien'kéha), *čhaŋháwata* (Lakota), and *oqiton* (Maliseet), among others. Moreover, some of these languages have more than just one word to describe canoes. For example, Maliseet, which Tappan Adney learned in his canoe-modelling career (see Chapter 4), distinguishes between birchbark canoes (*masqewuloq*), elm bark canoes (*wolokaskuloq*), dugout canoes (*walsoktahasik*), old canoes (*'kanuloq*), new canoes (*piluloq*), and skin canoes (*motekonuloq*). The canoes discussed in these pages are made not only of birchbark, dugout cedar, and poplar, but also of canvas, fibreglass, and Kevlar. They are the heritage of many nations. They traverse rivers, lakes, and rapids, and also city streams, ocean straits, and coastlines. They cross class boundaries as well as geographical ones. Most importantly, the canoes in this book are agents not just of romantic affiliation with wilderness but of protest, power, governance, social and environmental knowledge, history, cultural resurgence, and sovereignty. Their politics range from collective actions to intensely personal, individual ones.

The stories told in these chapters build on the work of scholars who are telling new stories about the canoe by showcasing the range of meanings canoes have long held, and continue to hold, for people both north and south of the border. Collectively, these stories shift the focus from the canoe as a pervasive Canadian national icon, revealing its far more diverse political valences as an agent in individual and collective action, in historical and contemporary narratives, in national and personal identities, in ecological and cultural knowledge and governance. Emanating from canoe builders, traditional knowledge keepers, and paddlers, as well as scholars from a range of disciplines, the multiple voices of our contributors register the local particularities that make "the canoe" meaningful in widely disparate ways, across times and places, nations and classes. There are, of course, many stories still left to be told. The effect of this book, we hope, will be to both engage canoe paddlers, builders, and researchers in new ways of thinking about the politics of the canoe, and prompt them to continue blazing new paths.

The Chapters

Indigenous Sovereignties

At the end of their journey of "discovery" across what we now know as the continental United States, Meriwether Lewis and William Clark realized they would need an additional canoe to travel back up the river. They were at the mouth of the Columbia River, in the territory of the Clatsop Chinookans. Not having any luck trading for one, they authorized four members of their expedition to steal one. What they did not recognize, as Jon Daehnke explains, is that "they were not just approving the theft of a carved piece of cedar: they were approving the theft of a living thing and a member of a family."[12] Canoes are a central part of Chinookan life, and the boats themselves are built into canoe families. The loss of that canoe was felt as the loss of a family member and has been remembered as such. During the planning of the bicentennial celebrations of Lewis and Clark's trip, descendants of William Clark learned from the Chinook Indian Nation about this theft and the importance of that canoe to the tribe. Using private funds, these family members arranged for a new canoe to be returned to the Chinook Indian Nation, where it was named and welcomed into the family through ceremony. The gift was a private donation, yet the journey of discovery that Lewis and Clark were on was an official expedition for the government of the United States. In the eyes of the Chinook, there is still a place for the government to step in and make good on this historic wrong.

While the act of reconciliation by the Clark family points us to the ways these histories can lead to renewed relationships between Indigenous people and settlers, it also illustrates the resilience of Indigenous relationships with canoes that existed long before the colonial encounter. The chapters in the first section of the book detail the central role canoes are currently playing in cultural resurgence, acting as agents of embodied sovereignty, decolonization, and healing by nurturing ancestral connections between communities and land. While many Indigenous nations are engaged in these kinds of canoe trips throughout North America and beyond, the examples in this book come from the Pacific Northwest coast and the Northwest Territories. These stories address the legacies of colonialism, but they also emphasize that despite the thefts Indigenous nations have suffered, the links that canoes forged between Indigenous communities and their territory, political practices, and cultural knowledge have not been lost. At the centre of these trips is the land the paddlers travel through, with canoes acting as agents of both community resilience and sovereignty. As Rachel Cushman writes in Chapter 2: "Our canoes and protocols are the fists of our Elders hitting the negotiating table at the Chehalis River Treaty Council of 1855."

Tribal Canoe Journeys, a yearly gathering of over 3,000 participants and eighty-five canoe families who travel throughout dozens of communities on the Pacific Northwest coast, started with the 1986 paddle to the Vancouver Exposition and the "Paddle to Seattle" trip in 1989. In Chapter 1, Frank Brown, Hillary Beattie, Vina Brown, and Ian Mauro recount the origins and transformative impacts of this annual gathering. Drawing from interviews with members of the Heiltsuk nation, they describe the canoe's role in repairing losses that Indigenous communities have suffered under colonialism. They show that by reconnecting the Heiltsuk with their ancestral ocean-going canoes, Tribal Journeys is also rebuilding relationships between people and their traditional territories, between youth and Elders, and among several Indigenous nations along the coast.

The revival of ocean-going canoes has also been vitally important for the Chinook Nation, through both Tribal Journeys and everyday practices. In Chapter 2, Rachel Cushman, Jon Daehnke, and Tony Johnson illuminate how these canoes function as agents of living heritage and embodied sovereignty. Cushman's personal descriptions of her "canoe family" and the profound responsibilities and relationships this family carries are woven through the chapter, revealing the intimate ties between people and their canoes who are, she emphasizes, not inert objects but living beings. The protocols and ceremonies that govern these canoeing practices, the authors show, are not a nostalgic re-enactment of the past, but rather living practices that solidify these links and create a "path to decolonization" that is " active, forward-looking and resilient."

Chapter 3 takes us from the West Coast to Tłįchǫ territories north of Great Slave Lake. Through the annual canoe trips of Whaèhdǫǫ̀ Etǫ K'è (The Trails of Our Ancestors), which have been running since 1995, Tłįchǫ are reviving connections between communities and the stories held in their lands and waterways. These journeys engage youth in the teachings that come from the land, reinforcing not only cultural knowledge but also their presence in and sovereignty over their territory. As John B. Zoe and Jessica Dunkin explain, the trips began in the context of the land claim process and they continue after the Self-Government Agreement as a way to implement that land claim. Being on the land is central to the Tłı̨chǫ vision of governance, and the canoe, these authors show, is a central part of that connection.

Building Canoes

The rise in recreational canoeing during the nineteenth century increased the numbers of non-Indigenous paddlers and canoe builders. This era also brought changes in canoe construction practices, one of which was the shift from free-form construction to building canoes on a pre-existing form. The building form acts as a guide that ensures both consistency of shape and efficiency of construction while relying less on the expertise of individual builders. This shift was precipitated by a number of factors, including increasing demand for canoes as recreational vehicles, declining numbers of suitable birch trees, and innovations in waterproof materials that could replace birchbark. The shift was also part of a changing economy of boat builders. In the factories that used this process, builders could be paid by the hour, not by the boat. Manufacturers such as the Old Town Canoe Company were established by entrepreneurs and managers who participated in industrial commodity markets. Canoes were no longer identified by their builder but by the company name. These changes reshaped canoeing culture. On the one hand, the cost-effectiveness of this method of building meant a significant drop in price for a canoe, resulting in "a more democratic canoe" that was not only available to elite sportsmen.[13] On the other hand, it also meant that Indigenous artisans no longer built the majority of canoes on lakes and rivers.

The resurgence of Indigenous canoeing includes canoe building. The Tribal Canoe Journeys celebrated in the first section were jump-started by a renewed interest in building traditional dugout canoes. Canoeing resurgences are connected not only to material practices of living on and learning from the land, but also to the cultural teachings that the canoe-building process imparts. The chapters in the second section of this book examine the construction of canoes in a variety of different settings, including sites of contact between Indigenous and non-Indigenous boat builders. The authors in this section highlight the material histories, relationships, and local knowledges that shape handcrafted canoes. Indigenous and non-Indigenous builders alike emphasize that canoes are more than just a mode of transportation and communication: they are also repositories of knowledge, holding in their forms and materials the histories, languages, teachings, and complex biological and social environments of the middle ground. They can be appropriated, but they can also build bridges between different canoeing communities.

The complex life of model canoes is the topic of Chris Ling Chapman's contribution to this volume. In Chapter 4, Chapman revisits the model canoes of Edwin Tappan Adney, an American-Canadian amateur naturalist and model–boat builder whose bark canoes, Chapman argues, represent not imitative relics or appropriations of fading cultures but rather material stories of Indigenous survivance amid complicated relationships with colonial settlers. Akin to Adney's writings on the Maliseet language, which he diligently learned and recorded, his model canoes are not silent objects. Their intricate craftsmanship speaks: as Chapman demonstrates, they tell "miniature local histories" closely tied to the land-based languages and practices that Adney learned from Indigenous community members and Elders, most notably the Passamaquoddy builder Peter Jo.

The survivance Chapman identifies in Adney's work is exemplified by the teachings that Chuck Commanda, Larry McDermott, and Sarah Nelson illustrate in the process of building a birchbark canoe, described in Chapter 5. Building a bark canoe is one way to enact *ginawaydaganuc*, the Algonquin law based on respect for natural law, as it holds the seven sacred teachings: love, honesty, humility, respect, bravery, wisdom, and truth. From these initial lessons, Algonquin builders have also used the teachings of canoe building to inspire their own communities and work toward reconciliation. By learning more about the materials, collection methods, and practices of construction, we can see how the birchbark canoe is folded into the cultural, spiritual, and political practices of Algonquin communities. In recent years, work by Algonquin builders, including Chuck Commanda, has brought these teachings to others, using the tangible practice of boat building for revitalization and reconciliation.

Jonathan Goldner learned to build birchbark canoes through both independent research and experimentation and apprenticeships. In Chapter 6, he recounts his process of learning to harvest bark in the forests near the Quebec-Ontario border. Like building boats, harvesting bark requires a complex set of physical skills and environmental knowledge. As Goldner describes, his personal pathways through the forests led him to develop a more acute sensory relationship with the shrinking ecology that sustains birchbark canoes, as well as a more intimate understanding of the land as both Indigenous territory and colonial resource. Harvesting bark opens up these landscapes and relationships, which are as replete with gaps, tensions, and conflicts as they are with possibilities for reconciliation.

Telling Histories

In 2011, the Royal Canadian Mint issued a limited edition pure silver commemorative coin featuring the front half of a canoe, perfectly mirrored on a glassy lake. In the canoe sits a child, reaching down into the water, as if to touch the world on the underside of the lake. We are told in the description of the coin that as the child "dips his hand in the water, it touches the past." The reflection in the water shows not the child but an adult figure leaning into their paddle stroke. With his long straight hair tied back and clearly defined muscles on his shirtless torso, the paddler is clearly meant to be Indigenous, and historical. The Indigenous paddler is a copy of the figure that appeared on the 1935 silver dollar, evoking both a monetary past (the old silver dollar) and a mythological past (the "early native paddler"). As the coin illustrates, the canoe is a vehicle of history. This is true not only when we think about the particular role the canoe plays in the history of North America, but also in the way that canoes help shape how we tell this history, among others.

From record-setting voyages and historic narratives to local activism and family histories, the chapters in this section bring a broad lens to the stories that we tell about and through canoes. These histories detail some of the political contexts that shaped the canoeing experiences they describe. More than this, however, these chapters also illustrate the choices that we make when we retell these stories. They refuse to let the canoe simply be a vehicle of convenience or innocence and illustrate the impact of canoes on the way we interpret these histories. This kind of historiography informed by the canoe allows us to see how our canoeing stories are shaped not just by colonialism but also by religious doctrine, class, gender, and environmental politics.

Chapter 7 re-examines the story of seventeenth-century French explorer Baron de Lahontan and the controversy surrounding his narrative of a remarkable trip into western North America. While Lahontan's published account of his American experiences proved immensely popular, European authorities soon tried to discredit his book, in part because its author was aligned against the French monarchy and Catholic papacy. To dismiss the entire work, critics often singled out as fabrication his story of an unlikely journey west of the Mississippi River, pointing to inconsistencies in Lahontan's geographic and ethnographic observations. Here, Peter Wood argues that we can verify Lahontan's voyage in part because of the types of log canoes he encountered, used, and learned about from Indigenous informants. This chapter illustrates how an awareness of canoe diversity and distribution can be a useful tool for modern-day historians. It also underscores the way the interpretation of canoe-filled narratives from the era of colonization can be shaped by distant and changing political climates. Experiences in canoes are part of the political and historical geography of the continent, but the way we remember those encounters can also be politically charged, as the debates over Lahontan's account illustrate.

In Chapter 8, Albert Braz discusses Don Starkell's famous canoe trip as recounted in *Paddle to the Amazon*. Starkell's trip, Braz argues, was "monumental" not only in its ambition but also in its disruption of prevalent Canadian narratives that mythologize canoeing as a genteel activity designed to bring paddlers closer to a northern wilderness landscape and national identity. Instead of exploring a wilderness of boreal forest and Precambrian Shield, Starkell, who learned to paddle in a creek not far from his Winnipeg foster home, navigated dangerous political and social landscapes south of the border in order to complete one of the longest canoe journeys in history. Yet as popular as his bestselling book may have been, these features of Starkell's journey make him something of an outlier. *Paddle to the Amazon* showcases the canoe as a vessel of highly individualized aspirations shaped by class, gender, and an ambition to eschew the traditional borders of Canadian canoe travel.

In Chapter 9, Cameron Baldassarra examines the paddling community that arose in the face of a proposal to build a dam on the Petawawa River.

Spawning a concerned community and a successful whitewater rodeo, the ultimately unsuccessful dam project ignited interest in a river that offers easy access to a large paddling community and yet still fits the aesthetic of a "wilderness" river. In a region of rivers altered by hydro development, the Petawawa is shaped by a unique confluence of histories. Its connection to Algonquin Park and the picturesque "Group of Seven" landscape meant that the Petawawa held special value, which paddlers were able to mobilize in their opposition to the dam. Although canoeists were not ultimately responsible for thwarting the dam's development, it was through their activism that the canoe rose to its current prominence as a central feature of the town's recreational culture and image.

Like many paddlers, Danielle Gendron developed a childhood obsession with the canoe as a way to imagine a different world around her. Drawing from her family's voyageur history, in Chapter 10 Gendron outlines how she connects, some 200 years later, to the same landscape her ancestors paddled through. She illustrates how the dynamics of colonialism, industrialization, nationalism, and urbanization have dramatically altered not only the landscape along the Trent Severn Waterway but also how she engages with that landscape, even when she is ostensibly paddling the same craft as her forebears used. Written as a meditation on planning a trip amid these changes to the landscape and the experience of canoeing, this chapter can also guide the rest of us as we plan our own journeys. The public image of the canoe may be dominated by nationalist stories of wilderness, but Gendron argues that it is possible to conceptualize our trips in other ways to experience canoe travel as a more complex historically rooted activity.

Conclusion

A paddler struggling to carry a seventy-pound Old Town over a tough, bush-and-mosquito-whacking portage may be hard pressed to see this boat as a political vessel. Yet almost everywhere we turn, and any way we look at it, the canoe both affects and is affected by complex political and cultural histories. This book covers ground in colonial and environmental history, Indigenous sovereignties, and national narratives, giving thoughtful canoeists new stories to ponder while they paddle the lakes, rivers, streams, and oceans of this watery world. Borrowing Gendron's metaphor of unpacking and repacking (Chapter 10), settler paddlers in particular need to ask: What baggage do our canoes carry? With what narratives do we deliberately or inadvertently pack them? How might we shift these stories, repacking our canoes in ways that push against the simplified narratives of colonial conquest, belonging, and nation building—or the sanitized ones of wilderness exploration and outdoor leisure—that have imprisoned these complex and vital objects, not just in museums but in many paddlers' minds? Across Canada and the United States, canoeing cultures have been born of activism and resistance as much as of adherence to the mythologies of wilderness and nation building. Canoes influence how we engage with and interpret our histories and physical environments. Agents of freedom and autonomy, they embody individual as well as collective expressions of—and interventions in—these histories. Canoes are more than objects; they are beings that animate our relationships to each other and to the world. As we hope this book shows, they amply reward critical reflection and inquiry.

The diverse concerns of our contributors show us that, just like the canoe's stories and meanings, its politics are neither singular nor unified. All the same, we wish to highlight that this book is as much the product of its own particular political moment as it is of the confluence of this unique collection of canoeists, builders, and scholars. In the making of this book, our interests converged on the kinds of stories that undercut the singular authority of the wilderness myth of the canoe that has been powerfully embraced by Canadians in particular. This book represents, among other things, a moment when Indigenous resurgences are gaining widespread recognition—when canoes increasingly carry the possibility of decolonization and reconciliation, and settlers are beginning to examine their complicity in cultural appropriation and dispossession. While colonialism and resurgence are focal points of this book, which brings together Indigenous and settler stories, topics as diverse as environmental history, historiography, and class identity are also included. The politics that each of our contributors foreground are sometimes overt, sometimes more subtle. What unites them is a collective interest in thinking about the canoe as a dynamic and multifariously meaningful vessel that can illuminate political and cultural histories. There is much more to be said on these topics, as well as on others—such as gender, race, and ethnicity—not explored in this volume; we hope that this collection opens the doors to further, far-reaching thinking and conversation.

This, we argue, is the value of a book on the politics of the canoe: not only can we learn more about these boats and their histories, but the way we regard the canoe can help us to think more broadly about national politics, identity, environmental and social history, wilderness, pleasure, and, of course, the colonial histories that mark Canada and the United States. As the chapters in this volume show, there are many ways to address the political life of objects. Like a good portage, these approaches are at once challenging and rewarding for those who embark on them.

Notes

1 Leanne Betasamosake Simpson, *How to Steal a Canoe*, directed by Amanda Strong (Spotted Fawn Productions, 2016), https://vimeo.com/188380371. Printed version of the poem: Leanne Betasamosake Simpson, "How to Steal a Canoe," in *This Accident of Being Lost: Songs and Stories* (Toronto: House of Anansi Press, 2017), 69.

2 Simpson, "How to Steal a Canoe," 70. One practice with bark canoes was to sink them in shallow water for later use. A sunken boat could be hidden from other travellers, a practice helpful in highly travelled and contested territories. See José António Brandão, *Your Fyre Shall Burn No More: Iroquois Policy towards New France and Its Native Allies to 1701* (Lincoln: University of Nebraska Press, 1997), 34.

3 Peter Cole, *Coyote and Raven Go Canoeing: Coming Home to the Village* (Montreal: McGill-Queen's University Press, 2006), 13.

4 Misao Dean, *Inheriting a Canoe Paddle: The Canoe in Discourses of English-Canadian Nationalism* (Toronto: University of Toronto Press, 2013), 160.

5 Ibid., 156.

6 "The Canoe Boom," *New York Times*, 19 July 1880.

7 Jessica Dunkin, *Canoe and Canvas: Life at the Encampments of the American Canoe Association, 1880–1910* (Toronto: University of Toronto Press, 2019).

8 Bruce Erickson, *Canoe Nation: Nature, Race, and the Making of a Canadian Icon* (Vancouver: UBC Press, 2013), 110.

9 Rose Hackman, "Seattle 'Kayaktivists' Take on Shell in Battle over Arctic Oil Drilling," *Guardian*, 16 May 2015, https://www.theguardian.com/us-news/2015/may/15/seattle-kayak-tivists-shell-arctic-oil-drilling.

10 Hunter Oatman-Stanford, "Love Boats: The Delightfully Sinful History of Canoes," *Collector Weekly*, 5 July 2012, https://www.collectorsweekly.com/articles/love-boats-the-delightfully-sinful-history-of-canoes/.

11 Liz Newbery, "Will Any/Body Carry That Canoe? A Geography of the Body, Ability, and Gender," *Canadian Journal of Environmental Education* 8, no. 1 (2003): 205.

12 Jon D. Daehnke, *Chinook Resilience: Heritage and Cultural Revitalization on the Lower Columbia River* (Seattle: University of Washington Press, 2017), 143.

13 Mark Neuzil and Norman Sims, *Canoes: A Natural History in North America* (Minneapolis: University of Minnesota Press, 2016), 203.

PART ONE

Asserting Indigenous Sovereignty

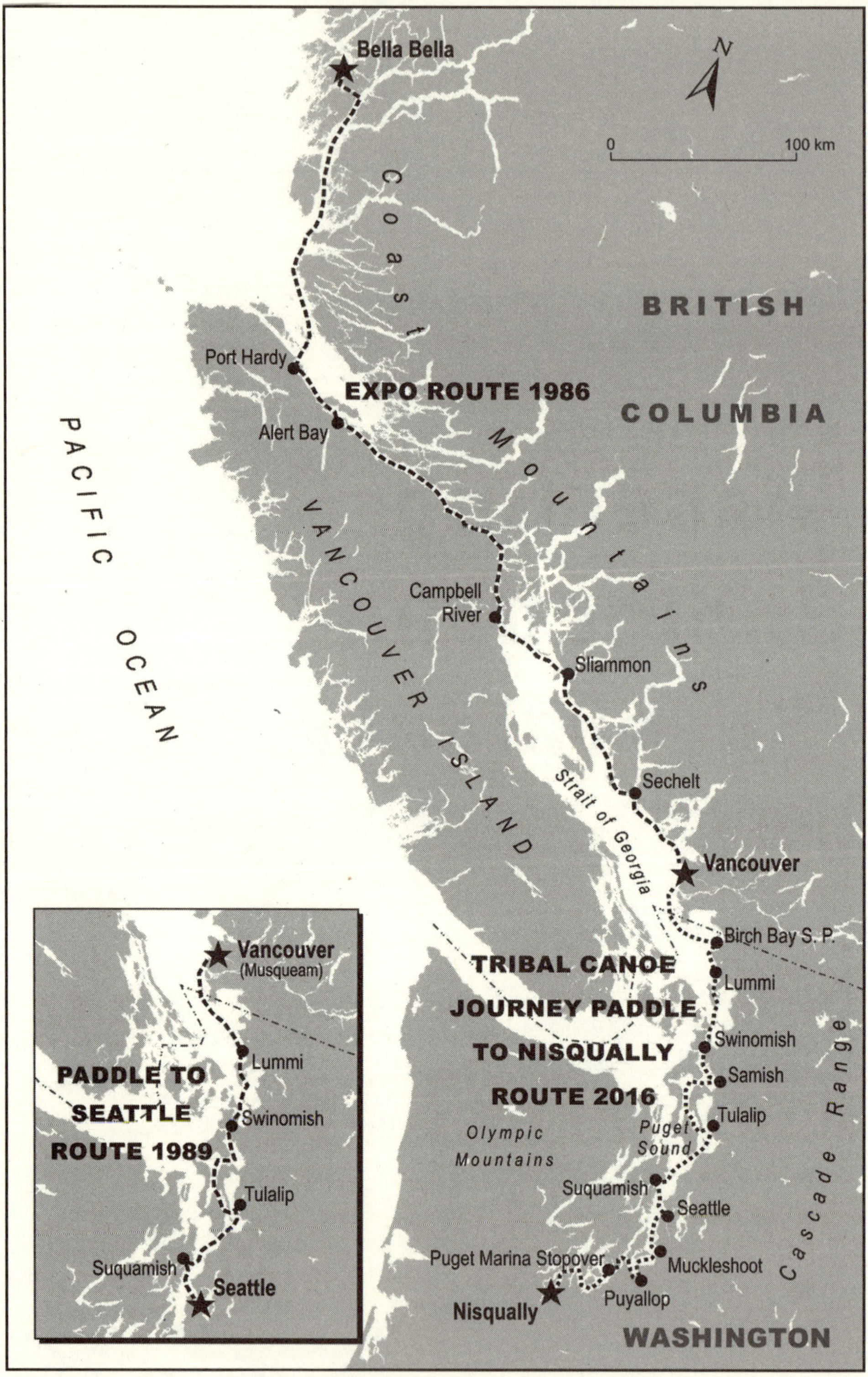

Bella Bella
N
0
100 km
Coast Mountains
BRITISH
COLUMBIA
Port Hardy
EXPO ROUTE 1986
Alert Bay
PACIFIC
OCEAN
VANCOUVER ISLAND
Campbell
River
Sliammon
Strait of Georgia
Sechelt
Vancouver
Birch Bay S.P.
TRIBAL CANOE
JOURNEY PADDLE
TO NISQUALLY
ROUTE 2016
Lummi
Swinomish
Samish
Tulalip
Puget
Sound
Olympic
Mountains
Suquamish
Seattle
Muckleshoot
Puget Marina Stopover
Puyallup
Nisqually
Cascade Range
WASHINGTON
Vancouver
(Musqueam)
Lummi
PADDLE TO
SEATTLE
ROUTE 1989
Swinomish
Tulalip
Suquamish
Seattle

CHAPTER 1

Tribal Canoe Journeys and Indigenous Cultural Resurgence: A Story from the Heiltsuk Nation

FRANK BROWN, HILLARY BEATTIE, VINA BROWN, AND IAN MAURO

Over the last three decades, a cultural gathering called Tribal Canoe Journeys has supported Indigenous community revitalization along the Pacific Northwest coast of Canada and the United States. The gathering involves "canoe families" from coastal communities paddling to host communities and sharing their cultural songs, dances, stories, and teachings with other participating canoe families. For decades these journeys have helped participants reconnect with their cultural traditions and heal from intergenerational traumas caused by residential schools, the potlatch ban, and other assimilation policies.

Many Indigenous scholars, including Leanne Simpson, Taiaiake Alfred, and Jeff Corntassel, argue that the root cause of these traumas is the disconnection of Indigenous peoples from their ancestral lands, cultures, and communities. For this reason, they believe Indigenous communities should focus on intergenerational knowledge sharing and on revitalizing their land and water-based practices, including canoeing. For Alfred, restoring these practices is "key to the reclamation of spiritual, physical and psychological health and to the restoration of communities characterized by peace and harmony and strength."[1] Scholars also argue that Indigenous cultural resurgence requires the renewal of land and water-based economies, languages, social and political institutions, and relationships between Indigenous nations.[2]

This chapter explores the ways that Tribal Canoe Journeys has helped the Heiltsuk Nation revitalize their culture from the perspective of community members who supported and witnessed its growth over the last three decades. The research was part of a larger project on Tribal Canoe Journeys between academics and the Heiltsuk, which also involved the production of a collaborative documentary film called *Glwa: Resurgence of the Ocean-Going Canoe*. This chapter is co-authored by Hereditary Chief Frank Brown, his daughter "copper canoe woman," or Vina Brown, a Heiltsuk and Nuu-chah-nulth scholar, and their non-Indigenous academic colleagues Hillary Beattie and Ian Mauro. It draws on fifty interviews conducted with Indigenous youth, leaders, and Elders between 2014 and 2016, along with the co-authors' experience of travelling with a group of Heiltsuk youth as they paddled to Nisqually Indian Tribe in Washington in 2016. This collaboratively developed chapter links scholarship on Indigenous cultural resurgence, traditional knowledge, and real-world experience from the Heiltsuk territory.

Heiltsuk History, Colonization, Residential Schools, and Cultural Loss

Prior to the arrival of European settlers, the Heiltsuk lived for millennia along the central coast of the Pacific Ocean in what is currently known as British Columbia, Canada. According to Western archeology, the Heiltsuk have lived there for at least 14,000 years, while according to Heiltsuk oral histories, they have lived there since time immemorial.[3] Prior to colonization, they lived in several different village sites in their traditional territories, which included over 35,000 square kilometres of mainland and islands. The Heiltsuk developed a rich culture with complex social, political, and economic systems, to which the potlatch is central. The potlatch is an important gathering where communities determine laws and transfer rights to land as well as fishing, gathering, and hunting spots. At potlatches, communities also negotiated trades and celebrated coming-of-age ceremonies, succession ceremonies, and marriages. The Heiltsuk relied on the canoe—known as a *glwa* in the Heiltsuk's traditional language of Hailhzaqvl—to travel through their territories and visit neighbouring communities for potlatches. These complex systems allowed the Heiltsuk to thrive for over 700 generations.[4]

In the mid-nineteenth century, European colonization began to impact the Heiltsuk. In 1862, gold miners from San Francisco carried the smallpox virus to Fort Victoria on southern Vancouver Island, causing an outbreak at the fort where Indigenous people were trading. When they paddled back to their communities, they unknowingly transmitted the disease and devastated Indigenous communities along the Pacific coast, including those of the Heiltsuk. This impacted the survivors not only physically and emotionally but also culturally: since Heiltsuk knowledge was passed down orally from generation to generation, the loss of population disrupted the transmission of this intergenerational knowledge, among other things. As a result, under the direction of hereditary chiefs, the Heiltsuk relocated from their ancestral villages to Campbell Island and amalgamated into a single community known as Bella Bella during the 1860s and '70s. In 1882, the Joint Indian Reserve Commission assigned thirteen reserves to the Heiltsuk, which represented a nominal portion of their traditional territory. However, the commission never established or signed treaties with many of the Indigenous communities in British Columbia, including the Heiltsuk. This means that the Nation's traditional territory remains unceded.[5]

Throughout the late nineteenth and early twentieth centuries, the federal government of Canada—with the support of Christian churches—implemented policies and practices designed to assimilate Indigenous peoples including the Heiltsuk. In 1880, Methodist missionaries entered Bella Bella to convert the community members to Christianity. Five years later, the Government of Canada outlawed the potlatch, in order to expedite the assimilation of coastal nations into Western culture.[6] Around this time, the federal government and churches also began establishing residential schools, which were designed to remove Indigenous children from their families and assimilate them into Western culture.[7] The overall effect of these assimilation policies was to disconnect Indigenous communities, including the Heiltsuk, from their land and sea, from traditional knowledge and cultural practices that had allowed their ancestors to survive in their territories for thousands of years.[8]

However, the Heiltsuk Nation did not passively accept federal and provincial assimilation policies and practices. In 1913, the Royal Commission on Indian Affairs for the Province of British Columbia—often referred to as the McKenna-McBride Commission—came to Bella Bella to settle what was considered to be the "Indian reserve question." The commission heard from a number of Heiltsuk chiefs and leaders, including Bob Anderson, who declared, "We are the natives of this country. . . . We feel we own the whole of this country, every bit of it, and we ought to have something to say about it."[9] This powerful statement—which was shared with the commission over 100 years ago—continues to inspire members of the Heiltsuk Nation to defend their traditional territories and advocate for their title and rights to the land.[10] Throughout time, the Heiltsuk people have demonstrated resiliency and have adapted through a variety of very challenging transitions into who they are today.

Restorative Justice, the Healing Power of Nature, and Tribal Canoe Journeys

In 1964, when Frank Brown was born in Bella Bella, the Heiltsuk were not encouraged to participate in their traditional cultural activities and were firmly confined within the Indian reserve system. Although the potlatch ban had officially been lifted in 1951, community members were still expected to assimilate into Canadian settler society. As a result of these policies and associated personal tragedies in his family, Frank had a challenging youth and was involved in a case of battery and assault of a local bootlegger when he was fourteen. The standard punishment for this type of crime was a sentence to a juvenile detention centre outside of the community in an urban area. However, Frank's aunt and uncle asked the judge to instead apply traditional Heiltsuk law, or *gvi'ilas*, based on ancestral teachings, and banish him to an island. The judge agreed and remanded fourteen-year-old Frank to an eight-month banishment on an uninhabited island near Bella Bella.[11] This was the first time in modern judicial history, and in the living memory of the Heiltsuk, that this traditional law had been applied in Bella Bella.

Frank believes this eight-month experience transformed his life. The banishment taught him about the profound power of nature and how to support and heal individuals and communities. Through this experience, he was able to separate his actions from his person, and recognized that he could transform his behaviour for the better. After much reflection, Frank shared that

> the four key elements in transformative change start with identification of the issue or problem. We move to acknowledge it, address it, and finally overcome it. We have challenges in each phase—for example, we can get stuck with an issue and not realize it. We have to, therefore, realize and acknowledge the problem, and then choose to deal with it or not. When we address the issue, we must reflect on the circumstances and make the decision to take action for change. The challenge within the final phase is not to be complacent but instead recognize this as a process or journey and continuum for a sustainable society."

In an interview, he observed that "it was through that time alone and through the teachings—the traditional *gvi'ilas* law of our people—that I had the opportunity to experience the healing power of nature in my life.[12]

In direct response to his banishment on the island, Frank helped start Tribal Canoe Journeys as a way to give back to his family and community, and reconnect them with the natural world. After high school graduation, he left Bella Bella and completed college programs in outdoor recreation and small business and tourism management, then started a successful ecotourism venture. Frank recalled that "all of this work was predicated on simply wanting to give back, share nature-based and particularly canoe experiences. And, wanting other people to have the opportunity to go through those amazing life experiences as an individual, as families, and as communities."[13]

Expo '86 and the Paddle to Seattle

In 1986, the City of Vancouver hosted the World Exposition, also known as Expo '86. Although the official theme of that year's fair was "Transportation and Communication: World in Motion—World in Touch," Frank did not believe that the first form of transportation along the coast—the ocean-going canoe—was adequately represented. For this reason, he and a group of Heiltsuk community members decided to carve a traditional dugout canoe—or *glwa*—to ensure Pacific Indigenous culture was present at Expo '86.

As this was the first time a *glwa* had been carved in Bella Bella in more than 100 years, the community was still in the early stages of renewing and revitalizing its ancestral knowledge and ceremonies relating to the harvesting

FIGURE 1.1. AND 1.2. Heiltsuk community members paddling to Vancouver for Expo '86. Source: Shirley Hall.

of a sacred cedar tree for this canoe. Traditionally, the community would have gone to the forest, recited prayers, made offerings, and felled the tree within a well understood and highly practised context of ceremony. Since over 100 years had passed since this was last done, community members were relearning these activities. They were doing much more than collecting material to build a canoe; they were using this opportunity to transport themselves back to the roots of their culture. Instead of "leaving the past in the past," as settler society was encouraging them to do, the Heiltsuk circled back to their traditions, renewing their sacred relationship with the land, waters, and all of life, which brought them back to their original teachings as a people: to have care, respect, and love for the earth and each other.

Frank and Heiltsuk cultural leader Chief David Gladstone ran a canoe-carving training program in 1984 and 1985 to teach community members about the process and meaning of making a *glwa*. They also asked Indigenous carvers from Haida Gwaii, Kwa Kwa Key Wak, and Coast Salish territory to help with the canoe-carving training program. In an interview with Tamara Marshall, Frank recalled, "Not only did our carvers carve canoes, but we were all brought back together with our ceremonial protocols that have always been associated with the canoe travel and had basically gone dormant."[14] After the *glwa* was completed, Frank and a group of fourteen community members paddled over 500 kilometres from Bella Bella to Vancouver, a route that their ancestors had also travelled. The canoe journey was historic: it brought people together to celebrate the *glwa*. In doing so, the *glwa* became a vessel for initiating a new era of cultural resurgence up and down the Pacific coast.

After Expo '86, a Native American committee, including the Suquamish Tribe in Washington State, invited coastal communities to participate in the "Paddle to Seattle" as part of the state's centennial celebration in 1989. Frank and a group of Heiltsuk community members accepted the invitation and paddled their *glwa* to Seattle.[15] While at the gathering, Frank emphasized how the canoe connected Indigenous communities all along the coast. During the Heiltsuk protocol time, he said: "The canoe is the cornerstone of our culture on the Pacific coast. The *glwa* or the ocean-going canoe is what binds us all together because we are an Indigenous maritime culture.... We are one people tied together through our ocean-going canoe and we bring you greetings from the north coast."[16] Prior to making these remarks, Frank

FIGURE 1.3. Heiltsuk community members carving a dugout canoe for Expo '86. Source: Shirley Hall.

FIGURE 1.4. Frank Brown speaking at Expo '86 in Vancouver. Source: Shirley Hall.

had phoned his grandfather Moses Humchitt and asked him what he should say. His grandfather replied, "You will know what to say." Frank's response was to challenge the coast Indigenous communities in attendance to paddle to Bella Bella for a gathering four years later in 1993, which the United Nations had declared the International Year of the World's Indigenous People. Frank's grandmother Maggie Hall named the gathering Qatuwas, which means "people gathering together" in Hailhzaqvl.[17] The communities accepted Frank's invitation and the Quileute Tribe from Washington State presented him with a paddle, which they said they would collect from him in Bella Bella.[18] Frank made this challenge and invitation because the Heiltsuk wanted other maritime Indigenous people to share in this experience and see the land and sea through the eyes of their ancestors.

The Growth of Tribal Canoe Journeys

In 1993, twenty-three canoe families from thirty different Indigenous communities along the Pacific Northwest coast of Canada and the United States accepted Frank's invitation and paddled to Bella Bella for Qatuwas. Approximately 3,000 participants showed up for the gathering, which caused Elders to cry tears of joy when they saw the canoes arriving on shore. Interview participants for this chapter spoke about the impact of Qatuwas on the Heiltsuk. Heiltsuk Elder Connie Newman said she was very emotional when she heard the singing and drumming and saw the canoes coming in, because her grandmother had worked hard to preserve their culture.[19] Christian White, a Haida man who attended the event, said Qatuwas "was something that really brought us all together as a family, as friends, and it was a statement by all the coastal First Nations that we were still here."[20]

Following Qatuwas in 1993, other Indigenous communities along the coast started hosting cultural canoe gatherings, and the gathering officially became known as Tribal Canoe Journeys. The gathering was hosted by a number of communities in Washington State, including LaPush, Puyallup, Quinault, Tulalip, Elwha, Muckleshoot, Lummi, Suquamish, Makah, Swinomish, and Squaxin Island. Several communities in British Columbia also hosted Tribal Canoe Journeys gatherings, including Ahousaht, Squamish, Chemainus, and Cowichan Tribes. Over a twenty-year period, the gathering grew significantly in size and now attracts thousands of participants from along the coast. Nowhere else are Indigenous people self-organizing in this way or at this scale. Tribal Canoe Journeys is now referred to by some people as the largest and most significant gathering of Indigenous people in the Americas today.

In 2014, twenty-one years after the Heiltsuk Nation hosted the inaugural Qatuwas Tribal Canoe Journeys, the community invited coastal nations to paddle back to Bella Bella for another gathering. For Frank, this represented Tribal Canoe Journeys' coming "full circle." To prepare, Frank and other leaders delivered local training programs and hired community members to harvest and prepare traditional foods. Local community members also made gifts for guests, and young people learned about their traditional songs, dances, teachings, and cultural protocols. In addition to helping Bella Bella prepare for Qatuwas, Frank believes, these training and employment opportunities helped community members learn about healthy lifestyles and develop new skills that could be applied to future jobs and opportunities. This work paid off when thousands of participants travelled from as far away as Alaska, Oregon, Hawaii, Japan, and New Zealand to celebrate and share their culture at Qatuwas.[21]

In addition to sharing their cultural songs, dances, and stories, a group of Indigenous leaders met at the gathering to discuss potential economic opportunities for their communities, which resulted in the establishment of an agreement known as the Qatuwas Accord.[22] The agreement acknowledged Indigenous communities' long precolonial history of trading and exchanging goods. It also emphasized the importance of Indigenous communities working together to investigate trade opportunities and to develop and renew commerce and trade networks. Frank believes this agreement helps reaffirm and strengthen social and economic relationships between maritime Indigenous nations.

This accord is one example of the many positive outcomes of Tribal Canoe Journeys that participants spoke about in interviews for this project. They also said that the journeys helped the Heiltsuk reconnect to land and water-based practices, learn and revive traditional canoe teachings, and learn their traditional songs, dances, stories, ceremonial canoe protocol, and language. It also helped the Heiltsuk revitalize their traditional maritime ecological knowledge and establish intergenerational relationships between Elders and youth. On the journeys, the Heiltsuk also re-established precolonial relationships with other Indigenous communities and reaffirmed their political authority in their traditional territories. In this way, Tribal Canoe Journeys is a gathering that reflects Indigenous histories, knowledges, governance, life-ways, and world views in practice.

Tribal Canoe Journeys and Indigenous Resurgence

During the nineteenth and twentieth centuries, systemic issues such as residential schools, the potlatch ban, and other assimilation policies disconnected Indigenous communities across Canada from their cultural traditions and practices. According to Alfred, the separation of Indigenous people from land and sea-based practices like trapping, hunting, and fishing remains a key issue in communities today.[23] In Bella Bella, community members spoke about how youth had not been connected to sea and land-based practices of canoeing and canoe building prior to participating in Tribal Canoe Journeys. For example, Mary Brown, who is the Director at the Heiltsuk Restorative Justice program and has organized multiple Tribal Canoe Journeys trips for Heiltsuk youth, shared that on one of the journeys, "when we departed Bella Bella, you could see that there was some fear of the unknown, of the water, because these young people haven't been on the water for a number of years, and the disconnect for them was huge."[24] Several Heiltsuk youth repeated this sentiment.

For Indigenous scholars like Alfred, Corntassel, and Simpson, the restoration of traditional cultural practices like canoeing is of utmost importance for Indigenous communities.[25] In an interview, Frank emphasized how Tribal Canoe Journeys helps reconnect youth to their ancestors' sea and land-based travelling traditions: "We bring our young people on the Tribal Canoe Journeys as a way of reconnecting to [the] tradition of travelling from our different sites, and our people travelled along the coast to trade food, to celebrate, whether it's feasts or potlatches or marriages or coming of age ceremonies. They spent a lot of time paddling between communities and gathering food."[26] Similarly, Krista Walkus, a Heiltsuk member and former youth participant on Tribal Canoe Journeys, explained that "being on the canoe kind of brings you back to our great-great-great-grandmothers, and great-great-great-grandfathers, who travelled these oceans through the canoe because they didn't have boats that we have today with motors. So [Tribal Canoe Journeys] gives you an experience of what they experienced hundreds of years ago."[27] The Heiltsuk have emphasized that Tribal Canoe Journeys allowed them to reconnect to their ancestors, homelands, and cultural practice of travelling to other communities on a *glwa*.[28]

By reconnecting participants to the canoe, Tribal Canoe Journeys also helps individuals heal from the intergenerational traumas caused by residential schools, which is an important part of personal and community revitalization.[29] Several young people spoke about how the journey allowed them to "release" some of their pain "into the water." Linda Humchitt, a former Tribal Canoe Journeys participant, said the journey "becomes a release to you. Like, you can release everything into the water, every stroke you take. It gets everything, like all the negativity away from you."[30] According to Heiltsuk spiritual beliefs, being on the ocean—between the water and the sky—allows a person to ponder and experience the space between life and death. Heiltsuk traditional knowledge teaches that the ocean is the medium through which the spirits of those who have passed away can cross over to the other side. This allows them to connect with the Creator and be among ancestors who have and will continue to walk the earth and paddle the oceans that comprise Heiltsuk territory and existence. By reconnecting to the water, the ancestors, and the meaning of existence itself, Tribal Canoe Journeys facilitates healing. Walter Campbell Jr., another former Heiltsuk participant, said that "it brings a lot of healing to me. Being on the water, hearing nothing but the paddle hitting the water . . . it's always a powerful experience for me."[31] In addition, participants indicated that Tribal Canoe Journeys improved their self-esteem and confidence. After completing a long, strenuous journey, youth felt proud of their accomplishments. Former youth participant Nevada Collins said, "After Tribal Canoe Journeys, it's just such a feeling of . . . self-worth and knowing that you're capable of doing something of that magnitude."[32] Heiltsuk adults and Elders also spoke about how happy and proud youth are when they arrive at the final destination. "You can see the strength and the pride, instantly," according to Mary Brown.[33]

On Tribal Canoe Journeys gatherings, Heiltsuk participants also learn about their traditional language, songs, dances, and stories that were passed down through generations for millennia prior to the introduction of the Canadian government's assimilation policies.[34] Significantly, all of the songs that Heiltsuk youth practise on Tribal Canoe Journeys are in the Heiltsuk

FIGURE 1.5. Heiltsuk youth paddling to Nisqually for Tribal Canoe Journeys in 2016. Source: Mark Wunsch.

language of Hailhzaqvl, which language teacher Frances Brown said helps "our youth to have confidence and [embrace] our language again."[35] Once the youth arrive at the final destination, they transition into the second part of the journey known as protocol, which can last for several days. This involves each of the canoe families sharing their cultural language, stories, songs, dances, and teachings with the other nations. Former participant Walter Campbell Jr. explained that this allows youth "to listen and watch and learn stuff they never seen before."[36] Other participants said this can inspire youth to get more involved in their own culture. As Linda Humchitt recalled, after being part of Tribal Canoe Journeys, "I started going to potlatches and I started dancing more and I started actually listening to the treasures that we have."[37] Overall, Heiltsuk community members believe that Tribal Canoe Journeys have inspired youth to learn more about their culture and language.[38] In her study of the journeys, Smethurst also found that they introduce traditional languages to Indigenous youth by encouraging them to "speak their language and find their own voice."[39]

The Heiltsuk have also spoken about how Tribal Canoe Journeys helped revitalize their traditional knowledge about the natural environment. This knowledge includes ancestral laws— known as *gvi'ilas* in Hailhzaqvl—that govern how the Heiltsuk interact with the natural environment. Kelly Brown, the director of the Heiltsuk Integrated Resource Management Department, said a simple example of these laws is "take a little, leave a lot."[40] Other Heiltsuk cultural teachings emphasize the connections between the Heiltsuk, the land, and the water. Heiltsuk social worker Mavis Windsor said, "There's no way that we can say that we're not connected to our environment. It's who we are, it's how we live our way of life."[41] During Tribal Canoe Journeys, youth learn about these teachings during conversations and protocol ceremonies. On the journeys, Kelly Brown said, Nations "share their treasures and talk about their relationship to the ocean and the rivers and the land."[42] In these ways, Tribal Canoe Journeys highlights the Heiltsuks' cultural relationship to their traditional territories and resources.

One way that these cultural teachings are shared is through the re-establishment of intergenerational relationships between Elders and youth. Heiltsuk Elders often accompany youth during Tribal Canoe Journeys, which multiple participants said was an important aspect of the gathering. Former youth participant Nevada Collins noted that "it's a good way for the Elders and the older people to get together with the youth to explain . . . the reasons behind what we do, and the history of our dances, our songs [and] the canoe."[43] In addition to passing on cultural knowledge, participants said that the Elders also help youth work through personal challenges. Tsinda Humchitt, a Heiltsuk youth, said that when someone feels like giving up, they can "just go and sit with the Elders, and you know, they bring you back up again."[44] Heiltsuk Elder Connie Newman emphasized the importance of this intergenerational connection: "The closer the youth and the Elders are, the stronger and healthier we are as a people."[45] Other scholars have also found that Tribal Canoe Journeys allows youth to connect with Elders and "to witness their knowledge, to learn from their teachings, and to hear their stories."[46]

In addition to establishing intergenerational relationships *within* communities, Tribal Canoe Journeys also helps re-establish precolonial relationships *between* distinct communities. Prior to colonization, many communities had treaties and formal diplomatic relationships with each other that governed how they worked together and resolved conflicts.[47] On the journeys, participants meet and form friendships with Indigenous people from other Nations. They build bonds with other communities through cultural sharing. Through this sharing, according to Frances Brown, "we develop lifelong relationships and we have new understandings about each other."[48] Community members have said these new relationships are especially important for Heiltsuk youth because Bella Bella is an isolated community. In addition to learning about other Nations' cultures, youth also witness other youth pursuing drug-free and alcohol-free lifestyles. Heiltsuk artist Ian Reid observed that "they interact with all these people and their circle of wellness and healthiness builds."[49] In this way, Tribal Canoe Journeys helps participants re-establish the political and social relationships that existed between distinct Indigenous communities prior to colonization.

Tribal Canoe Journeys supports the Heiltsuks' political efforts in other ways as well. Interview participants said that political issues and strategies are often discussed on the journeys, in both formal ceremonies and informal conversations. As Mavis Windsor emphasized, this inter-tribal sharing "raises awareness and gives an opportunity to share approaches."[50] Likewise, former youth participant Jessica Brown, whose name is also Qatuwas, said that Tribal Canoe Journeys allows individuals to learn about each other's political struggles and figure out how to work together. In addition, Tribal Canoe Journeys has allowed communities to reaffirm their title and rights to their traditional—and sometimes unceded—territories. When other canoe families arrive at the final destination, they obtain permission from the host community to land their canoe. In doing so, Frank has explained, they acknowledge the host Nation's title and rights to the waterways and that land. Further, because Tribal Canoe Journeys garners media attention, Nations can use the journeys to highlight their relationship to their traditional territories and their stewardship responsibility. For Kelly Brown, the 2014 journey was "about reaffirming our authority in the area [. . . and] making sure that other people are aware that we're still here and we're still strong."[51] In other words, Tribal Canoe Journeys helps the Heiltsuk Nation assert its traditional title and rights through practising *gvi'ilas* and ceremonial protocols in the potlatch spirit, harvesting resources from the land and sea to feed guests, and making ceremonial gifts to give to visiting canoe families.

Finally, the Heiltsuk have stated that by revitalizing culture, the journeys encourage individuals to stand up for and defend the environment in their traditional territories. Gary Wilson explained that Heiltsuk culture is based in the natural environment. If a marine species like herring becomes extinct, the Heiltsuk "could lose our language, lose our dances, our songs, because that's where they come from. It comes from the territory. It comes from the resources, the marine and the land."[52] Haida chief Guujaaw—who was instrumental in helping carve the *glwa* for the first canoe journey in 1986—also spoke about the important connection between Indigenous culture and the environment. Tribal Canoe Journeys, he said, instills a "love of culture" in youth, which can encourage them to stand up for their environment when it is threatened: "When we go into a fight with something, the strength in our heart is that strength of culture. And the people who are there, really on the land, on the water, feeling it, tasting it, and knowing it, you know, like being among the old people, they are the ones who are more inclined to fight for it."[53] In these various ways, Tribal Canoe Journeys has supported the cultural and political resurgence of the Heiltsuk Nation and, indeed, of Indigenous people and communities up and down the Pacific coast. During the 2009 International Year of Biodiversity, Frank helped co-author the book *Staying the Course, Staying Alive: Coastal First Nations Fundamental Truth: Biodiversity, Stewardship and Sustainability*.[54] This book's title uses a marine navigation metaphor that advises us to stay the course by maintaining the ancestral teachings that have sustained us throughout the millennia. According to Frank,

> The *glwa* ocean-going canoe is an important vessel that transports us, as Indigenous place-based peoples, on our journey toward reasserting self-determination. We must move forward upholding the following seven teachings: (1) honouring our ancestral creation stories; (2) connecting to nature for physical, emotional, and spiritual well-being; (3) showing respect to ourselves and all that's around us; (4) upholding our traditional knowledge; (5) continuing to exercise stewardship of our lands and waters for future generations; (6) sharing with others; and (7) adapting to change. How we validate these core values and teachings is through our Indigenous stories, languages, practices and maps.[55]

Conclusion

After three decades of Tribal Canoe Journeys, it is as clear as the most pristine waters of the Pacific coast that these gatherings have brought life back to the Heiltsuk Nation and highlighted the importance of their distinct culture, intergenerational knowledge, and inherent rights over their unceded territories. In reconnecting the community with the water, the canoe has helped the Heiltsuk revitalize their traditional songs, dances, stories, and language, and these practices are now central to guiding their larger cultural journey.

Traditional ecological knowledge and intergenerational relationships between Heiltsuk Elders and youth help orient the Heiltsuk in time and place and ground their understanding of where they have been and where they are going as a nation. Indeed, Tribal Canoe Journeys has played an important role in helping the Heiltsuk re-establish precolonial relationships with other Indigenous communities and reaffirm their political authority in their traditional territories. Importantly, Tribal Canoe Journeys has helped members of the Heiltsuk Nation heal from the intergenerational legacy of residential schools and at the same time been instrumental to their ongoing resurgence as a community.

Through the canoe journeys, the community has had decades to reflect on the past, specifically on the teachings that sustained the Heiltsuk through their experiences as an ancient maritime people, and how continuity of this knowledge is essential for helping them navigate their future in an era of ongoing colonial processes that continue to undermine Indigenous peoples and their environments. Despite efforts that acknowledge historical truths and seek reconciliation, settler society still engages in powerful economic and political forces that continue to subvert Heiltsuk knowledge, rights, and responsibilities regarding the lands and waters that make up their territory. However, Tribal Canoe Journeys stands as a dynamic response to this enduring colonial violence inflicted upon a people, and demonstrates that it is possible to reassert cultural and political agency by reconnecting with and protecting the land, ocean, and lifeways of past, current, and future generations of Heiltsuk. Thus the canoe represents a vehicle for practising respect, reciprocity, and resistance simultaneously. In reflecting on the overall impact of Tribal Canoe Journeys, Frank has suggested that the canoe is a reflection the Heiltsuk Nation's overall well-being: "It was the canoes that brought sickness to our people at the period of contact. And now, the canoe is bringing life to our people. So, for me, the significance of this gathering is it's kind of a barometer for where we're at as a society."[56]

Appendix A: Qatuwas Accord

Qatuwas Accord Preamble

Whereas the most complex maritime Indigenous societies in the world evolved along the Pacific Northwest Coast of North America; and

Whereas we, the Indigenous Peoples, have participated in profitable and beneficial trade and exchange relationships for thousands of years; and

Whereas we, the First Peoples, have utilized our water ways and our lands as transportation corridors to speed commerce and trade and between individuals, families and Nations linking communities from Alaska through British Columbia, Washington, Oregon and California to Mexico and beyond; and

Whereas we have un-extinguished Aboriginal and treaty rights; and

Whereas we are Indigenous persons who are proud to carry forward the traditions, rights and obligations from our Ancestors; and

Whereas we have gathered at the Qatuwas Festival to celebrate our Indigenous culture through the Canoe Journey, which affirms to us the need to enhance and grow our Indigenous commerce and trade for the wellness and prosperity of all our peoples; and

Qatuwas *"people gathering together"* Accord Memorandum of Collaboration

Work together to investigate opportunities (such as trade and investment agreements, missions, trade fairs, conferences and direct connections) to initiate and expand commerce and trade between our nations; and

Work together to seek out the supports and assistance made available by Indigenous and other agencies (including governments at all levels) to immediately begin work to develop commerce and trade networks among the Indigenous persons and our nations of the Pacific Northwest with the goal of setting up a formal organization to explore multilateral trade agreements; and

Work together to form our own networks of Indigenous business leaders and practitioners to promote the development of the entrepreneurial skills required for success in commerce and trade; and

Work together to utilize our networks to collaborate in "lessons-learned" and "best practices" so that all our Indigenous nations and individuals can benefit from the wellness and prosperity that come from increased commerce and trade; and

Work together to build stronger economic and social relationships with other Indigenous peoples of the Pacific Rim and beyond; and

We recognize that this Accord can produce many opportunities, some of which will be developed jointly, some of which will be developed independently, and some of which will be developed by others. This Accord is intended as a statement of general intent for collaboration among Pacific Northwest Indigenous groups and not intended to create any legal or financial obligations. We commit to one another through communication, collaboration and planning efforts.

Agreed to in principle at Bella Bella, British Columbia during Qatuwas "people gathering together" 2014. **WE HEREBY AFFIRM AND AGREE,** as Indigenous persons and members of our sovereign Indigenous nations.

Notes

1 Gerald Taiaiake Alfred, "Colonialism and State Dependency," *Journal of Aboriginal Health* 5, no. 2 (2009): 44, https://doi.org/10.18357/ijih52200912333.

2 Leanne Simpson, *Dancing on Our Turtle's Back: Stories of Nishnaabeg Re-Creation, Resurgence, and a New Emergence* (Winnipeg: Arbeiter Ring Publishing, 2011).

3 Duncan McLaren et al., "Terminal Pleistocene Epoch Human Footprints from the Pacific Coast of Canada," *PLoS ONE* 13, no. 3 (2018), https://doi.org/10.1371/journal.pone.0193522; Alisha Gauvreau and Duncan McLaren, "Stratigraphy and Storytelling: Imbricating Indigenous Oral Narratives and Archaeology on the Northwest Coast of North America," *Hunter Gatherer Research* 2, no. 3 (2016), https://doi.org/10.3828/hgr.2016.22.

4 Herbert Moody-Humchitt and Marilyn Slett, *Declaration of Heiltsuk Title and Rights* (Bella Bella, BC: Heiltsuk Tribal Council, 2015), http://www.heiltsuknation.ca/wp-content/uploads/2015/11/Heiltsuk-Declaration_Final.pdf.

5 Paul Tennant, *Aboriginal Peoples and Politics: The Indian Land Question in British Columbia, 1849–1989* (Vancouver: University of British Columbia Press, 1990); Cole Harris, *Making Native Space: Colonialism, Resistance, and Reserves in British Columbia* (Vancouver: University of British Columbia Press, 2002).

6 Douglas Cole and Ira Chaikin, *An Iron Hand upon the People: The Law against the Potlatch on the Northwest Coast* (Madeira Park, BC: Douglas and McIntyre, 1990).

7 Truth and Reconciliation Commission of Canada, *Honouring the Truth, Reconciling for the Future: Summary of the Final Report of the Truth and Reconciliation Commission of Canada* (Winnipeg: Truth and Reconciliation Commission of Canada, 2015).

8 Nancy Turner, Marianne Boelscher Ignace, and Ronald Ignace, "Traditional Ecological Knowledge and Wisdom of Aborginal Peoples in British Columbia," *Ecological Society of America* 10, no. 5 (2000): 1275–87, http://www.jstor.org/stable/2641283; Menno Boldt, *Surviving as Indians: The Challenge of Self-Government* (Toronto: University of Toronto Press, 1993).

9 Ian Gill, *All That We Say Is Ours: Guujaaw and the Reawakening of the Haida Nation* (Madeira Park, BC: Douglas and McIntyre, 2009), 31.

10 Moody-Humchitt and Slett, *Declaration of Heiltsuk Title and Rights.*

11 Phil Lucas and Frank Brown, *Voyage of Rediscovery*, VHS video (Vancouver: Moving Images Distribution, 1990); Bruce Barnes, "An Overview of Restorative Justice Programs," *Alaska Journal of Dispute Resolutions* 1, no. 1 (2013), https://www.narf.org/nill/documents/2013-ak_jrnl_dispute_resolution_pp101-120.pdf.

12 Frank Brown, interview with Hillary Beattie, Bella Bella, 21 June 2015.

13 Ibid.

14 Tamara Marshall, "A Tribal Journey: Canoes, Traditions, and Cultural Continuity" (Master's thesis, Royal Roads University, 2011), 24.

15 Ibid.

16 Leslie Jeanne Lincoln, "Paddle to Seattle: A Native Washington Movement to 'Bring Them Canoes Back Home'" (Master's thesis, University of British Columbia, 1990), 154.

17 David Neel, *The Great Canoes: Reviving a Northwest Coast Tradition* (Madeira Park, BC: Douglas and McIntyre, 1995).

18 Ibid.

19 Connie Newman, interview with Hillary Beattie and Vina Brown, Bella Bella, 5 July 2015.

20 Christian White, interview with Hillary Beattie and Vina Brown, Bella Bella, 27 June 2015.

21 Marilyn Slett, *Qatuwas 2014: Tribal Journeys to Bella Bella, People Gathering Together* (Bella Bella, BC: Heiltsuk Tribal Council, 2014).

22 See Appendix A: Qatuwas Accord.

23 Alfred, "Colonialism and State Dependency."

24 Mary Brown, interview with Hillary Beattie and Vina Brown, Bella Bella, 24 June 2015.

25 Alfred, "Colonialism and State Dependency"; Simpson, *Dancing on Our Turtle's Back.*

26 Frank Brown, interview with Hillary Beattie, Bella Bella, 21 June 2015.

27 Krista Walkus, interview with Hillary Beattie and Vina Brown, Bella Bella, 24 June 2015.

28 Marshall, "A Tribal Journey: Canoes, Traditions, and Cultural Continuity"; Tania Suarez, "Tribal Journeys: An Integrated Voice Approach towards Transformative Learning" (PhD diss., University of Victoria, 2012); Bruce Johansen, "Canoe Journeys and Cultural Revival," *American Indian Culture and Research Journal* 36, no. 2: 131–42; Hillary Beattie, "'Resurgence of the Ocean-Going Canoe': An Exploration of the Impacts of Tribal Canoe Journeys on the Heiltsuk Nation through Participatory Video" (Master's thesis, University of Manitoba, 2017).

29 Michelle Jacob, *Yakama Rising: Indigenous Cultural Revitalization, Activism, and Healing* (Tucson: University of Arizona Press, 2013); Truth and Reconciliation Commission of Canada, *Honouring the Truth, Reconciling for the Future: Summary of the Final Report.*

30 Linda Humchitt, interview with Hillary Beattie and Vina Brown, Bella Bella, 10 July 2015.

31 Walter Campbell Jr., interview with Hillary Beattie and Vina Brown, Bella Bella, 10 July 2015.

32 Nevada Collins, interview with Hillary Beattie and Vina Brown, Bella Bella, 24 June 2015.

33 Mary Brown, interview with Hillary Beattie and Vina Brown, Bella Bella, 24 June 2015.

34 Leanne Simpson, ed., *Lighting the Eighth Fire: The Liberation, Resurgence, and Protection of Indigenous Nations* (Winnipeg: Arbeiter Ring Publishing, 2008).

35 Frances Brown, interview with Ian Mauro, Bella Bella, 18 July 2014.

36 Walter Campbell Jr., interview with Hillary Beattie and Vina Brown, Bella Bella, 10 July 2015.

37 Linda Humchitt, interview with Hillary Beattie and Vina Brown, Bella Bella, 10 July 2015.

38 Hillary Beattie, "'Resurgence of the Ocean-Going Canoe.'"

39 Tania Smethurst, "Well-Being and Ethnic Identity Promotion for Aboriginal Youth: A Community Based Mixed Methods Study of Tribal Journeys" (Master's thesis, University of Victoria, 2012), 60.

40 Kelly Brown, interview with Ian Mauro, Bella Bella, 18 July 2014.

41 Mavis Windsor, interview with Hillary Beattie and Vina Brown, Bella Bella, 26 June 2015.

42 Ibid.

43 Nevada Collins, interview with Hillary Beattie and Vina Brown, Bella Bella, 24 June 2015.

44 Tsinda Humchitt, interview with Hillary Beattie and Vina Brown, Bella Bella, 24 July 2016.

45 Connie Newman, interview with Hillary Beattie and Vina Brown, Bella Bella, 5 July 2015.

46 Marshall, "A Tribal Journey: Canoes, Traditions, and Cultural Continuity," 87.

47 Leanne Simpson, "Looking after Gdoo-Naaganinaa: Precolonial Nishnaabeg Diplomatic and Treaty Relationships," *Wicazo Sa Review* 23, no. 2 (2008): 29–42.

48 Frances Brown, interview with Ian Mauro, Bella Bella, 18 July 2014.

49 Ian Reid, interview with Hillary Beattie and Vina Brown, Bella Bella, 11 July 2015.

50 Mavis Windsor, interview with Hillary Beattie and Vina Brown, Bella Bella, 26 June 2015.

51 Kelly Brown, interview with Ian Mauro, Bella Bella, 18 July 2014.

52 Gary Wilson, interview with Ian Mauro, Bella Bella, 18 July 2014.

53 Guujaaw, interview with Frank Brown and Hillary Beattie, Bella Bella, 26 June 2015.

54 Frank Brown and Y. Kathy Brown, *Staying the Course, Staying Alive: Coastal First Nations Fundamental Truths: Biodiversity, Stewardship and Sustainability* (Victoria: Biodiversity BC, 2009). Available at www.biodiversitybc.org.

55 Ibid.

56 Ibid.

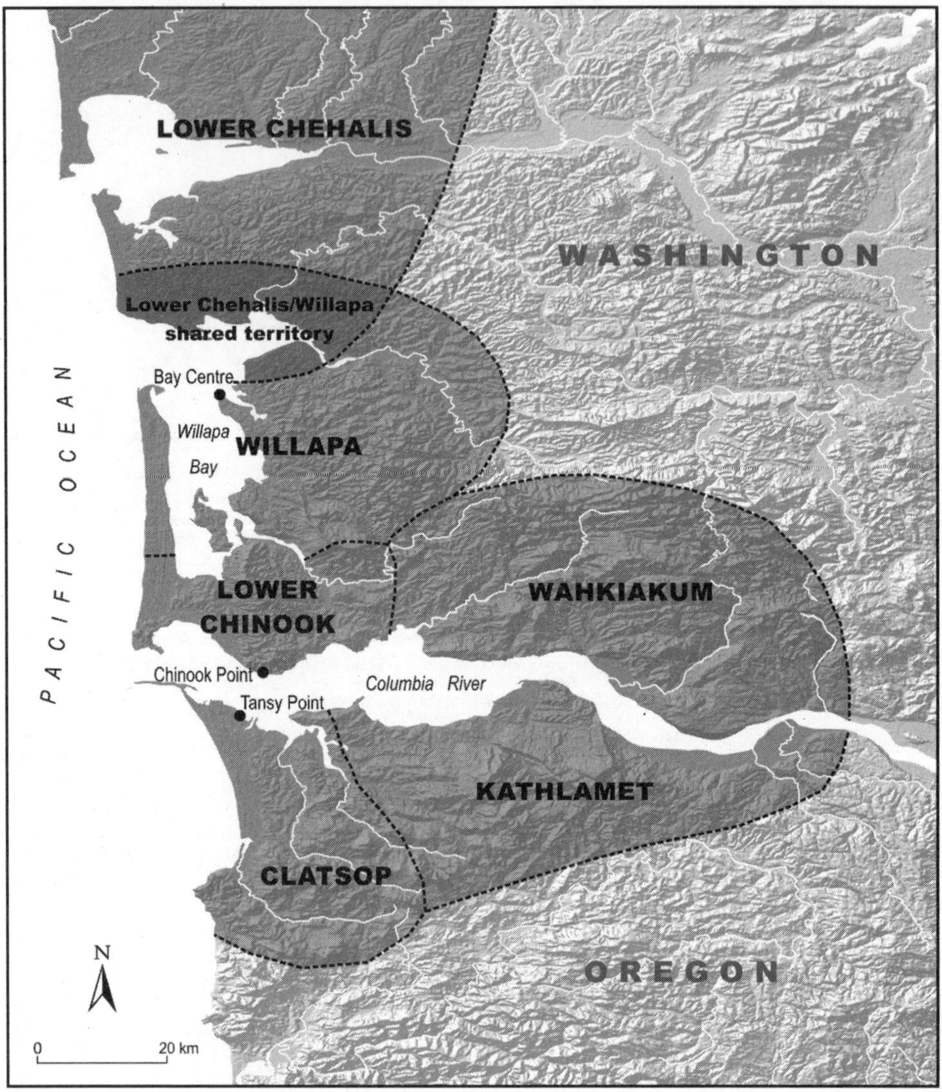

LOWER CHEHALIS
WASHINGTON
Lower Chehalis/Willapa shared territory
PACIFIC OCEAN
Bay Centre
Willapa Bay
WILLAPA
LOWER CHINOOK
WAHKIAKUM
Chinook Point
Columbia River
Tansy Point
KATHLAMET
CLATSOP
N
OREGON
0
20 km

CHAPTER 2

This Is What Makes Us Strong: Canoe Revitalization, Reciprocal Heritage, and the Chinook Indian Nation

RACHEL L. CUSHMAN, JON D. DAEHNKE, AND TONY A. JOHNSON

I've never felt more comfortable, more at home, than I do in the canoe. I was made to pull. It's in my DNA. *My body was designed for the canoe—long torso and short legs. My build comes from thousands of years of my family travelling by canoe. I remember the first time I ever got into a Chinookan- style canoe with a Willapa Bay paddle. They stuck me in the lead puller's seat and told me to set the pace. They kept me there. I've been a lead puller for my family for many years now. Nothing can keep me from getting into the canoe and pulling with my family, not even being nine months pregnant and in labour.*

On 28 July 2013, I paddled the six-mile pull from Bay Center to Georgetown, WA. *I was nine months pregnant, and in labour with my eldest son. Many people were sceptical about me getting into the canoe. I had no fear. I hoped that I would give birth on the shores of my homelands. That day, I pulled every stroke of that leg. I was hoping that the pull would move the labour along, but it didn't. My contractions slowed during the pull across Willapa Bay. After arrival protocol, I got out and my contractions started. The nurse and midwife who were travelling with us had to leave, so my husband talked me into heading home as well. As*

I was taking my leave, I waddled by the skippers' meeting. They started freaking out when they realized I was out on the water with them. Our family skipper said, "Too bad she didn't give birth out there."

The birth of my eldest son ended up being more difficult than intended. I was in labour for several more days, until 2 August at 3:30 a.m., when the doctor suggested that I have a Caesarean birth. I was afraid and disappointed in myself. I had dreamt of having a natural birth out on the spits out in Willapa Bay, not in a surgical room in a hospital. After crying and trying to reason with my doctors, my mother, and my husband, I called my canoe family's skipper at 4 a.m. He answered the phone and told me, "It doesn't matter how he comes into the world, just make sure he comes into the world." I decided to have the C-section.

My son was delivered at 6:15 a.m. that morning. I didn't know it at the time, but I delivered him while my family was on the protocol floor, singing our songs and sharing our dances. They brought onto the floor with them a very old song. It was the first time that the song had been shared publicly in decades. The song was about Thunderbird and his mom.

After resting, I called the canoe family to let them know that their youngest puller had made a safe journey into this world. I told them about the birth and when it had happened. They shared their story about protocol. I knew at that moment that my son's name would be Kanim, the Chinookan word for canoe. He would always be connected to the canoe culture. He would have no memory of his first time in the canoe.

Rachel Cushman—Chinook Indian Nation

Canoes and the protocols attached to them have played a central role in cultural revitalization, community resilience, and embodied sovereignty for many Indigenous nations across the Pacific Northwest.[1] Historically, cedar dugout canoes were the most ubiquitous and one of the most recognizable manifestations of Indigenous culture in the region, and it has even been suggested that once there were perhaps as many canoes as there were people.[2] But like many aspects of Indigenous culture, canoes—and the cultural practices and protocols tied to them—were negatively impacted by colonial invasion and its associated polices of assimilation and cultural genocide. The colonial imposition of a sedentary wage economy—instead of a traditional economy based on regular travel for fishing, hunting, and trading—diminished the role of canoes, as did the outlawing of cultural practices like the potlatch that were integrally tied to canoe travel (see Chapter 1). Additionally, privatization of land and large-scale industrial timber harvesting separated Indigenous communities from the western red cedar from which canoes were made. Finally, the twin colonial forces of introduced disease and introduced alcohol led to the loss of many Elders who were knowledgeable in the ways of the canoe, which in turn led to a disruption in the cultural mechanisms for passing down that knowledge.[3] Although canoes and the extensive and interwoven cultural practices associated with them never entirely disappeared in the face of colonial pressure, the combination of economic imposition and cultural assault led to their near disappearance on waterways and shorelines in the decades following white invasion.

In recent decades, however, canoes have made a dramatic return to the land/waterscape of the Pacific Northwest. Canoes are most notably and publicly visible in Tribal Journeys, a weeks-long paddle and gathering of Indigenous nations that annually brings together thousands of Native American/First Nations citizens in the Pacific Northwest, an event that has garnered substantial media and public attention.[4] The resurgence of canoes, however, is not confined to Tribal Journeys.[5] Canoes have become integral to Indigenous events and ceremonies—both public and private—throughout the year. They are again a common presence on waterways and shorelines, and a part of the Indigenous everyday. It should be unsurprising that canoes play such a central role in Indigenous cultural revitalization in the Pacific Northwest, since in many ways they are the material manifestations of the resilience of Indigenous nations. We argue that this is the case because canoes and the protocols attached to them reflect a decolonized vision of heritage, one based in tribal cultural values of place and reciprocity. Canoes therefore represent a form of reciprocal heritage, one that is lived and enacted through canoe culture and where the terms of the reciprocal responsibilities between humans and humans, and humans and non-humans, are defined in the performance of protocols, the rules of behaviour that come from the past but which must be followed to ensure the future. As a result, rather than being backward-looking and nostalgic, this form of reciprocal heritage is instead tribally relevant, based in current and ongoing relationships and responsibilities, and thus active, forward-looking, and resilient.

In this chapter, we look at the importance of canoe revitalization specifically through the lens of the Chinook Indian Nation, a tribal nation that has approximately 3,000 enrolled citizens and whose headquarters are located in Bay Center, Washington. Two of this chapter's authors (Cushman and Johnson) are Chinook citizens and both are active in Chinook tribal government as well as the Chinook Nation canoe family. Present-day Chinook citizens are the descendants of Chinooks who lived for generations along both shores of the lower Columbia River, as well as north and south along the Pacific coast at the river's mouth. They numbered in the thousands. Today, citizens of the Chinook Indian Nation live throughout the Pacific Northwest and the United States, although most still reside near traditional Chinookan lands in Washington and Oregon. Citizens of the Chinook Indian Nation are direct descendants of the people that made up the five westernmost Chinookan tribes: Lower Chinook, Clatsop, Willapa, Wahkiakum, and Kathlamet. Despite the invasion and theft of their lands by colonial outsiders, the devastation of introduced disease, and efforts at forced assimilation, the Chinook survived and continue to this day to maintain a distinct Indigenous identity. Currently, the Chinook Indian Nation is not recognized as a tribe by the government of the United States.[6] In the face of this non-recognition, however, the Chinook not only survive but remain culturally strong and resilient, and canoes and protocols are a central reason for this. Canoes are an everyday reaffirmation of Chinook presence on the land/waterscape and their asserted sovereignty as a people.

Canoe Revitalization and Tribal Journeys

Although canoes are present in many Indigenous events, their resurgence has become most popularly visible in Tribal Journeys. The origins of Tribal Journeys are multiple, as the canoe revitalization efforts of a number of individuals and the legacies of a number of tribal revitalization efforts coalesced. But the event that is most often directly credited for the creation of Tribal Journeys is the "Paddle to Seattle" that happened in 1989 in conjunction with the centennial celebrations of the state of Washington. In July of that year, canoes from the tribal communities of Hoh and La Push in

Washington State left their Pacific coast homes and paddled into the Salish Sea (Puget Sound). There they met up with canoes from the Heiltsuk, Lummi, Tulalip, and Suquamish nations, and the flotilla of canoes travelled together to Golden Gardens Park, located just outside of Seattle. Here participants delivered a letter to the people of the state of Washington. The letter, signed by representatives of twenty-one tribal communities from the state of Washington, contained the words of the famous Duwamish and Suquamish leader Si'ahl (Seattle) and asked the residents and government of the state of Washington to fulfill their obligations as responsible stewards of the earth.[7]

At the "Paddle to Seattle," a member of the Heiltsuk Nation canoe invited all of the canoe nations that were present on that day to meet again in four years in Bella Bella, the home of the Heiltsuk Nation. After some discussion the other canoes accepted the invitation, and the proposed gathering in Bella Bella came to be called the Qatuwas Festival—Qatuwas meaning "people gathered together in one place" in the Heiltsuk language. News of the upcoming Qatuwas Festival quickly spread and canoe nations up and down the Pacific coast began preparations for the gathering. The direct result of this was that more Indigenous nations were building canoes, revitalizing protocols, relearning songs, and paddling once again. In the summer of 1993, twenty-three canoes landed at Bella Bella and were welcomed on shore by Heiltsuk Nation Tribal Chairman Edwin Newman, who noted that "Native people are regaining their strength and culture, and this gathering is a sign that things are changing for our people."[8] Close to 2,000 people attended the Qatuwas Festival, and those who were in attendance quickly recognized the importance of the event and the potential that canoe resurgence and the gathering together of multiple Pacific Northwest tribes spanning both Canada and the United States had for cultural revival and the healing of tribal communities. They decided to gather together again four years later—in 1997—at La Push, Washington. The La Push gathering was also tremendously successful and powerful, and at this point Tribal Journeys became an annual event.

The Centrality of Protocols

Acknowledging and carrying out protocols is very important on Tribal Journeys, as well as year-round. Our protocols are what makes us Chinook. Our protocols are the teachings that have been passed down from generation to generation, and they encompass all aspects of our lives.

Our storytelling time and religious ceremonies begin at the first frost. During the warm seasons we are supposed to be working hard, but during the colder months we pass down our traditional knowledge. Every winter our community holds a winter gathering where we share songs and dances and acknowledge our neighbours who have supported us throughout the year. It was at this celebration that my community found out that I was expecting Kanim. We have many protocols around pregnancy and caring for infants. Chinook women are not to wear jewellery when pregnant. We have many superstitions about how wearing jewellery can affect the growing baby. We also have strict rules about death. Babies in utero and young children are not to be exposed to death, because they are still closely connected to the spirit world. There had been a loss in the community and memorial songs were to be shared at the gathering, so as a Chinook woman, expecting, I wrapped my belly with a shawl. When the community saw me with no jewellery and the shawl they knew I was expecting.

It is very important that people follow the rules associated with each of our songs and dances. We have been taught to never sing a song without acknowledging what it is, where it comes from, and most importantly, why we have the right to sing it. When we don't follow protocols for our gifted and inherited songs, it reflects poorly on our community. Many songs are owned by families and are protected closely by them. These songs are the wealth of our community and should always be treated that way. When it comes to singing songs, if you don't know whose song it is, where it comes from, or why you have a right to sing it, you should not sing it publicly.

Rachel Cushman—Chinook Indian Nation

Protocols are the rules and ways of behaving that come from the past that guide life in the present, and if followed, lead to cultural strength, resilience, and well-being. They guide nearly every aspect of Chinookan life, from annual community celebrations, major life events and transitions, to day-to-day activities. To outside observers the ever-present nature of protocols can appear to be almost overwhelming. But to the Chinook and other Indigenous nations in the Pacific Northwest, following the rules of protocol is essential. Canoes carry with them their own associated set of protocols, and the recognition and enactment of these protocols is evident in Tribal Journeys.

Anyone who has participated in or attended the activities surrounding Tribal Journeys knows that it is defined by powerful images and events. One of the central and most powerful events is the final canoe landing at the shores of the Tribal Journeys host community. The spectacle of dozens of beautifully decorated canoes and the hundreds of paddlers they carry arriving at the beach, rafted together and waiting for permission to come ashore while thousands more watch from the shoreline, is awe-inspiring. This unforgettable and powerful image of each Tribal Journey is inextricably tied to protocol; one of the central protocols in Tribal Journeys is the request to come ashore. As the canoes and the travellers they carry come to the shores of the host community, they must get permission from that community before landing. While there is no exact formula for this protocol of permission, it usually includes the following: a statement of identity by a canoe family representative; a declaration that they have arrived peacefully; an account of the day's travel, noting that the members of the canoe are tired and hungry, and that they are there to share songs and dances; and then finally the request to come ashore. A representative of the host community then welcomes and recognizes the canoe family and gives them permission to come ashore. In many cases this protocol is done in the traditional languages of the participants and often notes family and community ties. In the case of the final landing, when there are dozens of canoes waiting to come ashore, this protocol can last for many hours.

Protocols continue in the evening after everyone has been fed. At this point each community shares its songs and dances with the other communities present, and especially with the host community (Fig. 2.2). Typically, the community that has travelled the farthest distance from its home is the first to take the floor. This exchange of songs and dances is done as an act of reciprocity, a gift of thanks to the host community that has fed and housed all of its visitors. As is the case with the coming ashore protocols, this exchange of songs and dances can go on for hours and well into the night, and may continue for five or more days. Protocol ends with the dances and songs of the host community, who in perpetuation of potlatch traditions offer additional gifts to their visitors. These protocols are not exclusive to just the final landing and final host community; they are regular and required, and are performed each time a canoe arrives at the homeland of another tribal community during the course of their days-long travels.

The importance of protocols to Tribal Journeys and their role in cultural revival and resilience in the Pacific Northwest cannot be overstated. Protocols are central to the reassertion of tribal primacy and sovereignty on the landscape: they are the most important manifestation of the revitalization of the ancient highways that connected villages and peoples, they serve to recognize Indigenous occupation of the land (both of the hosts and the visitors), and they help to foster the renewal of Indigenous ceremonies, language,

FIGURE 2.1. Mary R. Johnson leads dancers for the "Willapa Bay Welcome Song" during the 2018 Paddle to Puyallup, Chinook Indian Nation protocol. Photo: Amiran White.

and knowledge. Perhaps most importantly, protocols accomplish all of this explicitly outside of the framework of the colonial nation-state. The rules of protocol predate colonial invasion and they reflect connections, ceremonies, and land/waterscapes that are centuries old. They also reflect a way for tribal nations to move forward and heal from the legacies of colonialism. In this sense the performance of protocol is not just an aspect of culture, it is fundamentally an act of decolonization.

Canoe Revitalization and the Chinook Indian Nation

The Chinook Indian Nation has been involved in Tribal Journeys and canoe revitalization from the very beginning. Emmett Oliver, a foundational figure in organizing the "Paddle to Seattle," was typically identified as Quinault, but he has strong ancestral ties to Chinooks and Chinookan homelands.[9] Additionally, Tony A. Johnson, the current chair of the Chinook Indian Nation and one of the authors of this chapter, was part of the Cedar Tree Institute that was started by many of the people central to canoe revitalization—people like Tom Heidlebaugh, Philip Red Eagle, Connie McCloud, Mary McQuillen, Tom Jackson, and Clint Hackney, among others. Johnson's participation in this institute drove his interest in carving, creating art, and ultimately building canoes. At this early stage Johnson's interest in canoe resurgence was happening principally within the scope of his personal life. But beginning in 2005, the Chinook as a community partnered with the Confederated Tribes of Grand Ronde and started travelling on Tribal Journeys. The Chinook already had a few canoes at this point, and the Grand Ronde had some financial resources and additional paddlers, and their partnership into the world of Tribal Journeys led to what would become an annual tradition and a restructuring of community timetables, to the point where the Chinook calendar is now in some ways structured from journey to journey (Fig. 2.2).[10]

Chinook and Grand Ronde participation in Tribal Journeys has only increased in the years since that initial partnership in 2005, so much so that the two nations no longer need to officially travel together on the journeys (although they still often paddle together and perform protocols jointly). Additionally, the growth in participation in Tribal Journeys has occurred despite the fact that travelling in the journeys can represent a substantial

FIGURE 2.2. Chinook Nation Canoe Family pulling in the canoe Kłmin during the Paddle to Nisqually in 2016. Photo: Amiran White.

FIGURE 2.3. Late Hereditary Chief Phillip A. Hawks enjoying the Annual Chinook Indian Nation Story Telling Gathering at Chinook Point. Photo: Amiran White.

financial hardship: no one gets paid to go on the journeys, and it can be extremely challenging to take that much time off from your regular work. Additionally, canoes are now also an everyday part of Chinook life and are essential actors beyond the window of Tribal Journeys. They are central to Chinook events like the First Salmon Ceremony and the annual Bay Center-Georgetown Paddle, as well as to numerous private and personal uses. Ultimately, canoes have again become essential to Chinook identity itself.

Healing Communities through Canoe Revitalization

Living our protocols and travelling in the canoe saves lives. One of the most important rules on Tribal Journeys and for our canoe family is to do no harm to self or others. We strictly prohibit the use of drugs and alcohol. Over the years many people have achieved sobriety and healing from trauma by way of involvement with our cultural protocols and canoes. No one exemplified the power of this cultural healing more than our late Hereditary Chief Phillip A. Hawks (Fig. 2.3).

Phillip was a very important member of the Chinook Indian Nation. He was the last Chinook baby born at the old village in Bay Center, WA, *at Goose Point. He was born in the home of his great-grandmother, Annie Victoria Lewis Hawks, and raised through much of his adolescence by her. In his younger years Phillip battled with alcoholism, but he found the strength to put down the bottle by taking up his birthright and leading his people. Phillip was a proud member of the Chinook Canoe Family, and he set a high standard for our youth. When he turned seventy years old, he paddled from Squaxin Island to Lummi Island, paddling every stroke of every leg. In the years to follow, he pulled every stroke of every leg that he travelled, always with a good attitude.*

When Phillip passed away in April 2017, our community lost a treasure. During the Paddle to Campbell River in 2017, the Chinook Canoe Family did not put our canoes in the water, because our hearts were mourning. A small group from our canoe family travelled to Campbell River to acknowledge the invitation and explained that we would put our canoes back in the water when our year of mourning was over.

Rachel Cushman—Chinook Indian Nation

An important element of Tribal Journeys and canoe revitalization overall is the effect that it has had on healing communities, especially in terms of combatting drug and alcohol abuse among both adults and youth. Unfortunately, the rates of drug and alcohol abuse are very high among American Indians, and while the causes for this are multifaceted and vary from community to community, they are ultimately tied to the impacts of colonialism.[11] It is a devastating and rampant issue, and one of central concern for many Indigenous communities. Involvement in canoe culture, however, has had a dramatic and positive impact, as numerous participants have returned from journeys clean and sober, leaving drugs and alcohol behind for good. The positive impact that Tribal Journeys and canoe resurgence have had in this area is not merely a fortunate yet unexpected side effect. When Tony Johnson was working with the Cedar Tree Institute, it was his experience that those who were leading canoe revitalization at the time—Philip Red Eagle, Connie McCloud, Tom Heidlebaugh, Tom Jackson, Mary McQuillan, Clint Hackney—were expressly dedicated to addressing problems in Indigenous communities through direct activism with the youth. These leaders, who were involved with canoe resurgence at the very beginning, expected that revitalizing canoe culture and following the protocols attached to canoes would provide a positive and tribally specific avenue for addressing problems associated with drug and alcohol abuse, and that it could do so among the youth. This was a primary reason for pushing for increased community involvement with canoes.

A central reason why Tribal Journeys is so effective in combatting drug and alcohol abuse is because it is an intervention method directly rooted in tribal values. Most previous attempts to address the problems of drug and alcohol abuse among Native Americans used intervention methods that had been successful among non-Native populations. But these methods tended not to work in tribal communities because those attempting to intervene assumed that the causes of abuse were the same in Indigenous populations as they were in the general population. They failed to look at the specific histories and cultures of each tribe, and they failed to consult with and include the communities affected. Tribal Journeys, however, springs directly from tribal values, of which the most central is the view of canoes as the hub for the family, whose members are committed to working together, who depend upon each other, and who are accountable to each other.

Every canoe travelling on Tribal Journeys has a canoe family associated with it. Some canoe families care for multiple canoes, and some tribal communities have multiple canoe families. Canoe families are typically comprised of canoe(s), a skipper or skippers, pullers, water support, and ground crew. Every person in the canoe family has a job to do, and no job is more important than the next. Members of the canoe family are expected to learn the protocols of their family, which include the protocols associated with travel as well as the protocols of the community from which the canoe comes. As part of these protocols, canoe families typically meet every evening to talk about the day, to pray, and to speak truthfully about any issues that may have arisen. If there are issues in the family or with other families, they are discussed at the meeting so that they can be taken care of. Bad feelings and bad behaviour are not to be taken into the canoes. This is not just to provide a harmonious experience while travelling, but also because canoes themselves feel any tensions in the family. Paddling a small craft in large bodies of water can be dangerous, and in order to ensure that the canoe takes care of its family, good feelings must be maintained. These values of family, truth-telling, and reciprocal responsibilities to others are emphasized to journey participants and encapsulated in the associated protocols. Furthermore, these values come directly from Elders and other leaders of the community. In this approach, culture and heritage are the routes for healing and they are the only things that effectively address the problem of abuse and addiction over the long term.[12]

In focusing on tribal values and protocols, Tribal Journeys and canoe resurgence assert a decolonized and enacted form of heritage. They present a world where actions are guided by Indigenous notions of reciprocity and truth-telling, and the paths to healing from drug and alcohol abuse are rooted in Indigenous ceremonies and values. One of the goals of colonization was to strip away from tribal populations all of those things that made them Indigenous—a view expressed in the well-known statement by Carlisle Indian school founder Richard H. Pratt, "kill the Indian, and save the man."[13] Whether it was through boarding schools and efforts to remove Native children from their families, the attempted separation of tribal communities from their lands and languages, or direct efforts at eradicating Native populations, colonialism worked to "kill the Indian." For the Chinook Indian Nation, however, Tribal Journeys and the return of canoes provide a path to decolonization, a way to remind people of their Indigeneity and resilience, something that Tony Johnson refers to as "feeding your Indian."[14] Tribal Journeys and being in the canoes do exactly that: feed your Indian.

Tribal Journeys and the return of the canoes are a way of reclaiming heritage that is explicitly an act of decolonization. It recognizes and celebrates pathways and connections that predate colonial invasion. It asserts Indigeneity through language and protocols, and by actions that remind everyone of who the original inhabitants of that place actually are. And all of this is done by communities that are living in the present on the landscape, demonstrating continuity, resilience, and a promise of future existence, even in the face of all they have had to survive. In Tribal Journeys, federal and state governments fade into the background, the colonial dictates of who is and isn't "authentic" or "recognized" fall away, and the boundaries of tribal communities as drawn and determined by colonial actors mostly disappear. This is not the heritage of a settler colonial nation. It's the heritage of sovereign tribal nations who were here before colonists arrived and who know that they will be here after the colonists are gone. This is something controlled by the tribes and is for the tribes, a sentiment nicely reflected in the words of Chinook citizen and vice-chair Sam Robinson when he states that "there's an ownership in Tribal Journeys. This is yours, this is your journey. You know, you do what's meant to be done . . . on the Journeys this is about you, and about all of the tribes along there."[15]

Reciprocal Heritage and Canoe Revitalization

Our kənim, our canoes, aren't empty vessels that we simply use to travel. They are members of our family. They have names. They have hearts. They have a job, like every member of the canoe family. We give them the same respect we'd give any member of our family. When Kɬmin came into the Chinook family and received his name, we came together as a community and gave thanks to him—we fed him. We had witnesses there, like we would during the naming of any other person. The community bathed him with cedar and prayers to protect and carry our nation forward.

Our canoes take care of us when we are out on the water. If the water is rough, we don't try to "correct" its movement with our bodies. We stay seated, with our hips against the gunnel and pull. Our canoes are built to keep us safe, and they will if we allow them to do their jobs.

We don't leave our canoes out in the winter to weather. We shelter them. We protect them. During the warmer months we clean them and paint them and prepare them for travel. After a long day on the water, we put them to rest in safe place and we don't leave them dirty—we clean them before we clean ourselves (Fig. 2.5).

Rachel Cushman—Chinook Indian Nation

For the Chinook Indian Nation, as well as other Indigenous nations of the Pacific Northwest, there is a strong recognition that non-human objects (both animals and things) have an existence outside of humans. Non-human objects are not merely created by humans or placed here for human use; they exist independently of us. The canoe provides an example of this world view. While the final shape of the canoe may be realized through the craftsmanship and the hands of a human, the life of the canoe is not given to it by humans; its life was already there. Chinook people believe that old-growth trees, which contribute to the creation of a canoe, are the source of the canoe's spirit. These trees hold the intergenerational knowledge of people and the land. Furthermore, the canoe is a being that has agency: it can feel happiness, disappointment, and pain. Although canoes and humans exist independently of each other, their lives are entangled by a sense of kinship and a series of reciprocal responsibilities; they are reliant on each other to make an appropriate path through the world. For the Chinook Indian Nation this form of reciprocal heritage is codified in the rules and performance of protocols. Protocols are the requirement for appropriately fulfilling reciprocal relationships, they are central to Chinookan views of heritage, and they ensure the well-being of canoe families and the recognition of Indigenous sovereignty on Tribal Journeys. Protocols, therefore, are more than simply a set of rules. They are the bridges that ensure reciprocity between humans and humans, and between humans and non-humans.

While protocols themselves can be considered as a form of intangible heritage, this does not mean that material objects are irrelevant to Chinookan views of heritage. In fact, quite the opposite is true: for instance, the physical canoe itself is vitally important. But beings are only as important as

FIGURE 2.4. Pullers and ground support carrying Kłmin to his resting place after the 2018 Paddle to Puyallup final landing. Photo: Amiran White.

the relationships between them. And it is the requirement of reciprocity in these relationships that holds everything together, and thus the intangible protocols, whose purpose is to ensure reciprocity between material agents, serve as the lynchpin to heritage. For the Chinook, a view of heritage that focuses solely or principally on the preservation and categorization of material objects—a view that tends to underlie much of Western cultural approaches to heritage—is simply not as meaningful, because it disconnects material culture from the intangible webs of reciprocity as defined in protocols. The Chinook approach to heritage, by contrast, destabilizes any easy dichotomies between the tangible and intangible, the natural and cultural, and the human and non-human. Furthermore, since heritage is attached to the *ongoing* relationships between entities that are necessary for well-being—rather than residing in static artifacts and objects from the past—heritage in this view is forward-looking. As heritage scholar Rodney Harrison notes, "Heritage emerges not as a process concerned with the past and present, but a future-oriented, emergent, contingent and creative endeavour. It is not a process of meaning-making that exists only in the human mind, but one in which multiple actors, both humans and non-humans, are equally implicated in complex processes that bind them across time and space."[16]

Conclusion: Protocols, Performance, and Nostalgia

In this chapter we have consistently used the term "performance" in connection with protocols. Use of the term "performance" within the broader context of heritage is certainly nothing new to the field of critical heritage studies. For example, heritage scholar Laurajane Smith has argued that "heritage" really does not consist of material things but rather is an ongoing process and negotiation that uses the past to construct identities, meanings, and belonging in the present, and as such all heritage then consists of ongoing cultural performance.[17] While Smith makes her argument within the context of heritage more generally, other scholars focus specifically on the role of performance within the realm of Indigenous political and legal claims. Laura R. Graham and H. Glenn Penny, for instance, discuss the "self-conscious, reflexive public performances of Indigeneity" that became increasingly common in the second half of the twentieth century and which are driven by Indigenous assertions to "recognition, self-determination, and cultural sovereignty."[18]

Our discussion of canoe revitalization and the role of protocols in that process certainly reflects elements of these scholars' views on performance and heritage. We want to be clear, however, that when we use the term "performance" in the context of canoes and protocols we are using it in a very specific way. It does not indicate merely a discursive negotiation of meanings tied to the past, nor describe an action that is explicitly performed for others in the way that an actor consciously performs for an audience. Rather, the term is used in the sense of how one carries out a duty, the action of fulfilling required responsibilities. This is an important distinction, especially within the context of twenty-first-century Indigenous claims to heritage. There can be a tendency to present these types of claims to heritage as something artificial, as invented political creations primarily constructed to convince others of the rightfulness of the claims. For the Chinook Indian Nation, however, the performance of protocols is not an act created or designed to convince others of the rightfulness of their heritage claims or their Indigeneity. Instead, it is simply behaviour done to ensure that the requirements of the reciprocal relationships between actors, both human and non-human, are fulfilled. And it is required behaviour that is done both in events open to the public and in Chinook private ceremonies conducted only in the presence of individuals or the community.

The nature of performance as the process of fulfilling responsibilities, rather than behaviour done expressly for the benefit of an external audience, also explains why the Chinook and other Indigenous nations in the Pacific Northwest tend not to view canoe revitalization and Tribal Journeys as historical re-enactment or a form of enacted nostalgia. Bruce Erickson argues that the promotion of recreational canoeing in Canada, especially to the white population, pushes a heritage narrative that celebrates and re-enacts the emergence of the colonial nation. In this sense canoeing "resurrects the voyageur period not through historical investigation of a very particular sphere of colonialism, but through a form of 'colonial nostalgia' . . . that celebrates the exploration of the continent as the discovery of a nation. While often taken to mean nostalgia by the colonists for that which colonialism destroyed . . . colonial nostalgia also functions as a yearning for the period of colonialism itself."[19] But the protocols attached to Indigenous canoe revitalization, while guided by the past, operate fully in the present and are guided by the maintenance of ongoing relationships and responsibilities. They do not represent a nostalgia for the past or a re-enactment but rather are a central part of a present-day process of healing and decolonization. As Misao Dean notes, "When indigenous people canoe, whether for recreation, cultural revival, or work, they do not imagine themselves to be voyageurs, or even the guides of explorers: they imagine themselves in the present, fighting the ongoing consequences of colonialism as enacted in the present."[20]

The Chinook Indian Nation certainly wants to remind others that they continue to exist, that they remain as a nation despite non-recognition and centuries of colonialism. This is a central message that is often repeated at both public and private events at which there is an element of audience-directed performance. The rules of protocol, however, that are attached to Chinook canoes were not created for the purposes of political theatre or as a type of nostalgic re-enactment. Rather, they exist independently, and humans are responsible for recognizing and following them. For this reason, the performance of protocols in gatherings like Tribal Journeys are not self-marketing performances of Indigeneity for the benefit of non-Indigenous people. They are simply a required responsibility and, as such, embody the most fundamental aspect of heritage. And it is this form of enacted and lived heritage—centred on the responsibility of the performance of protocols—that produces cultural resilience and that connects the Chinook Indian Nation's past to its present to its continued survival in the future.

Kanim's First Leg

My sons know who they are and where they come from. If you ask my eldest who his people are, he responds, "I am Chinook. My name is Kanim and it means canoe in chinuk. My brother is Isik and that means paddle in chinuk. We are Chinook." My children were born into a postcolonial world. They are the product of the United States government's broken treaties, boarding schools, relocation policies, termination era policies, and corrupt federal Indian recognition processes. We weren't supposed to survive. We aren't supposed to be here. According to some, we aren't here. Our existence is resistance. Our canoes and protocols are the fists of our Elders hitting the negotiation table at the Chehalis River Treaty Council of 1855. We would not give up our identity then and we will not give it up now. We will continue to teach our children. We will continue to represent our people as our ancestors have instructed us to. We know who we are. We sing our songs. We dance our dances. We tell our stories. We know our land and travel our waters. We honour our ancestors by continuing to teach and practise our protocols with our children (Fig. 2.5).

On 23 July, 2018, ten days before Kanim's fifth birthday, he travelled his first leg in the canoe, during Tribal Journeys, since his birth. This was his fifth Tribal Journey, but he had not travelled in the canoe. He was excited for his first leg. He was prideful, and finally, he was a big kid. When it came time to carry Kɬmin down to the water, Kanim found his place along the gunnel with all the other pullers and helped carry the canoe down. He then got in the canoe, found his seat and patiently waited for permission to leave the shore from the Samish community. He sat quietly, with his head held high. As per Chinook protocols, five is a very important number in our community. For me, Kanim's first leg was a monumental moment. This was Kanim's fifth journey, on the cusp of his fifth birthday. I was unable to be in the canoe with him on his first leg, but he carried me with him. I couldn't have been prouder. I know our ancestors were too. This is what makes us strong.

Rachel Cushman—Chinook Indian Nation

FIGURE 2.6. Councilwoman Rachel L. Cushman with husband, Chance White Eyes, and children, Kanim (right) and Isik Cushman-White Eyes (left). Preparing for the 2016 Paddle to Nisqually, Chinook Indian Nation Protocol. Photo: Amiran White.

Notes

1 The term "embodied sovereignty" comes from Brendan Hokowhitu and refers to "a critical bodily practice that brings into question those subjugating forces written upon the Indigenous body, that is, the very materiality of Indigenous existence, while affirming the complexity, diversity, and multi-dimensional ways of being Indigenous." Hokowhitu, "Haka: Colonized Physicality, Body-Logic, and Embodied Sovereignty," in *Performing Indigeneity: Global Histories and Contemporary Experiences*, ed. Laura R. Graham and H. Glenn Penny (Lincoln: University of Nebraska Press, 2014), 295–96.

2 Tony A. Johnson, "The Chinook People Today," in *Chinookan Peoples of the Lower Columbia*, ed. Robert T. Boyd, Kenneth M. Ames, and Tony A. Johnson (Seattle: University of Washington Press, 2013), 14.

3 Misao Dean, *Inheriting a Canoe Paddle: The Canoe in Discourses of English-Canadian Nationalism* (Toronto: University of Toronto Press, 2013), 164–65.

4 For example, see Lynda V. Mapes, "Tribes around Northwest Gather in Suquamish for Canoe Journeys," *Seattle Times*, 8 August 2009; William Yardley, "A Northwest Journey by Canoe to Reconnect with the Old Ways," *New York Times*, 24 July 2011.

5 There are many names for the Pacific Northwest canoe journeys. They have been referred to as Tribal Canoe Journeys, Canoe Journeys, Journeys, Tribal Journeys, etc. And sometimes they are referred to by their final destination (e.g., "Paddle to Nisqually," "Paddle to Bella Bella," etc.). Choice of terminology is often community and context based, but ultimately the different terms all refer to the same thing. The Chinook Indian Nation Canoe Family tends to use "Tribal Journeys" and that term is consistently used in our publications on the topic, so we continue that practice here.

6 The Chinook signed the Tansy Point treaty with government officials in 1851, but that treaty was never ratified by the U.S. Congress. New treaty negotiations in 1855 broke down, and as a result the Chinook were non-recognized. In the twentieth century, the Chinook filed for recognition through the Federal Acknowledgement Process (FAP) and on 3 January 2001, U.S. Assistant Secretary of the Interior Kevin Gover signed documents granting the Chinook Indian Nation formal recognition. Recognition was later rescinded under the Bush administration, and the Chinook remain unrecognized today. For further details, see Jon D. Daehnke, *Chinook Resilience: Heritage and Cultural Revitalization on the Lower Columbia River* (Seattle: University of Washington Press, 2017), 48–59. See also Andrew Fisher and Melinda Marie Jetté, "'Now You See Them, Now You Don't': Chinook Tribal Affairs and the Struggle for Federal Recognition," in Boyd, Ames, and Johnson, *Chinookan Peoples of the Lower Columbia*, 288–306.

7 David Neel, *The Great Canoes: Reviving a Northwest Coast Tradition* (Vancouver: Douglas and McIntyre, 1995), 2–4; David Neel, "Bella Bella: The Rebirth of the Northwest Coast Canoe," *Native Peoples Magazine* 7, no. 2 (1994): 10–18.

8 Neel, *Great Canoes*, 3.

9 Emmett Oliver passed away on 7 March 2016, at the age of 102. His role in canoe revitalization and his positive impact on tribal nations is incalculable. For a brief history, see Richard Walker, "Emmett Oliver, Founder of Paddle to Seattle, Walks on at 102," *Indian Country Today Media Network*, 8 March 2016, https://indiancountrytoday.com/archive/emmett-oliver-founder-of-paddle-to-seattle-walks-on-at-102-iJvgWt9n_kWudKuoqJufQQ.

10 Johnson notes that "we [the Chinook and Grand Ronde] traveled together and had a heck of an experience . . . and from that point forward, I think everyone who paddled at that time, which was less than twenty people, just reset their calendars. And their calendars are now

basically journey to journey. That's what my wife would tell you, that our calendar is just Tribal Journeys to Tribal Journeys." Tony A. Johnson, interview with Jon Daehnke, Ilwaco, WA, 22 January 2014.

11 See Fred Beauvais, "American Indians and Alcohol," *Alcohol Health and Research World* 22, no. 4 (1998): 253–59; Dakotah C. Lane and John Simmons, "American Indian Youth Substance Abuse: Community Driven Interventions," *Mount Sinai Journal of Medicine* 78 (2011): 362–72; Maria Yellow Horse Brave Heart and Lemyra M. DeBruyn, "The American Indian Holocaust: Healing Historical Unresolved Grief," *American Indian and Alaska Native Mental Health Research* 8, no. 2 (1998): 56–78.

12 The importance of canoe culture in efforts to combat drug and alcohol abuse, as well as collaborations between Native American communities and health care researchers and providers, is discussed in several publications. See Elizabeth H. Hawkins and C. June La Marr, "Pulling for Native Communities: Alan Marlatt and the Journeys of the Circle," *Addiction Research and Theory* 20, no. 3 (2012): 236–42; Heather S.V. Lonczak et al., "Navigating the Tide Together: Early Collaboration between Tribal and Academic Partners in a CBPR Study," *Pimatisiwin: A Journal of Aboriginal and Indigenous Community Health* 11, no. 3 (2013): 395–409; June La Marr and G. Alan Marlatt, *Canoe Journey Life's Journey: A Life Skills Manual for Native Adolescents* (Center City, MN: Hazelden Publishing and Educational Services, 2007); Lisa R. Thomas et al., "The Community Pulling Together: A Tribal Community-University Partnership Project to Reduce Substance Abuse and Promote Good Health in a Reservation Tribal Community," *Journal of Ethnicity in Substance Abuse* 8, no. 3 (2009): 283–300; Lisa R. Thomas, Dennis M. Donovan, and Robin L.W. Sigo, "Identifying Community Needs and Resources in a Native Community: A Research Partnership in the Pacific Northwest," *International Journal of Mental Health and Addiction* 8, no. 2 (2010): 362–73. See also the "Healing of the Canoe Project," a collaboration between the Suquamish, Port Gamble S'Klallam, and the University of Washington's Alcohol and Drug Abuse Institute (ADAI), at healingofthecanoe.org.

13 "'Kill the Indian, and Save the Man': Capt. Richard H. Pratt on the Education of Native Americans," *History Matters*, http://historymatters.gmu.edu/d/4929/.

14 Tony A. Johnson, interview with Jon Daehnke, 22 January 2014.

15 Sam Robinson, interview with Jon Daehnke, Vancouver, WA, 25 July 2010.

16 Rodney Harrison, *Heritage: Critical Approaches* (London: Routledge, 2013), 222.

17 For example, Smith argues that museum visitation is really a form of heritage performance, where the visitor emotionally engages with the past in order to negotiate and reify a contemporary sense of identity and place. Rather than serving as a learning experience, museum visitation is actually a performance that reinforces a sense of belonging. See Laurajane Smith, *Uses of Heritage* (London: Routledge, 2006), especially 66–74; Laurajane Smith, "The 'Doing' of Heritage: Heritage as Performance," in *Performing Heritage: Research, Practice and Innovation in Museum Theatre and Live Interpretation*, ed. Anthony Jackson and Jenny Kidd (Manchester: Manchester University Press, 2011), 69–81; Laurajane Smith, "Theorizing Museum and Heritage Visiting," in *The International Handbooks of Museum Studies: Museum Theory*, ed. Andrea Witcomb and Kylie Message (Hoboken, NY: John Wiley and Sons, 2015), 459–84.

18 Laura R. Graham and H. Glenn Penny, "Performing Indigeneity: Emergent Identity, Self-Determination, and Sovereignty," in Graham and Penny, *Performing Indigeneity*, 1–2. The collected essays in *Performing Indigeneity* provide an excellent overview of the themes and directions in scholarship on Indigenous performance.

19 Bruce Erickson, "Embodied Heritage on the French River: Canoe Routes and Colonial History," *Canadian Geographer* 59, no. 3 (2015): 324. See also Bruce Erickson, *Canoe Nation: Nature, Race, and the Making of a Canadian Icon* (Vancouver: UBC Press, 2013).

20 Dean, *Inheriting a Canoe Paddle*, 175.

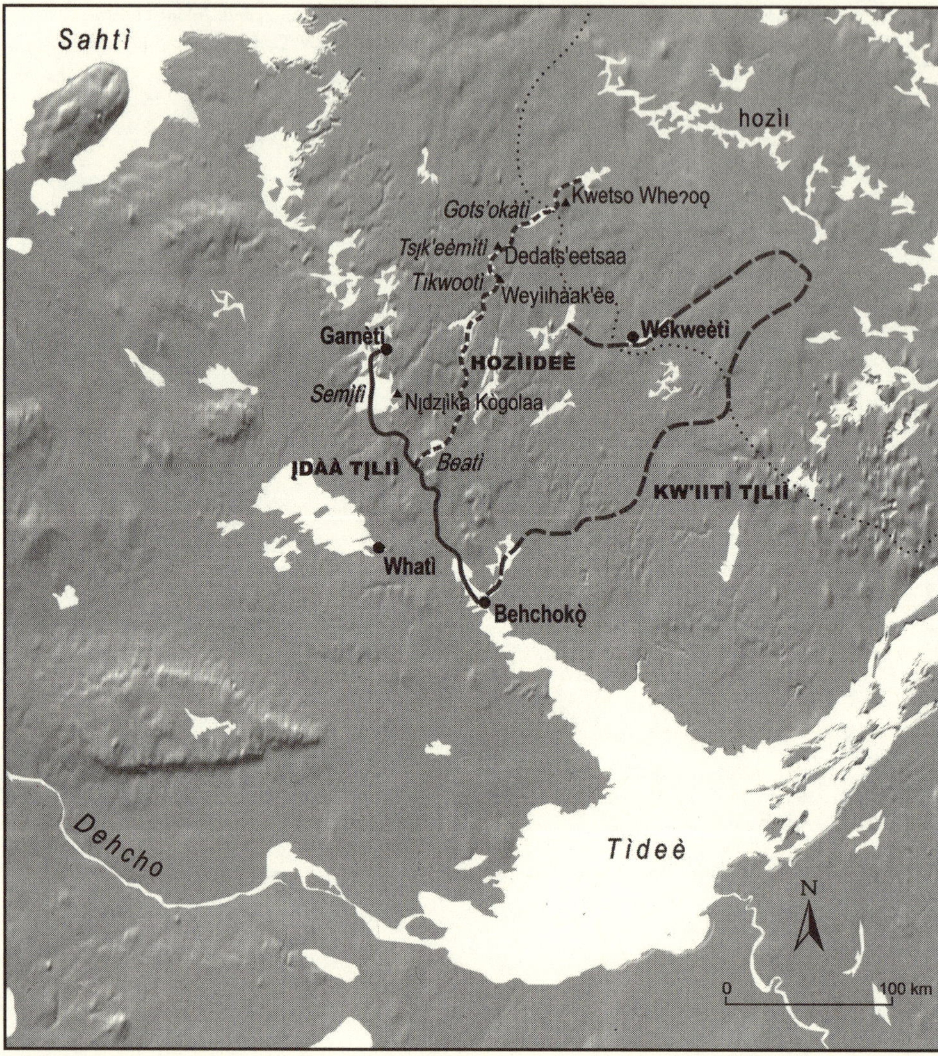

Sahtì
hozìı
Kwetso Wheʔoǫ
Gots'okàtì
Tsı̨k'eèmìtì
Dedats̨'eetsaa
Tıkwootì
Weyìıhàak'èe
Wekweètì
Gamètì
HOZÌIDEÈ
Semı̨fı
Nı̨dzı̨ika Kògolaa
Į̀DAÀ TĮLIÌ
Beatì
KW'IITÌ TĮLIÌ
Whatì
Behchokǫ̀
Dehcho
Tìdeè
N
0
100 km

CHAPTER 3

Whaèhdǫǫ̀ Etǫ K'e

JOHN B. ZOE AND JESSICA DUNKIN

The fleet of thirty-odd big canoes carrying the flag of the Tłı̨chǫ Nation stretches out across the water, bows pointed toward land.[1] Spread along the shoreline are fathers, aunties, brothers, and grandmothers, awaiting the arrival of the canoes bearing their daughters, uncles, wives, and grandsons. They are also welcomed by drummers, their voices rising up above the crowd, calling the travellers to the community. A volley of gunshots announces the arrival of the boats, an echo of the fur trade when gun salutes preceded hunters coming to deliver their furs. As the canoes reach the shore, the paddlers tumble onto the beach. Emotions are high. Tears are shed. Those on land feel the energy the travellers bring with them. They pass it on as they shake hands and are welcomed to the gathering. They also bring news of the trail.

Whaèhdǫǫ̀ Etǫ K'è (The Trails of Our Ancestors) began in 1995 as a way to return Tłı̨chǫ to the land, and also to bring the experience and energy of the land into the meetings and discussions happening as part of the Tłı̨chǫ Annual Gathering. The trips continue today. Every summer, groups of five to six canoes, each carrying six paddlers, travel from each of the four Tłı̨chǫ settlements (Behchokǫ̀, Whatì, Gamètì, and Wekweètì) in what is now known as the Northwest Territories, arriving at the host community just in time for the opening of the gathering.

The importance of the canoe to Tłı̨chǫ lifeways past and present is visible in the myriad portage trails that criss-cross an area of more than 295,000 square kilometres stretching between Tìdeè (Great Slave Lake) and Sahtì

(Great Bear Lake). Canoes and canoeing also permeate Tłı̨chǫ oral tradition. Before contact, canoes enabled travel across a vast territory in search of sustenance. Canoes were also a vehicle for acquiring knowledge. Canoe trails link together named places "like beads on a string," each named place holding stories that transmit information about Tłı̨chǫ cosmology, governance, and lifeways.[2] It is no coincidence that Elder Harry Simpson likened Tłı̨chǫ nèk'e (literally, the place where Tłı̨chǫ belong) to a book. Travel is vital to Tłı̨chǫ ways of knowing, because stories that bring forward ancestral knowledge are best told in the places they belong. As Tłı̨chǫ travel and hear the stories, they become knowledgeable.[3]

With contact, the canoe became a tool of trade. The canoe was also appropriated by colonizers, used to gain access to the riches of Tłı̨chǫ territory. Canoe use among Tłı̨chǫ declined with settlement in the middle part of the twentieth century—fewer people were spending time on the land—but also with the arrival of outboard motors and planes.

During land claim negotiations in the 1990s, the canoe re-emerged as a way to not only bring Tłı̨chǫ together but also to revitalize the connection between the people and the land. Even after the Tłı̨chǫ Land Claims and Self-Government Agreement was signed with the Government of the Northwest Territories and the Government of Canada in 2003—among other things, the agreement recognizes Tłı̨chǫ authority over their lands and their right to travel and live as their ancestors have done since time immemorial—Whaèhdǫǫ̀ Etǫ K'è continued because leaders understood the importance of the canoe to implementing the land claim. Whaèhdǫǫ̀ Etǫ K'è provides participants with opportunities to visit sites and to hear the stories in place.

Taking the shape of a canoe journey, this chapter travels to key places in Tłı̨chǫ nèk'e. The result is a map of historical and contemporary relations of Tłı̨chǫ with the canoe. We begin at Dedats'eetsaa (Figure 3.1), an imposing rock promontory on the trail to Gots'ǫkàtì (Mesa Lake) between Tıkwootì (Brown Water Lake) and Tsı̨k'eèmìtì (Emile River). Dedats'eetsaa, which has an open crevasse at the top, has long functioned as a repository for Tłı̨chǫ travelling north, a place of safekeeping for valuable things not needed at that time. Dedats'eetsaa serves as an important metaphor for Tłı̨chǫ today as they retrieve knowledge from the land left by the ancestors to chart a way forward.

FIGURE 3.1. Dedats'eetsaa. Photo: Petter Jacobsen.

FIGURE 3.2. Weyìıhàak'èe. Photo: John B. Zoe.

Whaèhdǫǫ̀ Etǫ K'è[4]

Tłı̨chǫ nèk'e holds stories about the origins of Tłı̨chǫ. These stories from the time of Yamǫǫ̀zha tell Tłı̨chǫ about their relations with the animals and the land.[5] They describe a time of coexistence. When Yamǫǫ̀zha and his brother were young, they went their separate ways. They eventually reunited here at Weyìıhàak'èe (Figure 3.2) as older men. These stories from before contact, from the time when people lived by the rules of Yamǫǫ̀zha, continue to exist. Tłı̨chǫ are reminded of them whenever they paddle or walk past this place.

Prior to contact, most Tłı̨chǫ canoes were made of birchbark, though there were different styles.[6] The most popular was k'ıelà, a small hunting canoe suitable for one or two people travelling on inland waterways.[7] K'ıelà were so light a paddler could carry two across a portage at one time with a spacer between them to avoid rubbing. Owing to their size, k'ıelà were relatively easy to make and repair. The latter fact was important because punctures were common during portages. For travel on larger bodies of water, Tłı̨chǫ used k'ıts'ı, large freighter canoes that measured five to seven metres in length and carried six people.

Tłı̨chǫ passed the summer at locations with proven fisheries. In late July or early August, families would load up their canoes and begin the long journey to hozìı (the barrenlands) to harvest caribou. K'ıelà were only large enough for people and gear, so dogs travelled on the land, following the calls of the canoeists. The going was slow because Tłı̨chǫ travelled close to the shorelines, in part to stay connected to their dogs.

The ancestors carried in their memories the migration patterns of ekwò (caribou). Having lived alongside ekwò for millennia and depended on them for survival, Tłı̨chǫ had intimate knowledge of the routes the ungulates travelled and also the timing of their migrations. The first sighting of ekwò was significant, prompting hunters to weigh the location of the caribou against their knowledge of the routes and make decisions about travel over the coming months. As fall drew to a close, Tłı̨chǫ followed ekwò back below the tree line to their wintering grounds. The final harvest happened in the spring before the ice was off the lakes.

Tłı̨chǫ built canoes as the sun returned and the snow melted but while lakes were still frozen. The spring ice made it easier to walk to different sites and gather the necessary materials: birchbark, spruce poles and roots, and spruce gum.[8] It was also easier to harvest birchbark in the spring when the sap was running.

Building canoes was a communal practice; canoe-making sites were often in shouting distance of one another. Women and men worked together to build canoes. Children were enlisted to chew the gum used for sealing and to gather moss to line the frame. A serviceable canoe could be built in as little as five days, though more commonly it took twice that long.

Today, the trained eye can find evidence of the sites used for construction and harvesting.[9] Construction sites are usually inland, because canoes were often made at winter and spring camps. Typically, there's a small depression, about four to five feet in length, filled with football-sized rocks. The bottom of the canoe would rest in the depression lined with moss. Some rocks were placed inside the frame to weigh it down, while others were placed along the outside to hold the sides in. A closer look at stands of birch near to the construction sites and beyond—birchbark was one of the items Tłı̨chǫ travelled further afield to find—might reveal trees with squares of bark missing. Tłı̨chǫ were careful to harvest only the outer layer of bark, so the tree could continue to give bark for future craft.[10] Birch stands are one of the named places in Tłı̨chǫ nèk'e.

There are a few of the old canoes left. John B. Zoe has seen some during his travels through Tłı̨chǫ nèk'e. While visiting Gamètì, John and Tom Andrews, then the territorial archaeologist, approached an older man who had heard they were looking for information about the old ways. He suggested they speak to his wife, Marie Mantla. Over a cup of tea, Marie told them about a trip to Behchokǫ̀ she made with her father and her brother, Harry Simpson, when she was a young woman. It was a memorable trip because she was married while they were in the community. On the return trip, the group travelled as far as Beatì, where they overnighted. When they woke the next morning, the lake was completely frozen, so they stowed their canoes by the shoreline and in time made sleds and harnesses for the dogs. They continued north by dog team when there was enough snow on the ground.

During archaeological surveys conducted between 1991 and 1994, John, Tom, and Harry camped on Beatì. Without prompting, Harry found his way to the place where his father had stored the canoes many years before. They were still there. Harry didn't remember the trip or the place, but Marie had shared details from the journey and explained the location of the canoes.

Harry explained: "I was too young, but my sister told me that this big one was the one that my dad and I paddled in. I sat behind him, pretending to paddle." The second canoe had carried Marie and her new husband.

One of the canoes had sustained a puncture during a portage, which Harry's father repaired with a strip of birchbark from a nearby tree. Harry, John, and Tom were able to find the tree that provided the bark. Records show the marriage took place in 1939, so the canoes were fifty-two years old. They did not look much like canoes at that point. They were flattened out and missing some of the scrolls of birchbark, but the frame and ribs were visible. In 2015, John returned to this same spot. The canoes, now seventy-six years old, were still there.[11] According to Harry, this was the last time that people had exclusively used birchbark canoes, in 1939. Until the arrival of motorboats in the 1960s, Tłı̨chǫ canoe builders used canvas instead of birchbark to cover the frame.

Concerned that the knowledge and skills used to build birchbark canoes would be lost, Tłı̨chǫ partnered with the Prince of Wales Northern Heritage Centre on a canoe-building project in 1996.[12] At a bush camp near Behchokǫ̀, three youth apprentices assisted six Tłı̨chǫ Elders as they crafted a birchbark canoe. None of the Elders had built a birchbark canoe by themselves before, though all had watched and assisted with birchbark canoes when they were younger. They also had experience building canoes covered with canvas. The boat made during that workshop, which is of a more modern style, is now on display at Chief Jimmy Bruneau School in Edzo, Northwest Territories.

Tsàwò Nàedìı Adzà Tł'axǫ̀ǫ̀[13]

Kwetso Wheʔoǫ is a large granite rock on Gots'okàtì in the barrenlands near to the place where peace was made between Dene leaders Edzo and Akaitcho in the early 1800s, after a long and difficult conflict (Figure 3.3). The canoe played an important role in the talks that led to the brokering of peace between the peoples of Edzo and Akaitcho.

In addition to reshaping relations between Dene, the trade in furs changed how Tłı̨chǫ organized themselves as well as when and how they travelled. Trading chiefs transformed existing campsites into little villages. On the shore of Semı̨̀tì (Faber Lake) on Į̀dàà Tı̨lıì (Į̀dàà Trail), the remains of large stone fireplaces and cabin foundations are evidence of Nı̨dzı̨ìka Kògolaa

FIGURE 3.3. Pierre Judas, Johnny Eyakfwo, and Johnny Bishop at Kwetso Wheʔoǫ, 1988. Photo: John B. Zoe.

FIGURE 3.4. Robert Mackenzie, Jimmy B. Rabesca, and Johnny Eyakfwo at Nı̨dzı̨ika Kògolaa, 1995. Photo: Aaron Herter.

(Figure 3.4), the name given to the village of K'aàwıdaà, a well-known Tłı̨chǫ trader. People would spread out during the year. In the winter, they would bring their goods to the trading chief. The canoe was no longer just a vehicle for living and understanding more; it had become a vital tool for negotiating the rhythms and demands of the fur trade.

Treaty making provided another reason for people to gather, further altering travel patterns and seasonal cycles. Tłı̨chǫ, under the leadership of Chief Mǫhwhìı, are signatories to Treaty 11 (1921).[14] Beginning in 1922, Tłı̨chǫ travelled to Behchokǫ̀ by canoe every July to mark treaty days. Treaty days served symbolic, economic, and social purposes. They represented a yearly renewing of the relationship between Tłı̨chǫ and the Crown; they provided an opportunity for state representatives to distribute annuity payments; and, once officials left, they were a time of celebration.

Though Tłı̨chǫ had contact with capitalism through the trading post and the colonial state through treaty days, they continued to live much as they had before well into the twentieth century, following the same seasonal cycles that had given shape to their ancestors' lives since time immemorial. Life changed dramatically in the 1960s.

A growing interest on the part of the Canadian state in northern affairs because of the Cold War and a new approach to Indigenous issues prompted the federal government to initiate a number of new policies and services that had profound impacts on Tłı̨chǫ.[15] Compulsory schooling, medical services, social assistance, and housing programs all hastened the settlement of Tłı̨chǫ in communities. These policy changes coincided with a period of shortage: the caribou were not where they were supposed to be. This further reduced the amount of time that Tłı̨chǫ were spending on the land. Some people continued to travel to hozìı for caribou meat, which they hauled back to the community and placed in the community freezer. Increasingly, however, the journey to the tundra was made in planes. By the 1970s, canoeing or boating to the barrenlands had all but ended.

Dè Ghǫ Nàyaetıı[16]

In the 1970s, the Indian Brotherhood of the Northwest Territories (which later became the Dene Nation) and the Métis Association of the Northwest Territories joined forces to negotiate a single comprehensive land claim for the Indigenous peoples of the Mackenzie Valley, including Tłįchǫ. Their action was inspired by unfulfilled treaty obligations. In 1988, an agreement-in-principle was reached between the Dene and Métis of the Northwest Territories and the Government of Canada. The following year, Tłįchǫ chiefs asked John B. Zoe to step into the recently vacated position of regional negotiator for the Tłįchǫ. In the ensuing months, John travelled to the four Tłįchǫ communities, often by boat and snowmachine, to sit with and listen to the Elders. The purpose of his education was to make clear to government negotiators that the land belonged to the Dene and that they could no longer take resources without consideration for or consultation with the Indigenous peoples who had lived on this land since time immemorial.

The Dene-Métis Claim fell apart in 1990.[17] Later, John would become the chief negotiator for the Tłįchǫ when they decided to pursue a regional claim. For the time being, he busied himself with part-time work in the community and research out on the land. He made a point of continuing to spend time with Elders, listening to stories and documenting place names on maps.

Discussions of reinvigorating the claim at a regional level began in 1991. The following year, Tłįchǫ chiefs organized a gathering to gauge community interest in returning to the negotiating table. The assembly was held in the recently completed cultural centre in Behchokǫ̀. People travelled from the other Tłįchǫ communities by kicker boat. The next year, the Treaty 11 Council hosted a similar gathering in Wekweètì, followed by one in Whatì in 1994 and in Gamètì in 1995. Each year, motorboats brought people to the gathering from the other communities.

During the same period, John worked with the territorial archaeologist, Tom Andrews, on surveys of Tłįchǫ nèk'e. John served as the interpreter for the third member of the survey team, Elder Harry Simpson. The two men shared a tent, so there was no shortage of opportunities for John to learn from Harry. During their third summer out, Harry remarked that in all of that time, they had seen lots of non-Tłįchǫ people but none of their own people: "What happened to us? We're all stuck in the community. We're not on the trail anymore. We aren't running into our own people. Maybe it's time." There was also the matter of the ongoing land claim negotiations. In John's words: "If we're going to talk about the land and the land claim, we need to get people out on the land, living on the land. You can talk all you want, but you need context. You need to be on the land." Both men saw the utility in something that could connect Tłįchǫ with one another and with the land. The canoe seemed the perfect vehicle for that.

At the time, both Harry and John served on the school board, so they approached the superintendent about organizing a trip that would involve students. Harry and John were adamant that whatever they did, it had to involve paddling. Flying prevented travellers from seeing the places in between. Motorboats travelled too fast and weren't able to go into the shallows. There was also the matter of weight: gas and motors are heavy on the portage trail.

There was a precedent for these kinds of trips. In 1988, the Rae-Edzo Friendship Centre, with the support of an Elders group and the GNWT Department of Economic Development (a predecessor of the Department of Environment and Natural Resources), had organized a trip to Gots'okàtì.[18] With the exception of some Elders who went by plane, the participants, who came from Behchokǫ̀ and Gamètì, travelled by canvas boat and kicker. Hundreds of people participated. A similar project was organized the following year by the Dogrib Divisional Board of Education at a site near Wekweètì.

Whaèhdǫǫ̀ Etǫ K'è

The first Whaèhdǫǫ̀ Etǫ K'è trip ran in 1995. Over the course of fifteen days, five twenty-two-foot canoes, each powered by students from the local high school and directed by an Elder, paddled from Behchokǫ̀ up Hozìıdeè to Gamètì, returning on the Įdàà Tįlıì. Įdàà Tįlıì is an important travel route for Tłįchǫ. Comprising two rivers, the Marion and the Camsell, that link together Tìdeè and Sahtì, the trail was historically travelled by canoe in summer and dog team in winter, each using slightly different routes. There are forty-one portages along the route; the longest is just over four kilometres.[19]

John recalls landing in Gamètì that first year: "You can see the emotions of the people and the young people in the boats. You can feel the energy. You can never re-create it. It's like a powerful awakening. People would cry. Wow! This thing is really powerful, especially for young people connecting and for the community, bringing back memories."

The canoes arrived in time for the annual gathering. The timing was deliberate. By 1995, the annual gatherings had become an important occasion for Tłįchǫ to discuss issues related to community life. However, as John and others observed, these rarely had anything to do with the land. The leaders, who at that time were actively involved in land claim negotiations, realized that if they were going to talk about the land, they needed to bring the energy of the land into the meetings. Whaèhdǫǫ̀ Etǫ K'è did this. The leadership observed that participants felt a profound need to protect the land they had just been on. Not to mention that the trips made the place names and the stories that provided the context for the land claim real.

Because of the importance of the annual gathering to the decision-making process during the land claim negotiations, and because the canoe trips have preceded every gathering since 1995, the claim and Whaèhdǫǫ̀ Etǫ K'è have been intertwined from the acceptance of the framework to the agreement-in-principle to the signing of the final agreement in 2003.[20] Whaèhdǫǫ̀ Etǫ K'è was part of the widespread support for the land claim and Tłı̨chǫ self-government. Ninety-three percent of eligible voters cast a ballot at a special gathering on 27 June 2003. Eighty-four percent of those who voted supported the claim.[21]

The Treaty 11 Council commemorated the ratification of the Tłı̨chǫ Agreement with a short film, *Gonaèwo: Our Way of Life*, linking treaty and land claim negotiations with Tłı̨chǫ canoe travel past and present.[22] The accompanying booklet is even more explicit in making connections between the canoe and self-government. The booklet chronicles the steps of ratification, each represented by a different part of the canoe building process. Step one, Amèe Tłı̨chǫ ne sìı cha nı̨htł'è eghàlagìıde dǫǫ dǫ gı̨zì dek'enıgeetł'è (the eligibility committee begins enrolment), is represented by a canoe builder seeking out birchbark. In the drawing for step five, Dǫ ek'ètehtso ehtsì ha dıì-le ts'aata nı̨htłe whela (voters list ready), men and women are building the frame that will hold the canoe together. In the final step, Wexèhoıwı dzę̨ę̨ (effective date), a Tłı̨chǫ youth takes to the water in the newly completed k'ıelà.

The relationship between the land claim and the canoe is also evident in the Tłı̨chǫ flag, itself a visual representation of the Tłı̨chǫ Agreement. Designed by James Wah-shee, the flag features four tents, one for each of the four Tłı̨chǫ communities. The sun rising over a flowing river captures Chief Mǫhwhıì's words during the signing of Treaty 11: "As long as the sun rises, the river flows, and the land does not move, we will not be restricted from our way of life." This element also represents the relationship between the

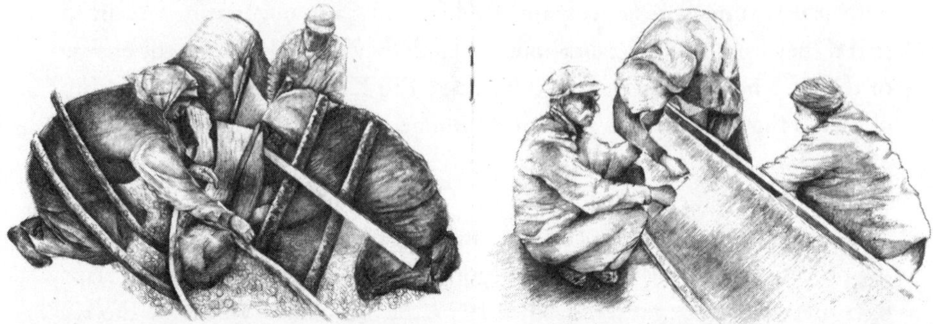

FIGURE 3.5. Step 5: Dǫ ek'ètehtso ehtsì ha dıì-le ts'aata nı̨htł'e whela (voters list ready) from *Gonaèwo: Our Way of Life* (2003).

FIGURE 3.6. Tłı̨chǫ flag. Designed by James Wah-Shee.

Tłı̨chǫ Nation and other nations, including Canada. The river creates a space for collaboration between nations that does not jeopardize the authority of any party. In the top right corner of the flag, the North Star, which signifies the coming generations, represents hope for the future. The royal blue background is Tłı̨chǫ territory, territory best travelled by canoe.

Even after the signing of the Tłı̨chǫ Agreement, the need for Whaèhdǫǫ̀ Etǫ K'è and canoe travel remained to aid in the implementation of the claim.

As in previous years, the paddlers brought the energy of the land to the annual gatherings and the people making important decisions.

The presence of Tłı̨chǫ travelling their territory is both a physical and symbolic act of resistance to colonial efforts to remove Tłı̨chǫ from the land. Being on the land has also had the effect of bringing back the memories of the old people and reinvigorating Tłı̨chǫ culture and traditions. Whaèhdǫǫ̀ Etǫ K'è has produced more modest benefits as well. It provides youth with structure, introduces them to new skills, welcomes them into a supportive community, and creates opportunities for personal growth and character building. There are more young people going out by boat now because they feel increasingly comfortable travelling in this way.

It was not just the timing of the Whaèhdǫǫ̀ Etǫ K'è that was deliberate but the choice of boats as well. Big canoes appealed for a number of reasons, not least because they recall k'ıts'ı, the large freighter canoes traditionally used by Tłı̨chǫ for travel on big lakes. They are also more stable, especially on larger lakes. Big canoes make it easier to keep the group together and allow people in the boats to communicate with each other. More canoes were purchased as time passed and interest in the trips increased. Today, five new canoes are added to the fleet each summer, while others are retired. The program administrators have worked with Western Canoe Kayak, the manufacturer of Clipper Canoes in Abbotsford, British Columbia, to develop canoes that meet the program's needs. New canoes are now fifty pounds lighter than the early Whaèhdǫǫ̀ Etǫ K'è craft, a fact that is appreciated by all!

Whaèhdǫǫ̀ Etǫ K'è continues to be a community affair. Elders make paddles. Mining companies provide lifejackets. Former participants serve as leaders. Today, the leaders receive training in water safety, bear safety, and gun safety. This is very different from the early trips, when the Elders were the guides. As they had lived and travelled on the land, the Elders were doing what was natural for them. The leaders of today only travel like this once a year, so they need extra supports.

Gonàowoò[23]

Whaèhdǫǫ̀ Etǫ K'è links past and present. It is a way of coming together annually that draws on traditional methods and strengths, but in a way that is always evolving to meet present needs. The energy gathered on the trail is shared with those who have come together for the annual gathering. This energy is also meant to carry the participants forward through the year until the next trip.

Whaèhdǫǫ̀ Etǫ K'è provides participants with a direct experience of Tłįchǫ nèk'e. They paddle the lakes and rivers. They walk the trails. They learn the place names and hear the stories held in those places. As they travel, they are following the trails of their ancestors, who had an intimate knowledge of the land and who survived because of this knowledge. Participants become more knowledgeable through travel, stories, and experience. Whaèhdǫǫ̀ Etǫ K'è is particularly powerful for young people who have not had the opportunity to spend much time on the land.

Whaèhdǫǫ̀ Etǫ K'è is vital, but there is more to be done. In the old days, many trails were used almost annually. With the current schedule, some trails are only travelled every four years and the growth of vegetation is such that travellers have to hack their way along portages. Whaèhdǫǫ̀ Etǫ K'è would also benefit from having portages with better landings. John likens the lineup of canoes at the beginning of some of the portages to planes waiting to depart LAX. A trail maintenance crew would provide people with employment. Just as importantly, it would provide them more time on the land, travelling the trails of the ancestors.

In an era of shrinking budgets and increasing concern for liabilities—not to mention the competition that exists for people's time and attention—it is no easy task to maintain initiatives like Whaèhdǫǫ̀ Etǫ K'è. If you rest, John observes, things go back to the way they were before, just like the trails travelled by the canoeists. In the old days, Tłįchǫ lived on and with the land. It was their way of life. Today, Tłįchǫ have many options as well as pressures that prevent them from spending time on the land. This makes initiatives like Whaèhdǫǫ̀ Etǫ K'è all the more important, not just because they maintain the connection between Tłįchǫ, the land, and the stories, but because activities like this also strengthen Tłįchǫ governance. Land-based programs empower the disenfranchised and maintain a balance between the people and the leadership.

In the old days, as Tłįchǫ paddled north to hozìı from their summer campsites, they stopped at Dedats'eetsaa to leave the things they did not need at that time. Later, they would return to this spot and retrieve their belongings. Named places throughout Tłįchǫ nèk'e serve a similar purpose, holding stories and knowledge about how to live as Tłı̨chǫ. Throughout the journey to and from the tundra, Tłı̨chǫ would stop at these named places to hear the stories. Over the course of this chapter, as Tłı̨chǫ have done for millennia, we have travelled northward, gathering stories about Tłı̨chǫ and the canoe. The canoe, we have seen, has been a feature of every chapter in Tłı̨chǫ history. It remains a vital symbol and tool in contemporary Tłı̨chǫ life. We have collected these stories so that we too can leave something for the future.

Notes

1 From the Tłı̨chǫ Constitution: "We are the Tłı̨chǫ. We are an Aboriginal people of Canada. We are a people of the North. We follow in the footsteps of our ancestors and acknowledge our Elders as the keepers of our living memory, self-determination, values and way of life... The Tłı̨chǫ Nation is one united Aboriginal People.... The Tłı̨chǫ Nation is composed of four communities—Behchokö (Rae-Edzo), Whatì (Lac La Martre), Gamètì (Rae Lakes), and Wekweètì (Snare Lake). Each community is a unique and valued part of the Tłı̨chǫ Nation." Tłı̨chǫ Constitution (2005), https://www.tlicho.ca/sites/default/files/documents/government/tlichoconstitution.pdf (accessed 27 September 2018).

2 Thomas D. Andrews and John B. Zoe, "The Dogrib Birchbark Canoe Project," *Arctic* 51, no. 1 (March 1998): 75.

3 Thomas Andrews, John Zoe, and Aaron Herter, "On Yamǫǫ̀zah's Trail: Dogrib Sacred Sites and the Anthropology of Travel," in *From Sacred Lands: Aboriginal Worldviews, Claims, and Conflicts*, ed. Jill Oakes, Rick Riewe, Kathi Kinew, and Elaine Maloney (Edmonton: Canadian Circumpolar Institute, 1998), 312.

4 "Whaèhdǫǫ̀ Etǫ K'è," in this context, means "the way of the ancestors" or "the old ways."

5 Yamǫǫ̀zha is the Tłı̨chǫ name for a powerful being, a traveller and lawmaker, who helped establish a relationship of respect and understanding between the Dene and the animals. Though known by different names in different Dene communities, Yamǫǫ̀zha is remembered by people across Denendeh (the land of the Dene).

6 According to Tłı̨chǫ oral tradition, spruce bark canoes were also built, though rarely. Andrews and Zoe, "The Dogrib Birchbark Canoe Project," 75.

7 K'ıelà typically measured three and a half to five metres in length. Ibid., 77.

8 A more detailed account of the construction of Tłı̨chǫ k'ielà can be found in ibid., 77–79.

9 During an archaeological survey in the early 1990s, John B. Zoe and Tom Andrews recorded the remains of nearly thirty k'ielà. Most were found near portages, where they had been stored in anticipation of future journeys. Ibid., 75. See also Thomas D. Andrews and John B. Zoe, "The Įdaà Trail: Archaeology and the Dogrib Cultural Landscape, Northwest Territories, Canada," in *At a Crossroads: Archaeology and First Peoples in Canada*, ed. G.P. Nicholas and T.D. Andrews (Vancouver: Simon Fraser University Press), 160–77. Forest fires make canoe-building sites easier to find. In recent years, forest fires have been more frequent in Tłı̨chǫ nèk'e.

10 Andrews and Zoe, "The Dogrib Birchbark Canoe Project," 80.

11 A better-preserved example of a Tłı̨chǫ birchbark canoe can be found at the Prince of Wales Northern Heritage Centre in Yellowknife. The canoe was made by the late Tłı̨chǫ Chief Jimmy Bruneau. "Canoe Object 973.027.001a," Prince of Wales Northern Heritage Centre, https://www.pwnhc.ca/item/canoe/ (accessed 4 May 2018).

12 The project was documented in print and film. Andrews and Zoe, "The Dogrib Birchbark Canoe Project"; and *Dogrib Birchbark Canoe Project* (Lone Woolf Productions, 1997), https://www.youtube.com/watch?v=fW1PAKPHam8 (accessed 1 May 2018).

13 "Tsàwo nàedìi adzà tłaxǫ̀ǫ̀" means "after they started selling furs." Tłı̨chǫ harvested furs for use prior to contact. The notable shift in Tłı̨chǫ lifeways came not with encountering Europeans but with the commercialization of the fur harvest.

14 Treaty 11 is the last of the numbered treaties. The Canadian government delayed treaty negotiations with northern Indigenous communities until it proved economically and politically expedient. The prospect of oil and gas development in the Mackenzie Valley provided the impetus for the government to enter into talks with the predominantly Dene nations in the North. Tłı̨chǫ understood the hastily negotiated treaties differently than the state did. Most importantly, they did not consent to surrendering their title to the land. In the words of Chief Mǫhwhìı, "as long as the sun rises, the river flows, and the land does not move, we will not be restricted from our way of life." Rene Fumoleau, *As Long as This Land Shall Last: A History of Treaty 8 and Treaty 11, 1870–1939* (Calgary: University of Calgary Press, 1973/2004).

15 Allice Legat, *Walking the Land, Feeding the Fire: Knowledge and Stewardship among the Tłı̨chǫ Dene* (Tucson: University of Arizona Press, 2012), 113.

16 "Dè Ghǫ Nàyaetıı" refers to the process of working through differences. In this case, it describes the land claim negotiation process that was ongoing in the 1980s to 2000s.

17 Peter Keith Kulchyski, *Like the Sound of a Drum: Aboriginal Cultural Politics in Denendeh and Nunavut* (Winnipeg: University of Manitoba Press, 2006).

18 The trip grew out of an Elders forum hosted by the Friendship Centre at which organizers asked, "What can we do to bring back our languages, our way of life, things that people used to do?" The Elders responded, "Go back to the barrens." The Elders knew that the history is out there in the land. Merely talking about history and the land in the community does not do it justice.

19 Andrews and Zoe, "The Įdaà Trail," 163.

20 Tłı̨chǫ Agreement (Ottawa, 2003), https://www.tlicho.ca/content/tlicho-agreement (accessed 4 May 2018). The Tłı̨chǫ Land Claims and Self-Government Agreement was signed on 25 August 2003, eighty-two years to the day that Chief Mo̧hwhìı signed Treaty 11. The Tłı̨chǫ Agreement was the first combined land claim and self-government agreement in the Northwest Territories.

21 "Do you approve the Tłı̨chǫ Agreement?," https://tlichohistory.ca/en/stories/do-you-approve-tłı̨chǫ-agreement (accessed 4 May 2018); Mary C. Hurley, *Bill C-14: The Tłı̨chǫ Land Claims and Self-Government Act*, (Canada: Parliamentary Information and Research Service, Library of Parliament, 29 October 2004), https://www.parl.ca/LegisInfo/BillDetails.aspx?Language=en&-Mode=1&billId=1406315 (accessed 30 June 2020).

22 *Gonaèwo: Our Way of Life* (Treaty 11 Council, 2003), http://film.tlicho.ca/films/tlicho-government/gonaewo-our-way-life (accessed 27 September 2018).

23 "Gonàowoò" translates as "our way of life." It refers, in this case, to the continuation of the Tłı̨chǫ way of life long into the future.

PART TWO

Building Canoes, Knowledge, and Relationships

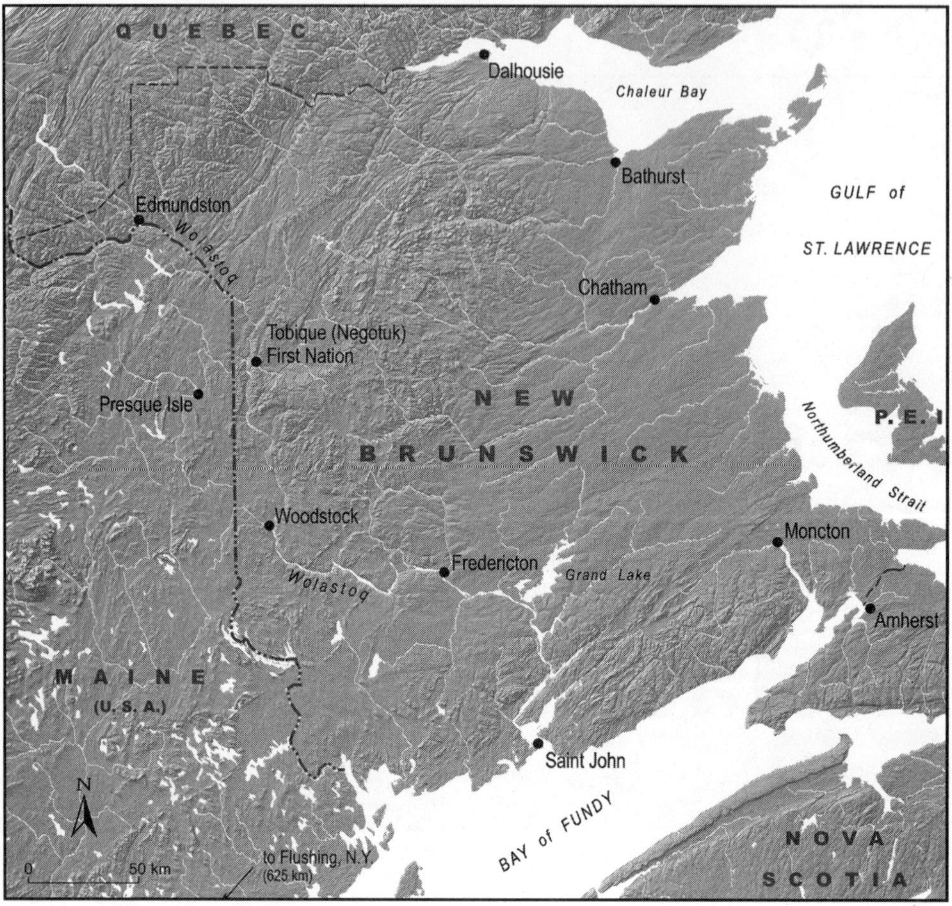
QUEBEC
Dalhousie
Chaleur Bay
Bathurst
GULF of
ST. LAWRENCE
Edmundston
Wolastoq
Chatham
Tobique (Negotuk)
First Nation
Presque Isle
NEW
BRUNSWICK
P. E. I
Northumberland Strait
Woodstock
Moncton
Fredericton
Grand Lake
Wolastoq
Amherst
MAINE
(U. S. A.)
Saint John
N
BAY of FUNDY
NOVA
SCOTIA
0
50 km
to Flushing, N.Y.
(625 km)

CHAPTER 4

Model Canoes, Territorial Histories, and Linguistic Resurgence: Decolonizing the Tappan Adney Archives

CHRIS LING CHAPMAN

I have only ever seen photographs of Tappan Adney's model canoes. One of these images stands out in my mind: Adney (1868–1950), the epitome of a Victorian sportsman in a white sportscoat and trousers, hunting boots and knee-high socks, perches awkwardly on a bed in a cramped study, examining a miniature canoe. It is a graceful birchbark hunting canoe, whose sides arch to perfectly symmetrical ends over a length of about two feet. The woodwork and lashing are visible even at a distance. On the floor next to him is a tiny toboggan, similarly scaled and impressively detailed. If these objects look foreign in his presence, it is the fault of photographic convention; the pair belongs to an extensive collection of scale models Adney spent decades building in the late nineteenth and early twentieth centuries. Today distributed across various North American museums,[1] Adney's models represent not only more than 100 birchbark, cedar, canvas, and skin canoes but a wide array of useful belongings of First Nations peoples living in Canada during his lifetime. Common objects like a simple fishing spear, hunting pouch, or broomstick[2] are given the same care and attention as the most intricate of canoes, to the point that considering them models—in the sense that the term denotes mere representation or imitation—does little to recognize them as living archives of cultural memory, language, and collective experience.

At the same time, the framing of the photograph is telling. If these objects appear as exotic curiosities in Adney's hands, it is because colonial and settler colonial societies have a reputation for making curiosities out of cultural Others. North American anthropologists working in the tradition known as salvage ethnography[3] made fetishes out of physical belongings and commodities out of intangible cultural heritage, such as Indigenous stories. Salvage archives, replete with racialized and grossly oversimplified imagery and writing, were used to advance the interests of Western societies at the expense of Indigenous ones. They are sometimes still used this way in our settler colonial present. The contemporary result is the same: the cultural and social lives of Indigenous belongings—both intellectual and physical property—are denied within Western structures of accumulation, examination, and display. Ongoing disputes surrounding cultural appropriation and repatriation tell us that these practices remain pressing concerns connected to larger issues of linguistic and territorial rights, as well as the affordances of basic dignity and humanity.

The Salvage Legacy

Adney's work is easily located in a lineage of well-known figures like Franz Boas, Edward S. Curtis, and Canadian anthropologist Diamond Jenness, a close contemporary of Adney's known for his Inuit ethnographies.[4] An American settler, Adney spent the majority of his life recording First Nations ethnographies in Canada, his interests having been captured first by the natural history of the region, then by the Maritime canoe cultures he encountered around Woodstock, New Brunswick. Consistent with the romantic ethos of the salvage era, his research was shaped by dominant tropes of tragic and inevitable cultural losses among Indigenous communities. His career as a popular journalist, photographer, and illustrator in addition to an ethnographer speaks to the ease with which mythologies about vanishing races and cultures were solidified for a Western reading public.

However, the methods involved in producing salvage archives often provided opportunities for just the opposite. Indigenous languages and other cultural practices could be remembered, and consequently were able

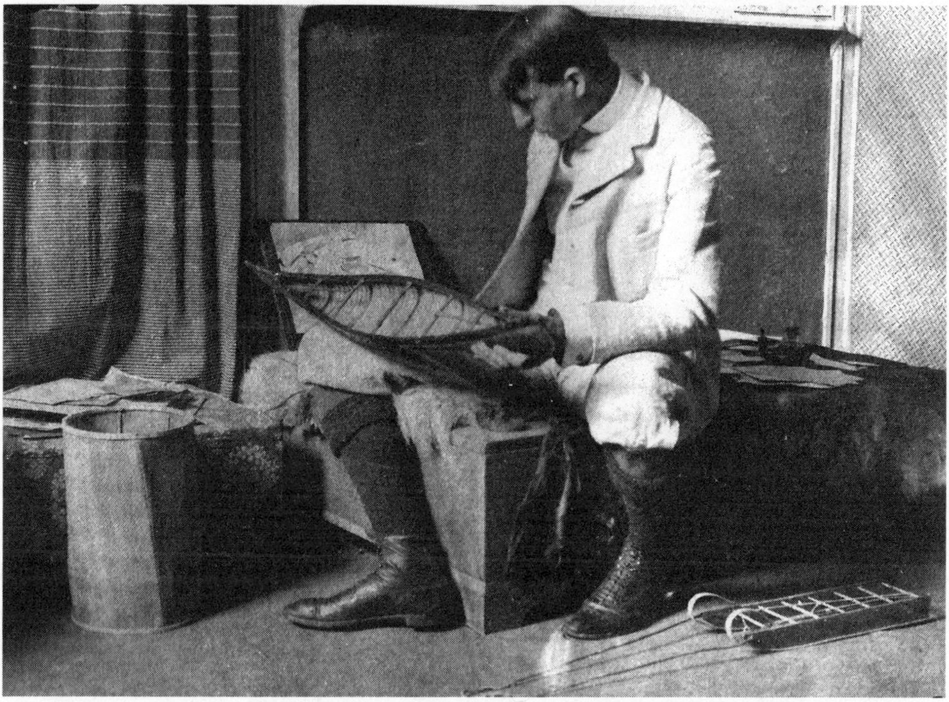

FIGURE 4.1. Edwin Tappan Adney in 1896 at his studio in Flushing, New York, with model canoe and toboggan. Source: Carleton County Historical Society.

to endure in and through these archives—sometimes exclusively through them, in cases where other ties between people, language, and land were broken. Because photographs, films, and other ethnographic documents were inevitably produced in collaboration with their subjects—Indigenous communities—they have aided in securing the transmission of vital cultural knowledge in the face of processes of cultural genocide. Adney's records of Native canoes are a clear example: models as well as photographs, illustrations, and countless notes and writings produced in the name of "salvaging" the birchbark canoe continue to be an important contemporary resource for Indigenous canoe builders. Besides enabling knowledge production of a more technical, canoe-specific kind, the canoe archives are important simply because they contain so many scenes of everyday life, work, and language—telling ethnographies not easily found on the colonial record. This argument follows a trend in archival research concerned with the protection and production of Indigenous knowledge. Legacies of individual authorship are rejected, so that archives can be recognized as the products of collective memory and ownership.

Indigenous writers and allies working with Maritime First Nations histories are already using Tappan Adney's archives in this way.[5] His extensive records of Indigenous languages and oral histories—especially records of Wolastoqiyik, the Maliseet language—are providing opportunities for the revitalization of Native words, names, and stories, and the recollection of family lineages. Travel journals Adney recorded during two lengthy New Brunswick expeditions have also been found to contain valuable information for recovering traditional territorial maps of hunting and fishing sites, as well as ancient trails and other travel routes.[6] The stories his canoe models tell appear to me to be natural extensions of this rich conversation and developing Indigenous archive. In evidencing relationships between people and places and the telling changes that took place in those relationships during Adney's lifetime, these objects do not represent a series of antiquated traditions or cultural remnants—as he and other proponents of the salvage project believed they did. Instead, they materialize traditional knowledge into a body of ever-adapting, resilient, and often resistant practices.

Objects and Language in the Adney Archive

Adney found his motivation for creating models of Indigenous objects in a typical assumption of his times: that the so-called material cultures of Indigenous peoples, including historic methods of subsistence and travel in which canoe building played a central role, would eventually disappear along with broader land-based oral traditions. Sharing the same lament one finds in Edward Curtis's writing, or in classical ethnographies like Jenness's *People of the Twilight* (1959), Adney's writings about canoe cultures urgently call for salvaging these apparently fading traditions and ways of life. None of these writers, however, tends to consistently reflect on the complicity of their own, dominant cultures in threatening the viability of Indigenous lifeways. Instead, the narrative of tragic cultural decline is an inevitable one—a product of natural, not social forces.

Maliseet historian Andrea Bear Nicholas, who hails from Tobique (Neqotkuk) First Nation, where Adney conducted years of research, reminds readers approaching this archive of its inherently problematic nature; she points out how Adney's very presence in the St. John River valley,[7] present-day New Brunswick, "amounts to a contradiction."[8] The non-Native companions appearing alongside Adney in his travelogues in Maliseet territories, she points out, were typically elites, "wealthy businessmen and politicians who created the conditions they sought to escape" by travelling with Native hunters and guides on wilderness expeditions.[9] Indigenous language represents perhaps the most potent contradiction of these journals. Without Maliseet oral traditions—the products of local knowledge embedded over time in relations between language and land—these expeditions would have been impossible. Yet the rapidly industrializing society signalled by the presence of Adney and his white companions was expropriating and destroying precisely those land bases Indigenous languages depend upon for continuity. The consequences reach into the present: Bear Nicholas has recently raised the alarming point that Wolastoqiyik, the Maliseet language, after facing centuries of settler colonial destruction, including through the operation of Indian residential schools, ranks as "critically endangered" on the UNESCO scale, having slipped two categories in only recent decades.[10]

Despite the clear complicity of a figure like Adney in structures of Indigenous dispossession, Bear Nicholas finds contemporary value in revisiting his archival practices with the present needs of her community and others he represented in mind. Her specific focus is linguistic revitalization.[11] Adney's archive is invaluable in this context because, like many ethnographers of his day, he went to great efforts to record and translate Indigenous languages he believed would vanish in his lifetime. He immersed himself for years in languages that are sometimes collectively referred to as Wabanaki[12] —focusing especially on Maliseet, Passamaquoddy, and Penobscot—and is known to have been a functional speaker of Wolastoqiyik (Maliseet). He compiled massive volumes of words, names, and phrases, leading him to a special interest in collecting Wabanaki stories and oral histories—what the nineteenth century and much of the twentieth dismissively termed "Indian folklore." Bear Nicholas tells readers how Adney's diligent record-keeping practices "gave me a direct communication to a grandfather and other ancestors I had never had the opportunity to know."[13] Reading her annotations of

Adney's descriptions of traps, deadfalls, moose shanks,[14] pirogues,[15] pitsnargans,[16] fishing spears, bear traps, steel traps, toboggans, and of course canoes of all kinds has convinced me that language—not objects, as is commonly assumed—represents the most important contribution of his archives.

Language, Linguicide, Model Canoes

The predominance of a history and politics of Indigenous languages in the Adney archive is reflected in his first recorded encounter with canoes, by way of a Passamaquoddy canoe builder named Peter Joe.[17] In a famous article published the following year, "The Building of a Birch Canoe" (1891), Adney recalled the spring day when he first laid eyes on "a certain canoe, whose graceful form . . . grew from day to day under the magic hand of its Indian builder":

> Along the St. John River, while there were many who in some fashion could build a birch canoe, those whose canoes were known for their model and substantial build could be counted on the fingers of one hand. One of these was Peter Joe . . . a kindly old man, willing to answer a boy's foolish questions about the names of birds and animals; explaining, while engaged at his labor, how to split and resplit the basket-ash, until it was but a thin, flat thread; how to bend the cedar without breaking, or how the jaws of the spear spring apart to grip the struggling salmon—everything a boy would want to know.[18]

Adney's memory of the old builder exposes a glaring contradiction. As one of the last people in his community who could remember how to build bark canoes in the "old way," with locally derived materials and tools, using ancient construction methods, Peter Joe also reflects the strained state of broader land-based oral traditions. This was as true in the Maritimes as it was in numerous Indigenous communities elsewhere in Canada at this time, though these effects were far from evenly experienced. Indeed, it can be said that Adney's first encounter with the canoes he dedicated his life to was also an encounter with the impact of Indigenous language loss resulting from a process known as linguicide.[19] A specific aspect of cultural genocide, the concept of linguicide posits that the connection between land and language in Indigenous contexts is irreducible. It recognizes how the destruction of traditional land bases is simultaneously the destruction of vital sources of spoken, embodied languages. On the one hand, "The Building of a Birch Canoe" exemplifies how readily local, land-based Indigenous knowledge is found within the Adney archives. But what is unsaid is equally important: that Adney's pastoral descriptions threaten to obscure harsher realities of everyday life for Wabanaki people, namely, how the interconnections between land and language encapsulated in the building of a canoe were increasingly unfeasible as traditional territories were violently reorganized.

The St. John River valley, known to Maliseets who have lived there from time immemorial as Wolastoq[20] or Wəlastəkw, historically supported a way of life defined by seasonal mobility for hunting, trapping, and fishing, established growing locations along the river, and extensive networks of villages. The centrality of canoes and canoe-building traditions cannot be overstated. But for more than a century before Adney visited the region, Wolastoq, or "the bright river," as it translates in English, had witnessed a dark period of colonial violence. The land had been settled rapidly around the end of the American War of Independence, at which time as many as 15,000 settlers, mostly soldiers, arrived en masse from Maine, New England, and surrounding states. The local beaver population, a prominent source of Maliseet income as well as a traditional food source, had been depleted long before during an initial wave of settlement, altering the lives of numerous families and displacing many. The new population influx also led to the destruction of traditional regional place names, a process that intensified in the years immediately following the war.[21] Bear Nicholas notes that by 1786, less than three decades after maps bearing Maliseet names for places first began to be noticeably anglicized, "virtually all Maliseet homelands along the St. John River from its mouth north to Woodstock were settled."[22]

The social history of the region helps to contextualize the state of canoe building as Adney found it. Bark canoes were still being built during his lifetime, but what were once numerous varieties even within the river valley had dwindled to only a handful by the end of the nineteenth century. There are clear reasons for the decline, most of all the availability of and access to traditional resources, increasingly affected by colonial reorganizations of time, space, and labour. As more Indigenous populations were relocated to townships and urban centres, the reserve lands allocated for them became smaller and more restrictively managed.[23] These spaces grew impoverished as the nineteenth century progressed. Adding to the dismantling of traditional land bases were assimilationist policies, including fish and game laws discouraging Indigenous sovereignty over resource access, widespread educational reforms, and the suppression or legal prohibition of traditionally spoken languages and numerous "customs" under the Indian Act.[24] Although canoe building was never banned explicitly, for many communities the land-based economies and the spaces they provided to practise oral traditions became less and less a part of daily reality. In some cases Indian Act–era prohibitions directly impacted building practices. Writing about Eastern Cree building around Great Whale River near James Bay, anthropologist Garth Taylor notes that traditional building songs disappear from descriptions of canoe construction in the early twentieth century: "The abandonment of building songs ... was probably related to intensive missionary influence around 1910. [Anglican missionary Reverend Walton] was responsible for suppressing a number of traditional practices, including drumming and singing."[25]

Considering the effects of linguicide on canoe cultures changes the stakes of an understated activity like building a miniature canoe. I would argue that in this context, the practice can be understood as a way for pressures placed upon Indigenous knowledge transmission to be actively resisted. Small canoes were part of the community and family structures of many Indigenous cultures long before Adney's lifetime. Miniature bark or carved wooden canoes were made as children's toys; more detailed and carefully decorated models served as gifts for diplomatic exchange.[26] Models more precisely replicating the designs of specific builders gained popularity in the eighteenth century, when Native craftspeople began to market their wares to tourists out of summer trading camps along the Eastern Seaboard. Considering that it was a marker of status for a trader, travelling soldier, or tourist to collect a bark canoe of a fully functional size, the portability and lower cost of a model canoe made it a popular, even commonplace commodity.[27] Indigenous builders working on commission for whites was thus a well-established practice by the nineteenth century, when Adney began his canoe research. For this reason, it is typical for vessels he documented to bear settler names and settler iconography,[28] while the Indigenous builders remain anonymous.

Miniaturization is a fitting metaphor for the commodification and consumption of Indigenous cultural heritage. There is no doubt that present examples of cultural appropriation continue a lineage of tokenizing traditional forms while ignoring their ongoing cultural lives. However, as the development of numerous Indigenous artforms attests, the appropriation-commodification story is never straightforward. For example, Abenaki filmmaker Alanis Obomsawin has described how the manufacturing of woven baskets by Indigenous women artists contributed to not only the survival but the prosperity of communities in Quebec during the late nineteenth and early twentieth centuries, difficult economic times for many Indigenous peoples in that region.[29] Similarly, Bear Nicholas points out that manufacturing baskets, canoes, and smaller items like moccasins and beadwork,[30] in addition to guiding parties of settler hunters and sportsmen, represented important means of survival for her community and others depicted in Adney's ethnographies.[31] And as in Obomsawin's example, Maliseet women, helped by children, assumed much of the responsibility for the production and sale of basketry to settler communities around Fredericton.[32] Given the disruption of family structures marked by the urbanization of Maliseet populations and loss of traditional lifestyles, material objects made for sale or personal use (often both) represent important instances of linguistic and cultural survival as well.

Territorial Histories

Adney's own model-building practice provides further insight into the complexities of knowledge transmission. Adney built his own models to a consistent scale of one to five at the recommendation of Peter Joe, a measurement he would also use in other scale models of Indigenous objects. Visible, physical construction details are practically and attractively represented at this size; it is easy to notice the intricate patterns of spruce root lashings or the subtle signatures in a particular builder's woodwork or decoration. But beyond physical considerations, the scale is important because of the way it allowed key building processes to be carried out in the same manner as with full-size canoes. An Anishinaabe canoe builder, Chuck Commanda,[33] explained to me that the one-fifth scale allows individual components of the canoe's overall structure to be handled using the crooked knife, a tool and associated way of working that is employed in not only canoe building but also basketry and carving of varying kinds by Indigenous artists across North America. Crooked knives are drawn toward the body with one hand and because of this action can be easily used without a workbench or vice—the builder's body provides the necessary bracing. The tool—and the technique it is synonymous with—is thus well suited to the portability necessary for canoe travel, something that required extensive maintenance because of the fragile nature of canoes made from bark. Crooked knives are also used by builders of dugout canoes in the Pacific Northwest. Adney's journals list the crooked knife in the travelling toolkit of Maliseet hunters. He also provides a description of the knife in "The Building of a Birch Canoe": "An implement used by woodsmen, . . . wherever in British North America I have been. In the East I was inclined to think it rather an invention of the lumbermen, until I saw in use by the Indians on the Klondike River a knife in every respect the same as that used by (my teacher in bark canoe construction) Peter Joe on the banks of the St. John. It consists of a thin, narrow blade, about three inches long . . . usually with a more or less distinct curve."[34] In short, the models provide not just an important visual representation but the tangible embodiment of an entire communicative process.

The same year Adney wrote "The Building of a Birch Canoe," he constructed a model of one of the canoes Peter Joe built.[35] Perhaps it was the vessel he described in the article, which had left in his mind the "first and most vivid impression . . . of the woods and wild things of the north."[36] If you look closely at the bow of this canoe, on a separate protective section of bark called a *wulegeiss*, you can make out "PETER JO" in block lettering. The canoe is perfectly symmetrical, fastened along its length by bright copper nails, while the rest follows the older conventional style of workmanship. Leaning across it are a paddle and a fishing spear—both of which are distinctly identifiable as Maliseet designs. The bottom of the canoe is adorned with long cedar strips notched near the ends, so that they may be temporarily fastened to the crosspieces by rawhide lashings. These were "cedar 'shoes,' used to protect the bottom of the canoe as it was being dragged up shallow rivers to avoid portages."[37] While not all of Adney's models physically bear names and signatures like this one, they all provide highly specific snapshots of localities. They are miniature local histories, accounting for changes in methods and material over time. In some models, for example, roofing asphalt and carpet tacks replace traditional spruce gum and roots,[38] remarking on a moment of industrialization and its impact on traditional land use.

These details linking people to place are especially potent considering the way other archival forms of the same period erased Indigenous histories of territorial belonging. Continuing her work on the regional dispossession of her ancestors, Bear Nicholas makes a convincing case in a recent essay that depictions of Maliseets in settler colonial artwork of the nineteenth century played a powerful role in severing them from their lands and cultures, as well as contributing to their ridicule in the urban spaces of settler communities.[39] Painters, especially landscape painters, "selectively highlighted the achievements of settler society and either ignored or misrepresented the tragic realities of the Maliseet experience."[40] A popular convention involved painting Maliseets in settings that were unnamed and/or removed of distinguishable territorial markers. "Effectively disconnect[ing] them from any specific geographical location, [and] thus avoiding the implication that they might, in fact, belong there,"[41] Bear Nicholas writes, these paintings carried real, tangible weight. She argues that in no minor way they enabled dispossession by making the violent contradictions of settlement easier to stomach by the public imagination. In a painting titled *Indian Camp, New Brunswick*, by a British officer,[42] she finds the only identifying markers of these Indian subjects in the distinctive style of their birchbark canoes.[43]

Authorship and Ownership

Adney's model collection provides archives of territorial presence that interrupt historical records characterized by representations of Indigenous absence. The social histories the models record can also be connected with broader work being done with Adney's archives, specifically community efforts involving linguistic resurgence and local histories in Maliseet First Nations. As with numerous other archives produced under similar circumstances, Indigenous scholars and allied researchers are shifting emphases from settler authorship and intentionality toward the production of Indigenous knowledge, in order to serve present and ongoing needs of Indigenous communities.

However, structures that have historically privileged settler colonial knowledge persist—and continue to threaten the stability of Indigenous knowledges. Relations between law, property, and ownership present ongoing challenges to processes of linguistic revitalization and cultural repatriation, among other avenues by which Indigenous communities pursue self-determination. A recent example involves a number of Maliseet families Bear Nicholas helped to legally represent in a decade-long dispute involving an anthropologist who collected a number of Maliseet oral histories in the 1970s and '80s. This collector refused to transfer copyright of the stories, translated for him by Maliseet elders, to the families involved. Bear Nicholas explains how Canadian laws "invest copyright in anyone who records or transcribes a story, rather than in the teller of a story (or his or her people) as originators of the intellectual content."[44]

Situations such as this one make critical practices of decolonizing archives all the more urgent. What those practices look like, however, is always varied and complex; in the case of Adney's archives, relating the intellectual products of a settler to Indigenous self-determination efforts is something that must be done cautiously and reflexively. If there is a shared thread among these diverse and often divergent practices, it is that the specificity of ties between people and place must be insisted upon.

Notes

1 The canoe models are housed together at the Mariners' Museum in Newport, Virginia.

2 The McCord Museum at McGill University in Montreal retains a miniature broom-stick Adney made from cedar and dried bound grass, replicating one that belonged to a Haudenosaunee family.

3 The term "salvage ethnography" was popularized by American anthropologists in the 1970s. See Jacob W. Gruber, "Ethnographic Salvage and the Shaping of Anthropology," *American Anthropologist* 72, no. 6 (December 1970): 1289–99.

4 Diamond Jenness, *People of the Twilight* (New York: Macmillan, 1928; Chicago: University of Chicago Press, 1959).

5 See Jason Hall, "Maliseet Cultivation and Climatic Resilience on the Welastekw/St. John River During the Little Ice Age," *Acadiensis* 44, no. 2 (2015): 3–25; Andrea Bear Nicholas, Foreword to *The Travel Journals of Tappan Adney Vol. 2, 1891–1896*, by Tappan Adney, edited by C. Ted Behne (Fredericton: Goose Lane Editions, 2014), 7–10; Andrea Bear Nicholas, "The Role of Colonial Artists in the Dispossession and Displacement of the Maliseet, 1790s–1850s," *Journal of Canadian Studies* 49, no. 2 (2015): 25–86; and Martha Walls, "Countering the 'Kingsclear Blunder': Maliseet Resistance to the Kingsclear Relocation Plan, 1945–1949," *Acadiensis* 37, no. 1 (March 2008): 3–30.

6 Adney, *The Travel Journals of Tappan Adney, Vol. 1, 1887–1890*, and *The Travel Journals of Tappan Adney, Vol. 2, 1891–96*, ed. C. Ted Behne (Fredericton, NB: Goose Lane Editions, 2010; 2014).

7 In her language this region is called Wolastoqiyik, meaning "the bright or beautiful river." Wolastoqiyik is also the Maliseet name for their language.

8 Bear Nicholas, Foreword to *The Travel Journals of Tappan Adney, Vol. 2,1891–1896*, 10.

9 Ibid.

10 Andrea Bear Nicholas, "Who Owns Indigenous Cultural and Intellectual Property?" Institute for Research on Public Policy: Policy Options. June 2017. http://policyoptions.irpp.org/magazines/june-2017/who-owns-indigenous-cultural-and-intellectual-property/.

11 Bear Nicholas served as a contributing editor of two volumes of Adney's travel journals. See *The Travel Journals of Tappan Adney, Vol. 1, 1887–1890*, and *The Travel Journals of Tappan Adney, Vol. 2, 1891–96*.

12 The Wabankai Confederacy of the seventeenth century was composed of five principal Nations: the Mi'kmaq, Maliseet, Passamaquoddy, Penobscot, and Abenaki. The Confederacy was formally disbanded in 1862 but the Nations remain closely connected. For contemporary usage of the word Wabanaki that is related to but also importantly distinct from this historical designation, see Michelle Lacombe, "More Than Where the Heart Is: Meeting Places in Wabanaki Poetry by Cheryl Savageau and Mihku Paul," *Journal of Canadian Studies* 49, no. 2 (2015): 133–49.

13 Bear Nicholas, Foreword to *The Travel Journals of Tappan Adney, Vol. 2,1891–1896*, 7.

14 Adney, *Travel Journals, Vol. 2*, 317. A footwear for moose hunters made from the animal's hind quarters.

15 Ibid., 82. A kind of crude canoe that can be fashioned quickly from a fallen log.

16 Ibid., 324 and 344. A tool bag; from pitsəakən, a Maliseet word for "pocket."

17 Adney mistakenly assumed Peter Joe was Maliseet.

18 Adney,"The Building of a Birch Canoe," *Outing, an Illustrated Monthly Magazine of Recreation (1885–1906)* 36, no. 2 (May 1900): 185–86.

19 Andrea Bear Nicholas,"Linguicide and Land Expropriation," *Briarpatch* 40, no. 2 (Mar/Apr 2011): 5

20 Adney refers to it in his article as Wallastook and to Maliseets as Wallastook people.

21 Andrea Bear Nicholas,"Settler Imperialism and Dispossession of the Maliseet: 1758–1765." In *Shaping an Agenda for Atlantic Canada,* edited by John G. Reid and Donald J. Savoie (Halifax: Fernwood Publishing, 2011), 27.

22 Ibid.

23 For a critical history of the formation of reserves in Canada, see Cole Harris,"The Joint Indian Reserve Commission, 1876–78," in *Making Native Space: Colonialism, Resistance, and Reserves in British Columbia* (Vancouver: UBC Press, 2003), 104–35.

24 Perhaps the most notorious instance of this was the Potlatch Law or Potlatch Ban of 1884.

25 Garth J. Taylor,"Canoe Construction in a Cree Cultural Tradition," *National Museum of Man Mercury Series, Canadian Ethnology Service Paper* 64 (1980): 33.

26 Great Lakes Research Alliance for the Study of Aboriginal Arts & Cultures,"Four views of a Model Canoe: Odawa Chiefs Assiginack & Mookomaanish". Curated by Crystal Migwans. *GRASAC EXHIBITS,* 2013. Digital exhibition. https://carleton.ca/grasac/exhibits/.

27 Ibid. A small item like this would end up in the"Indian corners" of the houses of amateur collectors of the Victorian era.

28 Tappan Adney and Howard I. Chapelle, *Bark Canoes and Skin Boats of North America,* 1-6. United States National Museum Bulletin 230 (Washington: U.S. Government Printing Office, 1964), 75. See, for example, a racing canoe commissioned by Lt. Col. Herbert Dibble of Woodstock, built by a Maliseet builder.

29 Banff Centre for Arts and Creativity,"Documentary Filmmaker Alanis Obomsawin's 40Years of Storytelling, Part 1". YouTube Video, 13:18, 4 January 2016, https://www.youtube.com/watch?v=nGULfS4rEKE.

30 Bear Nicholas,"The Role of Colonial Artists," 65.

31 Andrea Bear Nicholas,"Our History," St. Mary's First Nation, December 2005, http://www.stmarysfirstnation.com/history.html.

32 Bear Nicholas,"The Role of Colonial Artists," 64–66.

33 Chuck Commanda (Kitiga Zibi First Nation), conversation with Chris Chapman,"Politics of the Canoe" workshop, Winnipeg, 9 June 2018.

34 Adney,"The Building of a Birch Canoe," 187.

35 John Jennings, *Bark Canoes: The Art and Obsession of Tappan Adney* (Richmond Hill: Firefly Books, 2012), 39. Jennings's book, which documents all of Adney's models housed at the Mariners' Museum in Newport, Virginia, contains two detailed photos of this canoe (the photographer is John Pemberton).

36 Adney,"The Building of a Birch Canoe," 185.

37 Jennings, *Bark Canoes,* 39.

38 Ibid., 34.

39 Bear Nicholas, "The Role of Colonial Artists," 25–86.

40 Ibid., 28.

41 Ibid.

42 Ibid. Bear Nicholas notes that landscape painting was commonly part of a British Officer's field training.

43 Ibid., 60.

44 Bear Nicholas, "Who Owns Indigenous Cultural and Intellectual Property?"

QUEBEC
Kitigan Zibi
ONTARIO
Map Area
Kitchisippi
ALGONQUIN PROVINCIAL PARK
(Ottawa River)
Pikwakanagan First Nation
Asinabka
Ottawa
ONTARIO
Plenty Canada
Lanark
Mazinaw Forest
Ardoch
Perth
Sharbot Lake
Shabot Obaadjiwan
Murphy's Point Provincial Park
Bedford Tract
Indian Point Provincial Park
Brockville
Curve Lake First Nation
St. Lawrence River
Canoe Museum
(Peterbourough)
Kingston
Thousand Islands
N
U.S.A.
0
25 km
Lake Ontario

CHAPTER 5

Ginawaydaganuc: The Birchbark Canoe in Algonquin Community Resurgence and Reconciliation

CHUCK COMMANDA, LARRY MCDERMOTT, AND SARAH NELSON | WITH SPECIAL THANKS TO JULIANA LESAGE-CORBIÈRE

Omàmìwininì or Mamiwinnini people, also known as Algonquin, have lived in the watershed of the Ottawa River (the Kiji Sìbì, or Kichisippi) for thousands of years. There is archaeological evidence of Indigenous peoples living in the territory from at least 10,000 years ago.[1] It is likely that people moved to this area as soon as the glaciers retreated from the area between Lake Champlain (south of Montreal, in what is now Vermont) and Lake Huron. Algonquin histories show that Algonquin territory covered much of what is now eastern Ontario and western Quebec, long before the territory was divided by colonial governments into those two provinces.

Our chapter focuses on teachings surrounding the building of an Algonquin-style birchbark canoe. These teachings are connected with the revitalization of Algonquin practices and communities as well as with reconciliation; as other chapters in this book also demonstrate, these practice-based teachings have important links to family and community, legal traditions, language, and relationships with land. Currently, birchbark canoe building is an important part of efforts to move toward both reconciliation and resurgence in Algonquin and other Indigenous communities. The canoe, being such an iconic symbol in Canada, also provides a means for people across cultures to connect with one other. Projects involving the canoe bring people together in a unique way; the canoe acts like a magnet for people of all ages and backgrounds, offering a chance for them to connect, share stories, and learn about one another in the context of a highly skilled Algonquin community practice.

Canoe building has important applications as a strategy for the revitalization of Indigenous cultures and community healing. Over the past several years, canoe building has experienced a resurgence in popularity in Indigenous communities. Birchbark and other types of canoes are being built in places where there have not been canoe builders for many years, and people are relearning how to build canoes. Chuck Commanda, who learned the craft from his grandparents, travels to various Indigenous communities not only to build canoes but to build the capacity of communities to continue to make birchbark canoes. In some cases, he returns multiple times to help improve people's canoe-building skills and pass on more knowledge of the craft.

Canoe building also helps to make people aware of ways in which climate change is impacting the environment, for example, by changing the texture of birchbark. According to the teachings of the medicine wheel,[2] Indigenous peoples around the world have special responsibilities for taking care of the land. Building a birchbark canoe, depending as it does on the natural environment for materials, can remind us of these responsibilities, reconnecting people with land. By healing ourselves through the canoe, we can also work toward healing the Earth.

This chapter examines the roles of the birchbark canoe in Algonquin family life, survival, and governance, as well as in reconciliation. We highlight some of the most important lessons of the Algonquin birchbark canoe, in particular *ginawaydaganuc*, a principle of Algonquin and natural law that teaches how all things on Mother Earth are connected. The teachings described here are those we, the authors, have learned from our Elders and from the canoe itself, as we have come to understand them through our own experiences. The ways in which we understand them are constantly adapting and changing, depending on the situation of our lives and the people and environments we are connected with. Thus, this chapter is a snapshot of our understanding at the current moment, from the places we are grounded in.

Ginawaydaganuc and Natural Law

> Algonquin Law, derived from the Creator, defines sacred responsibilities to others and to the Earth. A key principle of Algonquin law is *ginawaydaganuk*. The traditional Algonquin worldview conceives of physical, emotional, mental, and spiritual connections to all of life and the life-givers, including the plants, animals, water, air, earth, and fire. Under Algonquin law, there is a collective and individual responsibility to honour these sacred gifts and ensure that they thrive.... It also requires respect for the needs of those to come and consideration of the effect of each act that we take upon the next seven generations. Rather than a reductionist approach, Algonquin law requires consideration of the cumulative impacts of actions on the entire web of life.[3]

Ginawaydaganuc, or Algonquin law based on respect for natural law, recognizes that all creation is interconnected spiritually, emotionally, mentally, and physically. It reminds us of our first responsibility, which is to the continuance of life, and shows us that we have to live within Mother Earth's capacity to give.

As human beings, we need to be careful not to destroy our Mother Earth's capacity to give life—for example, by taking more than what she can give—and to recognize how dependent we are on the Earth for our survival. The recognition of our own dependency can lead to strong emotions when talking about taking care of the land, especially when principles of interconnectedness and responsibility come into conflict with colonial ideologies of ownership and resource use. It is also easy to misunderstand what *ginawaydaganuc* actually means. Sometimes we limit it to our responsibilities to each other as human beings, but the law implies much broader responsibilities to all beings. Even something as small as a blackfly is a part of creation that deserves our respect. We all hold the responsibility to ensure the survival of species into the future; this is another lesson that *ginawaydaganuc* teaches us.

Algonquin Elder William Commanda once said, "Respect for Mother Earth and all species and forms of life is fundamental to the true Indigenous way of life. Over the course of my own lifetime, I have witnessed our natural heritage damaged almost irrevocably at every level by unbridled greed, opportunism and development, and uncoordinated federal and provincial management."[4]

In order to correct the imbalances caused by this greed and mismanagement, it is necessary to recognize that "the land and the people are integrally connected and the protection of one is only found through respect of the other."[5] One way in which we are able to not only recognize but also experience this connection physically, emotionally, mentally, and spiritually is through the canoe. The birchbark canoe provides a way to remember and re-prioritize the fundamentally important connections that we all need in order to revitalize Indigenous communities and reconcile with one another. Many Algonquin, Anishinaabe, and other communities are drawn to this work and are turning to the canoe as a means of re-establishing and revitalizing spiritual connections to the land and water that in turn teach us and remind us about our own pre-existing principles and strategies of governance.

When describing *ginawaydaganuc*, Larry McDermott and Peigi Wilson write that "Algonquin law requires consideration of the cumulative impacts of actions on the entire web of life; this is how the Algonquin define sustainability."[6] Although Canada's "policies of divisiveness and exclusion frustrat[e] Algonquin efforts to practice [*sic*] *ginawaydaganuk* and sustain the biological diversity of their homeland,"[7] the canoe, in tandem with other practices that bring communities together and remind us of our collective responsibilities to one another and to Mother Earth, holds the potential for the revitalization of these fundamental elements of natural law.

The canoe teaches us from the four sources of intelligence—emotional, physical, mental, and spiritual—about the interrelatedness of the entire web of life. For example, when engaging with ceremonies related to gathering materials and building a birchbark canoe, the physical act of harvesting combines with spiritual and emotional connections to the canoe and to the Earth from whom the materials are provided. The work of building a canoe teaches ways of making these physical and spiritual connections, which in turn emphasize the interconnectedness that is a core part of Algonquin principles of sustainability and natural law.

Building a Canoe

Building a birchbark canoe is a creative act. It requires skill, knowledge, and empathy, and draws on the seven sacred teachings of love, honesty, humility, respect, bravery, wisdom, and truth. In order to connect with these teachings, it is important to take time. When we rush through a canoe build, often things go wrong. But when we take the time to take it all in—the quiet of the forest, the energy—and express kind words and thanks, things tend to go better. How we build a canoe reflects how we treat each other. When making a canoe, a person is acting in ceremony. When offering tobacco, other gifts, or kind words and thoughts as a ceremonial act, the spirits recognize a person's good intent. A person's intent can be off without their realizing it; therefore, it is important to have self-awareness when engaging in ceremony.

While collecting materials for the canoe, a person thanks the Creator for the specific trees, and the water, air, sun, and earth for giving those materials and for the knowledge to be able to build that craft. Giving thanks is an expression of both gratitude and reciprocity. Reciprocity is a way of expressing respect through giving something back while maintaining connections with Mother Earth, providing ways to connect to the seven sacred teachings. Expressing gratitude and developing relationships of reciprocity with everyone involved in building a canoe, including the Earth, teaches us how to honour the seven sacred teachings and how to honour all life.

Over time, things have happened to our people that have interfered with our abilities to work in ceremony and maintain these relationships of reciprocity with the land. Through disruptions to Algonquin communities, including displacement, division, and the imposition of colonial laws and policies, some Algonquin teachings about law and governance have been supplanted and need to be re-centred or revitalized. The Indian Act imposed a system of governance on Algonquin and other Indigenous communities across what is now Canada[8] and, together with other discriminatory colonial policies and regulations, has created abusive power relationships and divisions of power that cut through communities and even families, creating unsafe spaces for expressions of traditional Indigenous governance. This leads to harmful competition within communities for scarce resources and makes it difficult to remember and follow the seven sacred teachings and the ceremonies associated with them. Building a canoe is not always treated as a ceremony anymore.

One of the reasons for this loss can be traced to the impacts of colonialism in Algonquin territory and the ways it has separated Algonquin people from each other, from other Indigenous communities, as well as from the land. Ceremonies are not understood today as well as they once were. For example, we as Algonquin people understand the importance of offering tobacco, but not everyone still knows what the fundamental teachings related to tobacco are and why they are important. Many Algonquin people have grown up without being connected to ceremonies and only come to learn about them later in life. Ceremonies help balance us and connect us to each other and to *debwewin* (truth), but it remains the choice of an individual person whether to take on the teachings or not. Algonquin people know how to get the teachings back: we need to restore unity among our communities in order to be able to make the effort to bring the ceremonies back into our lives that can return us to the balanced life we once had.

The birchbark canoe offers one way of rekindling our connections with community and ceremony. In 2016, Chuck Commanda harvested materials for a canoe in the Thousand Islands area, where the St. Lawrence River meets Lake Ontario.[9] Part of this process involved praying for the water of the St. Lawrence and praying for the beings that inhabit the water, including spiritual creatures of the water that are portrayed in pictographs and legends. Praying for others—for the well-being of the water itself as well as for those who depend on the water—helps us to travel safely over the water and to find the materials we need. It is important to remember that we should not just pray for ourselves and the work that we are doing. When a person recognizes the interconnectedness of all things, we recognize that we can pray for others—for the ancestors or for the Elders, for example—as a way to receive what we need for ourselves. Remembering our connections to others and acting with awareness of our own "loving responsibility"[10] toward all beings in the world engages us with *zaagidowin* (love) and interconnectedness—some of the most important principles of Algonquin natural law.

Ceremony and principles associated with Algonquin law also need mechanisms by which they can be passed on from one generation to the next. One way of passing on knowledge in the canoe-building process is through teaching an apprentice. In the fall of 2017, Commanda took on an Anishinaabe youth apprentice to be his helper and to learn the craft himself. Teaching a young Indigenous person how to become a canoe builder can give them a path in life and a reason to have both hope for the future and pride in their people. Learning the art of canoe building made a difference in this young apprentice's life, giving him more reasons to stay on a good path.

Learning the art of canoe making benefits not only the builder and their apprentice but also the community as a whole. Building a canoe can provide opportunities for people to experience and embrace traditional Algonquin laws and governance and how they might look in terms of contemporary application. In the face of colonial systems that have displaced and divided communities—such as arbitrary, government-imposed splits between status and non-status people; geographical divisions among what were formerly shared territories; or the ways in which Christian religion and natural law are treated as mutually exclusive—unity among people becomes a key part of Algonquin (and other Indigenous) community resurgence and revitalization. Building a canoe together has the potential to bring a sense of unity to a community. Bringing the knowledge of birchbark canoe making back to a community can foster feelings of pride and bring the community together.

Often young Indigenous people, born into a society deeply affected by colonialism, question themselves and their purpose in life. One of the most important remedies to this is to come together as a community. To be able to work as a community and for the community, rather than focusing on the self and personal gain, is extremely important, and this is something that building a birchbark canoe can help teach to younger generations. Canoe building brings people together to work on a project that has meaning for everyone involved. The whole community can participate in the build, including people of all genders, Elders, youth, and children. For example, in 2013, three Algonquin communities from the Ottawa Valley came together to build two canoes with Chuck Commanda. Many youth participated, along with adults and knowledge holders from the communities. The group went out in the woods together, had lunch, and harvested spruce root and birchbark for the canoes as a big group. There was no radio or phones or television, so participants all talked, shared stories, and told jokes to entertain each other. The day began with ceremony, which unites everyone and calls in the ancestors and other spirits to help us, and finished in ceremony, which released those spirits. Going out on the land in this way promotes intergenerational knowledge sharing, and by taking away distractions and working in ceremony, participants are able to form better connections with the materials gathered, with one another, and with the land around them.

The canoe-building process helps to reinvigorate the Algonquin language as well, as people learn and remember Algonquin terms and concepts related to the canoe materials, ceremonies, and building process. After the canoe has been built, this process of language revitalization can continue through storytelling associated with the different uses of the canoe in community life, such as *pikodjamomin* (wild rice) planting and harvesting, shelter, transportation, and other knowledge about the waters and the lands.

As mentioned above, the process of building a birchbark canoe requires us to draw on the four sources of intelligence: emotional, physical, spiritual, and mental. Whatever a person has in their mind gets projected physically through their hands and will affect the canoe and the materials, as well as other people working on the canoe. Emotionally, a person cannot be in a state of anger to work on a canoe, because the anger will show through in the work. Spiritually, in order to do the work of canoe building properly, a person needs to act in ceremony and engage with the principles of *zaagidowin* (love) and interconnectedness. One needs to be in a good spiritual state and remain in that state while building the canoe. In order to achieve this good spiritual state a person needs to show respect: respect for the place the material comes from; respect for oneself and others; and respect for the tools being used. Through learning that we are not better than any other being on earth, we learn about loving responsibility.

Other important lessons of the canoe have to do with patience. Teachings about patience have been emphasized by Indigenous Elders in many nations across Canada.[11] Remembering to wait and to be aware of when the time is right, and most importantly, to be willing to wait if the time is not right, when harvesting materials, is a principle that can make or break a birchbark canoe. Rushing ahead in imperfect conditions only results in wasted materials—it is necessary to take the time to harvest properly and respectfully, and to accept that one will not always find what one is looking for right away. Another principle related to patience is that it is important to not take too much when harvesting and to leave some material for future generations. In the case of birch trees, those trees that are left for future harvesting cannot be too big. If they are big birch trees, this means that they are close to the

FIGURE 5.1. Designs etched on a canoe built by Chuck Commanda at Murphy's Point Provincial Park in the summer of 2018. Photo: Sarah Nelson.

end of their life; smaller trees will still be around in future years for others to harvest. Patience also means remembering not to put one person's priorities above others'—the priorities of the trees, of the natural environment, and of other human and non-human beings need to be given equal weight.

Working with the birchbark canoe also can inspire people to protect the natural environment. Leaders in Algonquin and other Indigenous communities who have participated in canoe building have become motivated to be more involved with forestry, expanding their roles in taking care of the land by being a part of the decision making to keep the forests healthy and adopt Indigenous priorities for certain species. Forestry policy does not always acknowledge these priorities. White birch, for example, is "on the house" in Ontario, meaning that any birch tree ten centimetres or more in diameter can be industrially cut without restriction. This type of policy fails to consider genetic diversity, species sustainability, or the high Indigenous cultural value assigned to this and other species.

The impacts of climate change as well as several generations of industrial logging can be seen in changes in birchbark, spruce root and trees, and in the quality of cedar trees. For example, a good way to tell when to harvest birchbark used to be by watching when the fireflies came out. Bark harvested before the fireflies appear is called winter bark—it has a darker inner layer of bark that can be scratched off to make beautiful designs on a finished canoe (see Figure 5.1). Because of changes to the climate, however, signs like these are not as reliable as they once were—winter bark can now be found long after the fireflies have come and gone. Spruce roots, used to sew the seams and gunwales of the canoe, are falling prey to a fungus that grows up into the root, discolouring and weakening the wood. Cedar trees, used for the ribs and sheathing of a canoe, have also suffered from over-harvesting. It is now more difficult to find cedar trees that are large enough to provide the gently curving circumference required to split the wood into thin sheathing to cover the inside of a canoe.

In many Algonquin communities, now diverse and spread out across colonially imposed boundaries, the knowledge to protect the environment, whether through government conservation practices or through time-honoured practices rooted in natural law, is often not readily available or has simply been replaced with colonial thinking. Bringing this knowledge back to life, community by community, is another contribution being made by the canoe.

The Canoe in Algonquin Family, Community, and Political Life

The birchbark canoe continues to be a link to Algonquin cultural strength, retaining the power to bring people together for a common cause. *Omàmìwininì* refers to "the people who gather," in a social sense; *mamiwinnini* means "nomad." The canoe embodies both of these meanings: by enabling movement throughout traditional lands, it helps Algonquin people to maintain governance structures, community ties, and connections to land. It also contributes to reconciliation through *zaagidowin*, the sacred teaching of love, as part of honouring *ginawaydaganuc* and the ways in which we are all connected.

Traditionally a family vehicle, respectfully constructed from materials in the surrounding environment, the birchbark canoe connects Algonquin communities with one another and with the land and water, as well as with newcomers. Knowledge of canoe craft and waterways within Algonquin lands has facilitated Indigenous resistance to colonial incursion, Indigenous resilience through maintaining family and community ties, and reconciliation through education and sharing of Algonquin teachings and histories.

Building birchbark canoes has always been a practice shared among the whole family. As with all aspects of life, you need to have balance. For example, in the teachings of the medicine wheel, children are at the centre, then women around them, then Elders, then the men around the outside. You need to have everyone doing their part in order to have balance. It is particularly important with the canoe to have women involved because of women's traditional relationships with water in Algonquin and other Anishinaabe communities. Water is the giver of all life, and our relationship with water begins well before we enter this world, in the womb. As carriers of the gift of this life-giving water, women are constantly in relationship with water and in Anishinaabe cultures are always the carriers of water in ceremony. All water, including the water we produce (such as tears) or the water we can't see (such as water in the air, or water underground), is acknowledged in water ceremony. Through women's responsibilities for bringing life into the world, in relationship with water, we learn about our loving responsibilities to one another and to all beings.[12] As Deborah McGregor writes: "Loving responsibilities and obligations flow from natural laws and thus are not mandated by governments through legislation, policies, funding or programs. Instead, knowing our responsibilities gives us power to act."[13] Water is the first medicine, and as the canoe travels along the waterways it is travelling along the veins of Mother Earth.

In old pictures showing Algonquin people with the birchbark canoe, often women and men are together, with children in the middle. Especially during a special gathering, children were included. Children are always listening, even if they are doing something else. By involving everyone in the community, the canoe can help to revitalize the Algonquin language and oral traditions (see Figures 5.2 and 5.3).

FIGURE 5.2. Mary and William Commanda, Chuck Commanda's great-grandparents, with a canoe they built. Source: Chuck Commanda.

FIGURE 5.3. Chuck Commanda with his grandmother, Mary Commanda, and a canoe they are building. Source: Chuck Commanda.

At the beginning of contact with settlers, Algonquin people used their skills and knowledge of canoe craft, waterways, and Algonquin lands to avoid danger and to find other places to practise our culture, especially in the face of settler hostilities. There are histories and genealogies that tell how settlers wouldn't have been able to survive without Indigenous peoples' help through the winter, in the early years of settlement of Algonquin territories. At least one of those histories/genealogies expresses lament over no longer seeing the Algonquin canoes travelling the Mississippi. Over time, however, settlers came to our territories bringing other ideologies, including different ideas about how to interact with land, based on ownership and extraction, and supercilious ideas about religion. When our communities began to be oppressed by these ideologies and threatened by settlement, we used the canoe to move to other places to avoid them.

In those times when we had to pack up and leave right away, the canoe was there and ready. The people we were running away from didn't have horses at the time; they would have had oxen and would have been slower. Settlers made the journey, for example, from Brockville on the St. Lawrence River to Perth, inland between Kingston and Ottawa, in ox wagons. These wagons would often bog down on the road, which was in very poor repair. The journey took a long time, and many settlers succumbed to illness, malnutrition, or exhaustion.[14] It was very difficult for settlers, to say the least, in the early years in this area.

Through these years, Algonquin communities would gather together, facilitating resistance and maintaining community ties. In the winter we dispersed to pursue snaring, trapping, and hunting in smaller groups, but there were spring and fall gatherings facilitated by the canoe. Such gatherings would include communities beyond the Algonquin. Indigenous peoples could cover long distances by canoe—it was nothing for someone from northwestern Ontario to come and visit with Elders in the local Algonquin communities in the Ottawa River valley. Even in the years when the French and English were fighting over territory, we as Algonquin peoples would still gather, to socialize, trade, and govern. And we got there by canoe.

Over the centuries, the canoe has brought people together to share stories, experiences, and histories. This is something that we have partially lost—as Indigenous communities and as a human race—but are working to regain. As part of our work, Chuck Commanda and Larry McDermott travel with canoes that we have made to demonstrate the power of the canoe. In all of the places we have gone with a birchbark canoe, it attracts people—there is something about it beyond the level of conscious thought that draws people in. Working on canoes also helps our ability to communicate orally. Around the world, all peoples have communicated orally to pass on traditions, histories, and other forms of information. As a society, through colonial experiences, we have in some respects un-learned this practice of oral communication—of sharing and listening with each other to learn about cultures, histories, peoples, and natural law. When observing a birchbark canoe being built, children, youth, and adults alike, instead of text messaging or focusing on their phones, actually tune in to what is happening, ask questions, and are thoroughly engaged with the canoe that is being created. This happened during Chuck Commanda's building of two canoes for the Canadian Canoe Museum in Peterborough, Ontario. The entire build was open to the public in the museum itself, and in addition there were several visits and educational Skype sessions with children from various schools, as well as a great deal of attention from the media. A group of youth from Curve Lake First Nation helped on the build as well. Overall, a large number of people were engaged both in person and virtually on this build, and children and youth showed their interest in and enthusiasm for this work by giving it their full attention.

Spiritually, the canoe represents creation. A birchbark canoe contains roots from the earth, bark from a tree that climbs toward the sky, and cedar as medicine which is a healer of people (see Figure 5.4). The canoe, being made up of all these things, is a connector that engages people through more than each individual material. The materials come together to make a whole that connects us to all of creation, including to one another. When we take down a tree to make a canoe, we ask the spirit of the tree to live on in the canoe. After the canoe has been created, that canoe then has a spirit. That spirit is honoured through ceremonies during the launching of the canoe and should be fed on a regular basis—both through feasting and through being taken on the water. Canoes should not remain in museums all the time—they need to be used. This is something that Indigenous communities could become involved with. Members of different communities could visit museums that house canoes to repair them and take them on the water—to nourish them and keep their spirits alive (see Figure 5.5).

FIGURE 5.4. Spruce root (wadab), peeled and prepared for use in a birchbark canoe build. Photo: Chuck Commanda.

FIGURE 5.5. Chuck Commanda and his apprentice paddling a canoe built at Murphy's Point Provincial Park in the summer of 2018. Photo: Sarah Nelson.

On the basis of these spiritual connections, the canoe helps Algonquin people to maintain governance structures through community ties and connections to the land. It helps us remember the time before colonial governance structures were imposed on our communities through the Indian Act; a time when we appreciated what we got from the land and used that to inform our governance structures and decisions. The canoe connects us with our traditional government, to what is healthy, and to what worked in a way that was sustainable, based on our relationship with Mother Earth. The canoe helps us connect to our history and our ancestors; it reminds us that we were self-governing people before contact; and it helps us in contemporary times to reconnect with that history and authority, and to connect with other communities on the basis of self-governance.

In helping us to understand governance, the canoe helps us to understand teachings and natural law in a way that is not abstract but tangible. When we use our hands, bodies, minds, and spirits to harvest materials and build a canoe, we are connecting the pieces together that represent our relationships with the natural world, the spirits, and other people. The process of sustainable harvesting reminds us to think about the future and future generations. This helps to re-establish connections with Mother Earth and with the future that we have sometimes forgotten. It also helps to re-establish family ties, as well as pride in our cultural history. When families work together and share our history, it fosters empathy for all of creation, and with that empathy comes respect, hope, confidence, and resilience.

Reconciliation and *Ginawaydaganuc*

Settlers adapted Indigenous canoes for their own purposes. The voyageur canoe, for example, was designed to carry large amounts of furs and other trade goods, people, and supplies—a thirty-six-foot canoe could carry up to six tons of goods as well as six people. Today, a large section of the Canadian population has had some experience with a canoe. The canoe has been appropriated as a symbol of settler Canadian culture, yet because it is a familiar symbol to so many, when we remember where the canoe came from, it can also be used as an important vehicle for reconciliation among communities.

Algonquin Elder William Commanda taught that it is both possible and essential in the work of reconciliation to get beyond false notions of separation between "us" and "them." When we bring our mind and our heart together, we can learn to connect with all of creation. It is not necessary to focus with one's mind on how to connect with creation; when one starts with the heart, the connection is like holding a baby—it just happens naturally. We are able to get more in touch with our inherent nature as human beings, with the rest of life, and with the loving responsibilities that come with that. Once these connections are made between the heart and mind, reconciliation and community revitalization become an honour, an act of love. At this point it is no longer "work"; it is not a burden to find these connections. Rather, it is a gift of *zaagidowin* to hold this loving responsibility for Mother Earth and all of us who inhabit it.[15]

During the summer of 2018, Chuck Commanda was commissioned to build a canoe at Murphy's Point Provincial Park, as part of the Ontario Parks 125th anniversary celebrations. This build, and the launch of the completed canoe, attracted hundreds of people. The partnership between Commanda and his helpers, together with the staff and management at Murphy's Point, resembled a mutually respectful form of co-governance. Materials were harvested locally, within the park, and the partners found that many park regulations aligned with Indigenous principles of natural law, or *ginawaydaganuc*. For example, the park enforces the rule that windfallen trees should not be harvested for firewood; instead, the fallen trees remain in the forest so that they can replenish the soil for the next generation of trees and other living creatures. This type of regulation implicitly recognizes the inherent interconnections among all things and honours the fact that even when no longer living, a tree or other organism has a vital role to play in the health and sustainability of the forest surrounding it. Historically, across Canada, conservation practices undertaken by national and provincial parks have frequently meant that colonial rules for conservation superseded Indigenous and natural laws and displaced Indigenous peoples from land. In this case, however, both partners on the project were seeking points where Algonquin law, natural law, and the regulations of the park were in harmony, and at no time did the park staff enforce their own rules at the expense of Commanda's understandings of good harvesting practices in accordance with natural law.

Reconciliation with the land and water, through living up to our collective responsibilities, is a critical step in the healing of human relationships. Canada is committed by treaty through the United Nations Convention on Biological Diversity and Climate Change to reverse declines in biodiversity. To this end, targets were set in 2010 in Nagoya, Japan, that included the expansion of protected terrestrial and inland waters to 17 percent. The process established to achieve this goal mandated inclusion of and co-governance by Indigenous peoples, which resulted in relationships of co-governance based on the concept of ethical space.[16] An Indigenous Circle of Experts (ICE) was established as part of this co-governance system, and in their report from March of 2018, *We Rise Together*, the ICE stated: "As noted throughout this report, ICE believes federal, provincial and territorial governments must take an integrated approach to meeting their domestic biodiversity goals and contributing to the public good. The twenty Aichi Targets and nineteen related Canadian biodiversity targets[17] are intended to work together. This approach aligns with Indigenous worldviews and thinking that have conserved biodiversity effectively for millennia."[18] Reconciliation with the land and water is also reconciliation with our children and other future generations, by honouring our ancestors, who cared for the land enough to give us a future, and their principles of caring for life with an eye to the well-being of seven generations into the future. Acknowledging our collective relationship with creation, not as a source of money and material wealth but as a relationship where we see the life within all species as interconnected—*ginawaydaganuc*—is at the root of Algonquin law. Within this law is the understanding of natural law and our responsibilities to limit our consumption to no more than Mother Earth can reproduce, to share, and to care for all life.

Conclusion

The goal of this chapter was to describe our understandings of some of the teachings involved with and brought out by building Algonquin-style birchbark canoes. These teachings are connected to the revitalization of Algonquin practices and communities as well as to reconciliation with settler and other non-Indigenous peoples, and as such they are linked to resurgence and revitalization of family and community, legal traditions, and relationships with land.

These teachings can be understood through the principle of *ginawaydaganuc*, or the interrelatedness of all life; a principle at the centre of Algonquin law. The canoe teaches us from the four sources of intelligence—emotional, physical, mental, and spiritual—about *ginawaydaganuc* and connects people to one another and to the Earth through the seven sacred teachings of love, honesty, humility, respect, bravery, wisdom, and truth. It does so in a tangible way, by bringing people together to work toward a common cause, as well as through the spiritual being of the canoe itself, fashioned as it is from living materials from the Earth that come together as a whole and become something altogether new.

During the process of building a birchbark canoe, family and community members are engaged with one other, Algonquin and Anishinaabe languages and traditions of oral communication are renewed, and people connect with and learn from the natural environment. This learning includes the ways in which the Earth is changing, the importance of leaving enough for future generations, and the essential role of patience. All of these teachings lead back to fundamental principles of Algonquin governance; principles grounded in *ginawaydaganuc* that have been disrupted by colonialism, including through the imposition of the Indian Act, but which can be restored through unity—within and among Indigenous communities, among all human beings, and with all life.

The revitalization or resurgence of Algonquin governance can also be achieved through reconciliation—understood as the recognition of our loving responsibilities to one another as people, but perhaps even more importantly, as the recognition and fulfillment of our responsibilities to the land. Just as it is important to recognize that environmental problems cannot be addressed without attention to social problems, reconciliation among peoples can only take place in the context of reconciliation with Mother Earth.

Appendix A

United Nations Convention on Biological Diversity, Aichi Biodiversity Targets (2010)[1]

STRATEGIC GOAL A: ADDRESS THE UNDERLYING CAUSES OF BIODIVERSITY LOSS BY MAINSTREAMING BIODIVERSITY ACROSS GOVERNMENT AND SOCIETY

TARGET 1
By 2020, at the latest, people are aware of the values of biodiversity and the steps they can take to conserve and use it sustainably.

TARGET 2
By 2020, at the latest, biodiversity values have been integrated into national and local development and poverty reduction strategies and planning processes and are being incorporated into national accounting, as appropriate, and reporting systems.

TARGET 3
By 2020, at the latest, incentives, including subsidies, harmful to biodiversity are eliminated, phased out or reformed in order to minimize or avoid negative impacts, and positive incentives for the conservation and sustainable use of biodiversity are developed and applied, consistent and in harmony with the Convention and other relevant international obligations, taking into account national socio-economic conditions.

TARGET 4
By 2020, at the latest, Governments, business and stakeholders at all levels have taken steps to achieve or have implemented plans for sustainable production and consumption and have kept the impacts of use of natural resources well within safe ecological limits.

STRATEGIC GOAL B: REDUCE THE DIRECT PRESSURES ON BIODIVERSITY AND PROMOTE SUSTAINABLE USE

TARGET 5
By 2020, the rate of loss of all natural habitats, including forests, is at least halved and where feasible brought close to zero, and degradation and fragmentation is significantly reduced.

---

1 Convention of Biological Diversity, "Aichi Biodiversity Targets," 5 November 2018, https://www.cbd.int/sp/targets/ (accessed 8 September 2020).

TARGET 6
By 2020, all fish and invertebrate stocks and aquatic plants are managed and harvested sustainably, legally and applying ecosystem based approaches, so that overfishing is avoided, recovery plans and measures are in place for all depleted species, fisheries have no significant adverse impacts on threatened species and vulnerable ecosystems and the impacts of fisheries on stocks, species and ecosystems are within safe ecological limits.

TARGET 7
By 2020, areas under agriculture, aquaculture and forestry are managed sustainably, ensuring conservation of biodiversity.

TARGET 8
By 2020, pollution, including from excess nutrients, has been brought to levels that are not detrimental to ecosystem function and biodiversity.

TARGET 9
By 2020, invasive alien species and pathways are identified and prioritized, priority species are controlled or eradicated, and measures are in place to manage pathways to prevent their introduction and establishment.

TARGET 10
By 2015, the multiple anthropogenic pressures on coral reefs, and other vulnerable ecosystems impacted by climate change or ocean acidification are minimized, so as to maintain their integrity and functioning.

STRATEGIC GOAL C: TO IMPROVE THE STATUS OF BIODIVERSITY BY SAFEGUARDING ECOSYSTEMS, SPECIES AND GENETIC DIVERSITY

TARGET 11
By 2020, at least 17 percent of terrestrial and inland water, and 10 percent of coastal and marine areas, especially areas of particular importance for biodiversity and ecosystem services, are conserved through effectively and equitably managed, ecologically representative and well connected systems of protected areas and other effective area-based conservation measures, and integrated into the wider landscapes and seascapes.

TARGET 12
By 2020, the extinction of known threatened species has been prevented and their conservation status, particularly of those most in decline, has been improved and sustained.

TARGET 13
By 2020, the genetic diversity of cultivated plants and farmed and domesticated animals and of wild relatives, including other socio-economically as well as culturally valuable species, is maintained, and strategies have been developed and implemented for minimizing genetic erosion and safeguarding their genetic diversity.

STRATEGIC GOAL D: ENHANCE THE BENEFITS TO ALL FROM BIODIVERSITY AND ECOSYSTEM SERVICES

TARGET 14
By 2020, ecosystems that provide essential services, including services related to water, and contribute to health, livelihoods and well-being, are restored and safeguarded, taking into account the needs of women, indigenous and local communities, and the poor and vulnerable.

TARGET 15
By 2020, ecosystem resilience and the contribution of biodiversity to carbon stocks has been enhanced, through conservation and restoration, including restoration of at least 15 percent of degraded ecosystems, thereby contributing to climate change mitigation and adaptation and to combating desertification.

TARGET 16
By 2015, the Nagoya Protocol on Access to Genetic Resources and the Fair and Equitable Sharing of Benefits Arising from their Utilization is in force and operational, consistent with national legislation.

STRATEGIC GOAL E: ENHANCE IMPLEMENTATION THROUGH PARTICIPATORY PLANNING, KNOWLEDGE MANAGEMENT AND CAPACITY BUILDING

TARGET 17
By 2015 each Party has developed, adopted as a policy instrument, and has commenced implementing an effective, participatory and updated national biodiversity strategy and action plan.

TARGET 18
By 2020, the traditional knowledge, innovations and practices of indigenous and local communities relevant for the conservation and sustainable use of biodiversity, and their customary use of biological resources, are respected, subject to national legislation and relevant international obligations, and fully integrated and reflected in the

implementation of the Convention [on Biological Diversity] with the full and effective participation of indigenous and local communities, at all relevant levels.

TARGET 19

By 2020, knowledge, the science base and technologies relating to biodiversity, its values, functioning, status and trends, and the consequences of its loss, are improved, widely shared and transferred, and applied.

TARGET 20

By 2020, at the latest, the mobilization of financial resources for effectively implementing the Strategic Plan for Biodiversity 2011–2020 from all sources, and in accordance with the consolidated and agreed process in the Strategy for Resource Mobilization, should increase substantially from the current levels. This target will be subject to changes contingent to resource needs assessments to be developed and reported by Parties.

Appendix B

United Nations Convention on Biological Diversity; National Targets specific to Canada (2010)[1]

REFERENCE	TARGET	RELATED STRATEGIC GOALS/ AICHI TARGETS
Goal A	By 2020, Canada's lands and waters are planned and managed using an ecosystem approach to support biodiversity conservation outcomes at local, regional and national scales.	18
Target 1	By 2020, at least 17 percent of terrestrial areas and inland water, and 10 percent of coastal and marine areas, are conserved through networks of protected areas and other effective area-based conservation measures.	11
Target 2	By 2020, species that are secure remain secure, and populations of species at risk listed under federal law exhibit trends that are consistent with recovery strategies and management plans.	12
Target 3	By 2020, Canada's wetlands are conserved or enhanced to sustain their ecosystem services through retention, restoration and management activities.	4, 5, 14, 15
Target 4	By 2020, biodiversity considerations are integrated into municipal planning and activities of major municipalities across Canada.	2

1 Convention of Biological Diversity, "Find National Targets: Canada," https://www.cbd.int/nbsap/targets/ (accessed 8 September 2020).

Target 5	By 2020, the ability of Canadian ecological systems to adapt to climate change is better understood, and priority adaptation measures are underway.	19
Goal B	By 2020, direct and indirect pressures as well as cumulative effects on biodiversity are reduced, and production and consumption of Canada's biological resources are more sustainable.	
Target 6	By 2020, continued progress is made on the sustainable management of Canada's forests.	4, 5, 7
Target 7	By 2020, agricultural working landscapes provide a stable or improved level of biodiversity and habitat capacity.	5, 7
Target 8	By 2020, all aquaculture in Canada is managed under a science-based regime that promotes the sustainable use of aquatic resources (including marine, freshwater and land based) in ways that conserve biodiversity.	4, 7
Target 9	By 2020, all fish and invertebrate stocks and aquatic plants are managed and harvested sustainably, legally and applying ecosystem-based approaches.	8
Target 10	By 2020, pollution levels in Canadian waters, including pollution from excess nutrients, are reduced or maintained at levels that support healthy aquatic ecosystems.	8
Target 11	By 2020, pathways of invasive alien species introductions are identified, and risk-based intervention or management plans are in place for priority pathways and species.	9
Target 12	By 2020, customary use by Aboriginal peoples of biological resources is maintained, compatible with their conservation and sustainable use.	18

Target 13	By 2020, innovative mechanisms for fostering the conservation and sustainable use of biodiversity are developed and applied.	3, 4
Goal C	By 2020, Canadians have adequate and relevant information about biodiversity and ecosystem services to support conservation planning and decision-making.	
Target 14	By 2020, the science base for biodiversity is enhanced and knowledge of biodiversity is better integrated and more accessible.	19
Target 15	By 2020, Aboriginal traditional knowledge is respected, promoted and, where made available by Aboriginal peoples, regularly, meaningfully and effectively informing biodiversity conservation and management decision-making.	18
Target 16	By 2020, Canada has a comprehensive inventory of protected spaces that includes private conservation areas.	11, 19
Target 17	By 2020, measures of natural capital related to biodiversity and ecosystem services are developed on a national scale, and progress is made in integrating them into Canada's national statistical system.	1
Goal D	By 2020, Canadians are informed about the value of nature and more actively engaged in its stewardship.	
Target 18	By 2020, biodiversity is integrated into the elementary and secondary school curricula.	1
Target 19	By 2020, more Canadians get out into nature and participate in biodiversity conservation activities.	1, 4

Notes

1 Brenda Kennett, "'Living by the Seashore, Watching a Lake Emerge': Indigenous Settlement around Big Rideau Lake" (Portland, ON: Big Rideau Lake Association, June 2017), https://www.bigrideaulakeassociation.com/htlw7; Lloyd B. Jones, *Living by the Chase* (Belleville, ON: Essence Publishing, 2002).

2 The medicine wheel or sacred hoop forms a part of many Indigenous philosophies; see, for example, Annie Wenger-Nabigon, "The Cree Medicine Wheel as an Organizing Paradigm of Theories of Human Development," *Native Social Work Journal* 7 (2011): 139–61.

3 Larry McDermott and Peigi Wilson, "'Ginawaydaganuk': Algonquin Law on Access and Benefit Sharing," *Policy Matters* 17 (2010): 205–41. McDermott and Wilson prefer to spell Ginawaydaganuk with a "k" but the authors prefer to use the spelling with a "c."

4 Ibid., 206.

5 Ibid., 214.

6 Ibid., 206.

7 Ibid., 207.

8 Government of Canada, Indian Act, 1985, http://laws-lois.justice.gc.ca/eng/acts/I-5/page-1.html.

9 This process was documented by a television crew from Germany for a promotional documentary about the Thousand Islands area.

10 Deborah McGregor, "Indigenous Women, Water Justice and *Zaagidowin* (Love)," *Canadian Woman Studies* 30, no. 2–3 (2015–2016): 71–78, http://www.sciencedirect.com/science/article/pii/B9780080449104003308%5Cnhttp://www.sciencedirect.com/science/article/pii/B9780080449104003308/pdfft?md5=c6d30af98554a4a65d3777fcba39ec74&pid=3-s2.0-B9780080449104003308-main.pdf.

11 R. Hoffman, "Perspectives on Health within the Teachings of a Gifted Cree Elder," *Pimatisiwin: A Journal of Aboriginal and Indigenous Community Health* 8, no. 1 (2010): 19–31; Ruth Couture and Virginia McGowan, eds., *A Metaphoric Mind: Selected Writings of Joseph Couture* (Edmonton: Athabasca University Press, 2013).

12 McGregor, "Indigenous Women, Water Justice and *Zaagidowin* (Love)."

13 Ibid., 13.

14 John McDonald, *Emigration to Canada: Narrative of a Voyage to Quebec, and Journey from Thence to New Lanark, in Upper Canada* (Edinburgh: Andrew Jack, 1825).

15 McGregor, "Indigenous Women, Water Justice and *Zaagidowin* (Love)."

16 Indigenous Circle of Experts, *We Rise Together: Achieving Pathway to Canada Target 1 through the Creation of Indigenous Protected and Conserved Areas in the Spirit and Practice of Reconciliation* (Ottawa, 2018).

17 These targets are included in Appendix A at the end of this chapter.

18 Indigenous Circle of Experts, *We Rise Together*, 19.

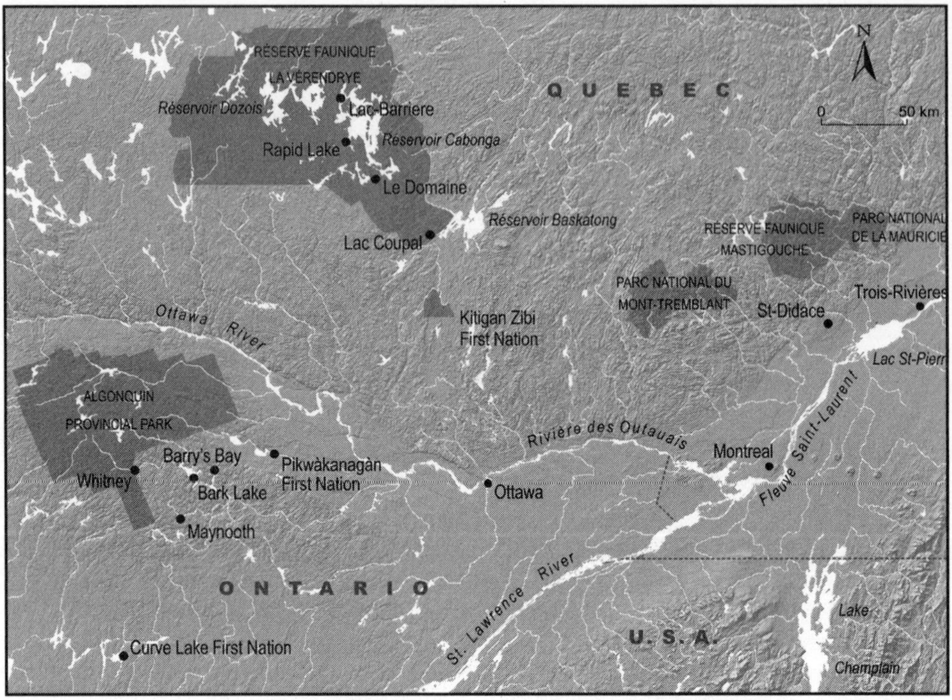

RÉSERVE FAUNIQUE
LA VÉRENDRYE
Réservoir Dozois
Lac-Barriere
Rapid Lake
Reservoir Cabonga
Le Domaine
Lac Coupal
Réservoir Baskatong
QUEBEC
N
0
50 km
RÉSERVE FAUNIQUE
MASTIGOUCHE
PARC NATIONAL
DE LA MAURICIE
PARC NATIONAL DU
MONT-TREMBLANT
St-Didace
Trois-Rivières
Lac St-Pierr
Kitigan Zibi
First Nation
Ottawa River
ALGONQUIN
PROVINCIAL PARK
Barry's Bay
Whitney
Bark Lake
Pikwàkanagàn
First Nation
Maynooth
Rivière des Outauais
Ottawa
Montreal
Fleuve Saint-Laurent
ONTARIO
St. Lawrence River
U. S. A.
Lake
Champlain
Curve Lake First Nation

CHAPTER 6

Pathways to the Forest: Meditations on the Colonial Landscape

JONATHAN GOLDNER

For millennia, harvesting bark has been part of the ongoing seasonal activities and an integral part of local knowledge for the people who inhabit the woodlands and boreal forest. The ethnobotanical evidence of birchbark harvesting and basket making among First Nations can be found in the archaeological record as far back as 4500 BP.[1] In many respects, the skills that are employed to make wooden-rimmed bark baskets used for containers can be scaled up to make larger rimmed vessels for floating people on water. Historic accounts of harvesting bark often focus on the expertise of the individual canoe builder and offer scant detail about the environment where good bark grows. This can give the impression that canoe builders simply deployed a skill set of harvesting techniques and returned home with canoe bark in hand. In reality it is much more complicated. This chapter begins with an account of what motivates me to learn to build birchbark canoes. Then through environmental storytelling, I reflect not only on what it means to harvest bark in this particular place and time where the ecologies of the forest can be immediately sensed, but also on the ways the colonial landscape has shaped the embodied practices of canoe builders.

Situating My Research: Living and Making

I begin by acknowledging my position here as a relative newcomer, a settler, a non-Indigenous, academically inclined male urbanite, and question how this has shaped my approach to harvesting bark and building canoes. I grew up in the small town of Kemptville in Leeds and Grenville County in southeastern Ontario, about an hour outside of Ottawa. Throughout my childhood, I was very keen on making things with my hands. I found the passivity in which students spent much of their day sitting, looking, and listening to a teacher at the front of the classroom completely uninspiring. I yearned for more time outside or in the workshop. Craftwork provided an opportunity to think through things in action and to anchor distant ideas and concepts that were not immediately obvious in the materiality of things. I can recall the moment when I moved from making scale models of trains and airplanes to hunting equipment and watercraft that belonged to First Nations. This move also coincided with a time when I was beginning to read in ethnography and archaeology and think more seriously about the ways our lives are heavily structured and shaped by material culture.

Before building birchbark canoes, I tried to make skin-on-frame kayaks. My first attempts looked more like cabinetry in the measured form of a boat. After a couple of laughable trials, I sought out apprenticeships to learn first-hand from more experienced builders. I remember reading a book published by the Alaska Native Heritage Center, *Qayaqs & Canoes: Native Ways of Knowing* (2001). Each chapter in this book tells a story about an Indigenous boat builder in Alaska. The eight watercraft that resulted from this initiative are on display at the Alaska Native Heritage Center in Anchorage.

In May 2003, I left Ottawa and hitchhiked to Alaska. I met with one of the Elders profiled in *Qayaqs & Canoes*, but plans to build a kayak with him in September later fell through. Along the way, I often slept under spruce trees, but never too far from a road or grocery store. I stopped at museums, archives, institutes, and cultural heritage centres to study ethnographic collections of kayaks and canoes. Edwin Tappan Adney's seminal work from the turn of the twentieth century on Indigenous watercraft provided a model with which to approach my own study, and I began learning how to survey and illustrate and build models in the same 1:5 scale. I used the computers at public libraries to email canoe builders (or authors of books about canoe building) to ask if I could meet with them. For years, I continued to pursue independent research. Though

I benefited from a fair amount of privilege, I had no personal savings or means to support my studies. Instead, I rid myself of the financial burden of having to pay rent and at peak efficiency, one year I slept upwards of 300 nights outside. There were times when I would put myself where the salmon were running, or where the blueberries or bakeapples were ripe, but for the most part I developed a capacity to live on the margins of an affluent society. Hitchhiking allowed me to travel and volunteer whenever possible on various canoe-building projects. I never owned a canoe or knew what it was like to paddle any great distance in one. Although my interest was in traditional crafts, the vast majority of the people I met and worked with over the years were non-Indigenous.

Eventually, I returned to school and enrolled at university in anthropology. Although the discipline of anthropology has a highly theoretical orientation, I was able to find traction for canoe building, not just as fieldwork but as research creation. Making a birchbark canoe as research creation challenges hierarchies of knowledge that conform to the standard academic genre of an analytic dissertation or essay. But I also did not want to sidestep the materiality of lived experience and to allow canoe building to be used as merely a site of academic investigation. I am interested in research that takes on multimodal forms that can be understood in their own context without the needless translation back into the terms of a dominant Western discourse. This practice of research creation taught me about the changing ecologies of the forests that have provided birchbark to Indigenous builders for millennia, and about the colonial landscape that all builders, both Indigenous and non-Indigenous, inhabit.

Pathways to the Forest

The apprenticeships that I have participated in over the years, with Don Gardner, Eugene Arima, and most recently, Chuck Commanda, have introduced me to the wide range of networks and collaborations between diverse communities of kayak and canoe builders in Canada. The richness of these exchanges comes, at least in part, from the different experiences each builder brings forth.

After completing several apprenticeships, I was eager to find some canoe bark and build a first canoe on my own. Sandra, a dear friend and partner, generously offered to help look for bark. At first, we looked close to home in the areas surrounding Ottawa and Montreal. When these searches turned up empty, we branched out farther afield, exploring the areas around Maniwaki and Golden Lake, where I had read that many Algonquin canoe builders lived. I remember the excitement that came with being in a forest that was predominantly populated with large birch trees. However, my excitement at being closer to my dream of building my first canoe was tempered by irritability from the constant harassment of airborne insects and the intolerable summer heat. East of Algonquin Park, the battery of biting insects was so thick that it was impossible to listen to our own consciences. The deerflies assault in orbit around the head with such furor that what is surprising is how infrequently one of them ventures a landing. The psychological torment is by far more severe than their bite. I promised myself that future bark reconnaissance would be done in the shoulder seasons of early spring or fall, when it is cooler and when we are less likely to be molested by bugs. Seasonal cycles also influence the times of the year that are best for harvesting different types of bark. Summer bark is honey blonde in colour and is typically harvested early to mid-summer when the sap is flowing. Winter bark, which doesn't benefit from the flowing sap underneath, is more challenging to peel but comes with an extra-thin membrane that oxidizes to a deep rust colour and allows for decorations to be etched in it. This bark can be harvested in the spring or late fall.

Sandra and I continued to look for bark over the next couple of weeks, exploring large swaths of forest adjacent to Algonquin Park. The terrain, roughly in the shape of a triangle formed by Maynooth in the south, Barry's Bay in the northeast, and Whitney in the northwest, encompassed a huge (and hugely disappointing) lake called Bark Lake. This lake, situated along the upper Madawaska River, is the result of a dam owned by Ontario Hydro. The Madawaska, a tributary of the Ottawa River, used to be a fast-flowing river with wild rapids, but over the last couple of centuries it has been drastically changed and tamed. The logging industry, with the assistance of government funding, began in the early 1800s to build slides, booms, and dams for sorting and triaging the trees before driving the logs further down to the Ottawa River to supply Upper Canada and the Royal Navy with timber. Later, hydroelectric generating stations were built to supply the burgeoning demand of the cottage industry in Renfrew Country for electricity. These dams turned land into lakes, and in the case of Bark Lake put over thirty-six square kilometres under water as deep as eighty-five metres. We nonetheless walked among thousands of birch and made little incisions to test the bark of between 200 and 300 trees. All of the mature trees we found were dry and brittle like parchment and, with the exception of one or two, delaminated. Bark that delaminates into thin sheets, often referred to as paper bark, falls apart, making it unsuitable for canoes.

Looking for bark on the east side and thus just outside the boundary of Algonquin Park is a search strategy that warrants further explanation. The default position of Canada's provincial parks (and national parks) is that harvesting plants and trees within the park is prohibited. And yet, to believe that the park was born out of the desire to preserve the natural landscape for its own sake would be naive and misguided. In the late nineteenth century, under the auspicious banner of conservation, private citizens—mainly sport anglers, hunters, and furrier associations—lobbied the Ontario government for a wilderness area to be set aside to safeguard fish and wildlife stocks.[2] Their efforts led to the creation of the Ontario Game and Fisheries Act (1892), and in the following year a wilderness preserve called The Algonquin Park.[3] Conservationists also argued for the protection of tree species, but it was never the provincial government's intention to sacrifice timber revenues.[4] Logging continues within the park at an alarming rate.

The conservation movement coincided with a growing antimodernist sentiment, which viewed the industrial revolution as not only damaging to the environment but also responsible for the detrimental effects of alienating people from it. Jean Manore explains: "As people increasingly shuffled papers and fastened bolts, they lost the day-to-day contact with the environment that farmers or hunters supposedly enjoyed."[5] Another related concern was that urban lifestyles, particularly for young men, rendered them "helplessly soft and luxurious" and "unfit for the battle of everyday life."[6] Campgrounds and paddle routes within the park were prepared so that an emerging urban and leisure class could restore their psyches and physiques by getting back in touch with nature through wilderness experiences and canoeing.

Meanwhile, the Algonquin people were forcibly evicted from the newly established park as state agents, including game wardens and park rangers, secured the activities of a select seasonal recreational clientele. The legacy of national and provincial parks is part of an ongoing colonial assault that seeks to claim land and resources and extinguish competing interests upon which many people's livelihoods are based. In 1894, Chief Peter Charbot (Sharbot) and a group of Algonquin requested a small parcel of land in the

Township of Lawrence (which was later incorporated into the park in 1911) be confirmed as a reserve, but their request was denied.[7] In 1896, Chief Charbot once again petitioned the government for permission to live near their traditional homelands, beyond the boundaries of the park on the south-east shores of Haye Lake in Sabine County, on a tract of land about which he thought "Crown Lands should have no objection because the timber there was all cut off and it was now a wasteland."[8] The government maintained that the Algonquin should move to Maniwaki or Golden Lake, where there was already land set aside for a reserve, far away from the game interests of the park. This calculated plan was made clear by the recommendations of Mr. Simpson, the Superintendent of Algonquin Park, in a report submitted to Indian Affairs in 1895: "You know the predatory habits of these people, how they roam about, and how difficult it is to keep watch of their movements in the forest or to get them to recognize that a law which applies to white people, with respect at any rate to the killing of game, should be made to apply to the Indian, . . . It would therefore be almost impossible to keep these Indians, thus situated, from hunting and trapping within the Park."[9]

Today, the Madawaska watershed remains dammed and flooded and the park, which celebrates the name of the people it displaces, remains heavily regulated and uninhabitable to First Nations hunters and foragers who endeavour to continue living with their land.[10]

Our First Bark Harvests

Before attempting the first harvest, Sandra and I needed permission from the landowners. The Ministry of Natural Resources informed us that we should ask the Bancroft Minden Logging Company, which has a 100-year lease on the cut rights to all the wood held on publicly owned Crown lands in the area. The logging company granted us permission to harvest and suggested we purchase a map showing all the parcels of land that belong to the Crown. They also advised us that Sabine County, just north of Maynooth, typically has high-percentage yields of mature white birch.

After a couple of weeks of only finding trees with dry, papery bark, Sandra and I eventually managed to come across an exceptional mature birch tree to the east of Papineau Lake that had nice healthy bark about 3/8-inch thick that did not delaminate. To test the bark, I cut into the tree with a small knife and removed a small piece which I then bent back and forth and pried at its edge with my fingernail. This piece felt almost rubbery and the edges stayed together and cut silky smooth like a piece of leather. When bent the other way, horizontally with the grain in the same direction as the lenticels, it stayed intact and the eyes did not crack open. Bark that is brittle and dry, with long, deep, open lenticels, will fall apart and make audible cracking noises under this kind of manipulation, which indicates that it would be unsuitable for canoes. This particular tree's profile also met a few other criteria in that it was of sufficient circumference (about thirty-eight inches), grew straight, and did not have any low-hanging branches or any significant branch scars (a defect or hole where an old branch once grew).

Using an axe and a three-foot bow saw, I cut a wedge out of the tree and then made one more cut on the back side to release it and send it falling. Once the tree was on the ground I made a vertical incision in a straight line along its length and slowly began to pry up on the edge of the bark using a knife and the flat surface of my axe. It was the end of July, somewhat late in the season, and the bark was stuck to the tree and lacked the moisture that would usually make it easier to peel. We continued to gently pry on the bark, pushing it slowly, a few inches at a time. We worked carefully and evenly with our hands along its length. Every once in a while, an audible crack would alert us to a small tear that occurred at the edge of the bark. These tears almost always happen at a lenticel and if left unattended could run and carry forward many inches, possibly ruining a good sheet of bark. To prevent this, Sandra used a small awl to punch little holes on either side of the tear and laced over it with a few stitches of waxed nylon.

The first sheet of bark presented a couple of challenges. Once the tree was on the ground, we noticed tiny little shoots with precocious buds sprouting right out of the side of the trunk. These grew on the sunny side of the tree and were too far up to have been spotted from the ground while the tree was still standing, yet not far enough up the tree to be beyond the sixteen- to eighteen-foot sheet we needed for the canoe. This might have been less of a problem had I made the vertical cut on the sunny side where these shoots were, since they would have likely been trimmed off in the excess above the gunwales during the building process, but I had already made the vertical cut (as is habitually done) on the rougher, shady side of the tree. This sheet of otherwise clean bark thus had about ten or twelve little holes, remnants of

FIGURE 6.1. First bark harvest, Hastings Highland Township, Ontario. Photo: Sandra Audet.

where the shoots had been sprouting, on what was destined to become the bottom of the canoe hull below the waterline. Undeterred, we flipped the bark over, white side facing up toward the sky, and beginning at the base of the tree we gently rolled it up. We were amazed that the skin of an entire birch tree could be rolled up like this. I had seen photos and videos of the process, but until you actually try it's hard to imagine just how well this works.

The following summer, Sandra and I returned to some forests in Lanaudière, Quebec, where we had previously sampled some bark. On the nearby road I flagged down a man driving a tractor and asked him who owned the land. He pointed me in the direction of a farmhouse. Here I met Mr. Brulé, an elderly French-Canadian gentleman who was using the forest as a woodlot and the adjacent agricultural fields to raise cows for beef. We explained that we would like to harvest the bark from a birch tree on his land and he immediately gave us permission. In fact, he said it was better we got to it first before it died, because he had noticed over the years that the health of all the mature birch was in decline.[11] He was so accommodating that he even gave us a tour of his property and showed us another spot with birch where he thought we might find some more bark. The tree we wanted to harvest grew on the edge of a steep rocky incline such that if we were to cut it down, it would fall to a precarious and damaging rest. Eager to learn a new harvest technique, we brought a few large nails, some rope, and a couple of small (one-inch) C-clamps along with a loud clanking aluminum extension ladder into the woods to attempt our second harvest.

Harvesting bark while the tree is still standing means the tree has a good chance of surviving the harvest. The steep slope, however, made working from a ladder difficult. The ladder needed to be constantly repositioned, extended, and collapsed so that our arms could reach the trunk. We worked our way up and down the tree a little bit at a time to make the vertical cut and slowly push the bark off the tree. When the bark remained attached by just a few inches on the back side, I went up to the top just above the sheet of bark and put a large nail into the tree. We then attached two C-clamps to the top edge of the bark, tied the thin rope to these clamps and looped the rope over the nail in the tree to secure it. We then pushed the bark completely off the tree until it hung free, suspended by the rope on the nail, and used this as a pulley system to gently lower the bark to the ground. In the end we were very pleased, and this tree yielded a nice sheet of bark with no delamination and only a couple of blemishes.

FIGURE 6.2. Bark harvest from ladder, Lanaudière, Quebec. Photo: Jonathan Goldner.

I spent another week searching the area for more bark, but only found more of the usual brittle and delaminating paper birch. I wondered what I might be doing wrong; some of the other, more experienced builders I had been in touch with reported finding better yields. I decided to give Rick Nash a call and ask him. Rick lives on the west side of Algonquin Park and has built many beautiful canoes over the years. I explained to Rick that I was having trouble finding bark. Rick listened as I told him that I could walk an entire slope for miles with tall, healthy, mature birch and test every single one of them, and they would all without exception delaminate. He asked, "Was the soil sandy?" I had no idea. While looking at the birch I hadn't even considered soil conditions, nor had I ever heard or read anything that correlated soil with bark quality. My ears tuned in as Rick said, "Oh yeah, they will do that, you might get lucky but hillside birch are usually in shallow soil with shallow roots where the sun can reach the trees and dry out the bark." He went on to advise me:

> Go deep into the woods, like two to three miles, pack a lunch, leave early, and come back by dark. You won't likely find any bark at the edges of roads or trails. Go deep [and] try to get yourself to flat terrain when things start to get dark and clammy in low-lying gullies. When you can feel the bugs crawling all over the place coming alive and getting more intense, you're probably getting close to finding some good birch. The ones I find around my place don't really grow in a mixed hardwood forest with maples, ash, or oak, they grow among the conifers like hemlock who help block out the light. These birch will grow really fast, they have to struggle to reach for the light at the canopy. They tend to be healthy and when you cut them down you will see nice fat growth rings and they have thick bark that doesn't delaminate. Now it's not easy—sometimes it takes me a few days other times it can take me a week or a little more, but if you look for these dark clammy damp buggy low-lying gullies, when you get in there you can almost get a feeling like you're going to find some birch.[12]

Rick called back one morning about a week later to say he had a look on a map and thought that if I could make it up a couple of hours north of Maniwaki to Rapid Lake or Barriere Lake, I'd probably be in a good spot to begin looking for bark. In his words, "One of the nicest pieces of bark I've ever seen on a canoe came out of the Gatineaus. The birch grow like roman columns on the north side of the (Ottawa) River."[13] I left for Rapid Lake that same morning and just as the sun was setting, I met a local man whose car had broken down on the side of the road. As I gave him a lift back to Rapid Lake, he recalled the days when many Elders in the community were building canoes and offered some tips on where to go look for bark. I inquired, "If I find a good tree, who should I ask for permission to harvest it?" He said, "Oh if anyone asks just tell them you need some bark; they might think you're working for a logging company since you're not from around here, but just tell them you want bark for a canoe and you should be all right."[14] His advice reflected a long history of colonial encroachment by logging interests, and the duty the Algonquin have to care for their land and protect it from ecological destruction.

This local, who showed me a great level of hospitality, was Jean-Maurice Matchewan, who I later found out was the former customary chief of the Algonquin at Barriere Lake (Mitchikanibikok Inik). I say "former" not because he was replaced under the customary governance code, where the Elders get together and decide who is best suited to guide the community in maintaining their way of life, but rather because he was supplanted through a process imposed by the Canadian government. In 2010 the federal government and its agents at the Department of Indigenous and Northern Affairs, flanked by armed police from the Sûreté de Quebec, set up a polling station on the outskirts of the community at which a mere ten ballots were cast, and in so doing forcibly replaced the traditional Algonquin way of governing with a newly elected band council by using an archaic section (74) of the Indian Act.[15] This was the first time this measure had been imposed on a First Nations community since 1924, and yet the federal government's claim was that it wished "to see their governance conflicts settled internally."[16] Under the customary code, chiefs usually hold the position for life. Part of the reason for this is that it takes a lifetime to develop the wisdom of how to lead and how to deal with the colonial government's tricks.[17] Matchewan had been chosen by the Elders because the community needed an intelligent and fierce leader who could defend the Algonquin and their territory from clear-cutting while also navigating the negotiations with government.[18] The Indian Act's provision for elected band councils not only serves to bring Indigenous communities in line with settler models of governance and legislation but also ensures that there is constant leadership turnover, with fresh ranks of inexperienced band councils that colonial governments can more easily take advantage of.[19]

The Algonquin of Barriere Lake have never ceded or surrendered title to their land. Their territory of roughly 15,000 square kilometres encompasses the La Vérendrye Wildlife Reserve. In 1991, the Algonquin of Barriere Lake signed a trilateral agreement to develop a resource co-management framework that harmonizes forestry activities with traditional Algonquin practices. In 2001, citing "escalating costs" and "lack of convincing results," the federal government reneged on this legally binding agreement—an agreement that the United Nations touted as an environmental trailblazer and model of coexistence.[20] The Algonquin continued to negotiate with political officials and tried to develop better relationships with the logging companies.[21] The illegal logging continued, sometimes under armed police protection. When the Algonquin organized peaceful protests, they were beaten, doused with tear gas, and arrested by riot police. In 2008, the Crown sought a one-year jail sentence for acting chief Benjamin Nottaway in order to "send a clear message" and to "make sure he has no desire to do this again."[22] A Quebec judge sentenced him to two months in jail for his role in organizing the protests. The government continued to issue clear-cut permits, including at Poigan Bay, a sacred location on the late customary chief Harry Wawatie's family lands. When his children sought a court injunction and set up a camp to protest the illegal logging, they were also arrested and charged.[23] Despite a resolution by the Assembly of First Nations to support the Algonquin of Barriere Lake and move forward with a process of reconciliation, the federal government remains embroiled in court battles while simultaneously in breach of its own legal obligations.[24]

After spending a couple of fruitless days looking for bark around Rapid Lake (in what must have been one of the most intense heat waves of the summer), I tracked down David Gidmark. He is the author of several books and has built canoes with local Algonquin, many of whom have now passed on. I found David living in Maniwaki, and he was happy to reminisce about the years he spent around Rapid Lake and Barriere Lake. He said he didn't know exactly where to go for bark nowadays because things have changed so much, but he shared a few stories: "The best haul of bark I ever found was by canoe on the far end of Lac Coupal. Jim [Jerome] and I got eight rolls."[25] I ask him if I were to hike in to that same lake whether there would be a small chance I might find just one roll of bark, but he said things have changed now; the whole area is being ripped up and cut by loggers.

David suggested that if I wanted to find forests that hadn't yet been disturbed by the logging industry, I could borrow a canoe to cross over to some of the islands in the middle of the Cabonga Reservoir. The idea that these were the only stands left untouched by the logging companies impressed upon me how dire the deforestation has become. I checked out Lac Coupal anyway, just to see if I could get a feel for the lay of the land and what may have made that particular location so special as to yield so many rolls of bark. Sadly, the lake is now attended by heavy machinery and the extent of the deforestation was disheartening. No longer could I walk in the shade among the trees; it was a huge mess of upturned roots, discarded and rejected wood, and sun-parched soil that would swallow my entire leg if I lost my footing scrambling over their spoils. A canoe isn't even required to access the far side of the lake anymore. You can drive in on the newly bulldozed logging road.

Early the next morning, farther north from Lac Coupal, before the heat had a chance to really set in, I found a patch of forest that was predominantly birch. The trees grew straight and the bark looked healthy, but they were widely spaced among other hardwoods, with underbrush of alders and willow where the sun could easily penetrate. As usual, the bark was dry and delaminated. Adjacent to this patch of birch, the land dipped and gradually descended into a bowl-shaped gulley filled mostly with spruce and hemlock, but there were quite a few birch that bled into the margins of these shady conifers. The conifer forest was cooler and darker and every once in a while, the contrast of a white birch would attract my eyes and lure me toward it. I kept going further into the woods, and once I was a little over a kilometre away from the access road, the ground levelled off and gave way to soggy moss that squished beneath my feet. In here was a cluster of five or six large healthy birch, each of them over fifty inches around. The test revealed a buttery smooth pliable bark that didn't show any signs of delamination, but the lenticels were deep and they were all prone to cracking. About another half-hour's walk away, I found a tree with really nice bark. Since I did not have a ladder with me, I had to cut the tree down. As I began to harvest the bark, it popped off the tree with loud, electrifying crackling sounds coming from underneath, travelling up and down the length of the tree as it came free with a slight encouragement from my hands. The entire sheet came undone and lifted off the tree in such a hurry that I had to wait for it to relax before I could roll it up. I had never heard that sound before. Perhaps that is the sound that summer bark makes when it is ripe for harvesting and wants to give itself up for a canoe.

Reflection

While the senses guide canoe builders through the topography and natural contours of the forest, the colonial landscape acts as a persistent mediator that continues to shape our embodied practices. Searching for bark is about learning to navigate the seasonality of the harvest, as well as the various land titles grounded in English and French concepts of property law. Walking down the hillside into the shady gully also means circumventing the scars of clear-cutting. The scorching summer's heat, which is getting stronger with climate change, is felt by all of the inhabitants of the forest; the bark is drier, like parchment, and the birch are weakened by disease and dying prematurely. The yellow birch, which is unsuitable for canoe bark, is also responding to climate change by migrating northward into white birch territory. Flooded lands are given natural names like Bark Lake to disguise their artificiality. The state uses forced relocation, political interference, and violence to try to silence Indigenous people as they assert their right to coexist, while factories turn entire forests on unceded Indigenous land into pulp and paper, cheap chipboard, and Popsicle sticks.

Engaging with the materiality of canoes provided an access point through which I became both observer and participant in colonial state ideology. The more I experienced in my bones what it was like to harvest a tree from the forest, to hold an axe or crooked knife in my hands, and to transform bark into canoes, the more I began to have doubts about what exactly I had convinced myself I was doing. I wondered how my own actions, replicating canoes that are recognizably Indigenous, might also be complicit in reproducing patterns of structural violence. On the one hand, harvesting bark allowed me to gain specific sensory insight into the forests, the tactile workings of materials, and the culture of canoe builders, which I knew so little about. But on the other hand, it was arrogant to assume that Indigenous land would be available for me to explore and that First Nations' material culture could be unproblematically appropriated in my reproductions of their processes. How different really is this behaviour than the other classic settler assumption that the Canadian wilderness is out there, available to use at our disposal? Furthermore, what privilege did I benefit from as I mobilized the services of state institutions: when I studied the collections of canoes in museums that profit from the loss of Indigenous cultural heritage, when I asked the Ministry of Natural Resources for a permit to harvest on Crown lands that were unceded Algonquin territory, and when I was able to drive unimpeded on roads cut right into the heart of Indigenous territory? What about the privilege of becoming a student at university, which gave me the time and funding I needed to be able to incorporate gathering materials and building canoes into my research practice? The story of building canoes in Canada is also the story of Indigenous-settler relations.

Canoes have crossed into cross-cultural spaces. But what happens to Indigenous knowledge when it is passed on, carried, and practised by non-Indigenous people? Indigenous people are powerful agents, disseminating their knowledge over a variety of different media and capable of deciding with whom to share it. Indeed, many people I've met over the years have developed close relationships while working with Indigenous communities and often (though not always) learned their craft from and alongside Indigenous people. A generous reading could highlight the multiplicity of meanings that emerge among various actors at different stages of engagement throughout the process of making and recreating. After all, cultures have mingled and interacted since time immemorial, and the nature of all knowledge that is produced through cultural exchange is syncretic. But syncretism and multiculturalism also have a particular liberal Western history that has been used to mask the conditions under which the dominant culture appropriates and assimilates Indigenous knowledge. Once this knowledge is passed on to non-Indigenous people (who in turn become connected in the ways this knowledge is shared), it becomes a different kind of knowledge altogether. My own embodied practice, though it is informed by a network of both Indigenous and non-Indigenous sources, is not directly connected to an ancestral lineage or a deep understanding of the communities from which much of this knowledge comes. If anything, my own apprenticeships and building and harvesting practices—arising from a secular and largely pragmatic interest in craft and in material knowledge—are undertaken in a completely disparate set of cultural experiences. Yet for me, the value of practising canoe building is not so much for its recreative potential but rather for its creative purposes, including the entirely new context for cultural exchanges that it opens up.

Colonialism isn't just an external phenomenon, something the Canadian government and its institutions or industry are doing to First Nations. It is settlers who colonize. Reconciliation doesn't just call for massive social and political changes in Indigenous-settler relations; it also calls for creative encounters that can effect change on the micro-political, individual, and local level. The compelling politics of canoe building is that it has always been a site of social gathering where the construction of canoes responds to the projected needs of the not-so-distant future. As such, it has the potential to create a powerful space that draws people from all nations into productive collaborations based on our shared and disparate experiences. It provides an opportunity to question some of our assumptions and to model and imagine other ways of being and inhabiting the world. Optimistically, canoes can help shift our sensibilities, and create new contexts for new conversations that lead toward decolonization. My own experience of harvesting bark for canoe building begins, I hope, to chart a modest path toward such a course. After all, in harvesting bark and building canoes the senses are not just re-attuned to the forest, the trees, and the bugs, but also to the people, their histories, and the colonial legacies of this place.

Notes

1 Shannon Croft and Rolf W. Mathewes, "Barking up the Right Tree: Understanding Birch Bark Artifacts from the Canadian Plateau, British Columbia," *BC Studies* 180 (2013): 88.

2 Gerald Killam, *Protected Places: A History of Ontario's Parks System* (Toronto: Dundurn Press, 1993), 6.

3 George Altmeyer, "Three Ideas of Nature in Canada, 1893–1914," in *Consuming Canada: Readings in Environmental History*, ed. Chad Gaffield and Pam Gaffield (Toronto: Copp Clark, 1995), 96–118.

4 Marijke Huitema, "Historical Algonquin Occupancy Algonquin Park," report prepared for Elders without Borders (undated), 50. See also Sayna Sadeghi et al., "Logging of Algonquin Provincial Park," UBC Student Research on Environment and Sustainability Issues, 2015, http://environment.geog.ubc.ca/logging-of-algonquin-provincial-park (accessed 16 July 2017).

5 Jean Manore, "Contested Terrains of Space and Place: Hunting and the Landscape Known as Algonquin Park, 1890–1950," in *The Culture of Hunting in Canada*, ed. Jean Manore and Dale Miner (Vancouver: UBC Press, 2008), 126.

6 Ibid.

7 Huitema, "Historical Algonquin Occupancy Algonquin Park," 45.

8 NAC (National Archives of Canada), RG10, V 2401, File 83-203, Chief Peter Charbot letter to E. Bennett, Indian Agent, Castile, Ontario, 1896/02/22, in Huitema, "Historical Algonquin Occupancy Algonquin Park," 47–48.

9 NAC (National Archives of Canada), RG10, V 2401, File 83-203, Aubrey White, Assistant Commissioner of Crown Lands to Hayter Reed, Deputy Superintendent General of Indian Affairs 1895/11/16: 108230:1–3, in Huitema, "Historical Algonquin Occupancy Algonquin Park," 46.

10 To this day, the Algonquin First Nations continue to be prosecuted under the Fish and Wildlife Conservation Act for unlawfully hunting in Algonquin Park. See *Ontario [Ministry of Natural Resources] v. Thomas Kohoko, Daniel Sarazin, Mervin Sarazin and Bruce Meness of the Pikwakanagan* and Appeal *Sarazin v. Ontario Ministry of Natural Resources* [2009] O.J. No. 4145; also Grant Tysick of the Kinouchepirini Ontario Court of Justice, Pembroke, 27 July 2015, and Appeal Ontario Court of Justice, Pembroke, 8 January 2016.

11 Laurent Brulé, personal communication with Jonathan Goldner, 26 June 2015.

12 Rick Nash, personal communication with Jonathan Goldner, 21 July 2015.

13 Rick Nash, personal communication with Jonathan Goldner, 27 July 2015.

14 Jean-Maurice Matchewan, personal communication with Jonathan Goldner, 27 July 2015.

15 Barriere Lake Solidarity, "Press Release – Barriere Lake Algonquins Mount Boycott of Government-Imposed Election Poll in Face of Threats of Arrest by Quebec Police," Barriere Lake, QC,11 August 2010, http://www.barrierelakesolidarity.org/2010/08/say-no-to-canadas-armed-imposition-of.html (accessed 20 November 2018).

16 Indigenous and Northern Affairs Canada, *Algonquins of Barriere Lake – Chronology 2009*, https://www.aadnc-aandc.gc.ca/eng/1100100016352/1100100016353#a3 (accessed 20 November, 2018).

17 Shiri Pasternak, *Grounded Authority: The Algonquins of Barriere Lake against the State* (Minneapolis: University of Minnesota Press, 2017), 164–66.

18 Ibid.

19 Ibid.

20 Indigenous and Northern Affairs Canada, *Algonquins of Barriere Lake – The 1991 Trilateral Agreement*, https://www.aadnc-aandc.gc.ca/eng/1100100016352/1100100016353#a3 (accessed 20 November 2018).

21 Canada, *Report of the Royal Commission on Aboriginal Peoples*, vol. 2, *Restructuring the Relationship – Barriere Lake Trilateral Agreement, Quebec* (Ottawa, 1996), 733.

22 Barriere Lake Solidarity, "Press Release – Quebec Judge Imprisons Algonquin Chief for Two Months for Peaceful Protest: Crown Asks for One Year to Send 'Clear Message' to Impoverished Community," Barriere Lake, QC, 10 December 2008, http://www.barrierelakesolidarity.org/2008/12/quebec-judge-imprisons-algonquin-chief.html (accessed 20 November 2018).

23 Barriere Lake Solidarity, "Press Release – Clarification from Barriere Lake Community Member Tony Wawatie," Barriere Lake, QC, 21 August 2012, http://www.barrierelakesolidarity.org/2012/08/clarification-from-barriere-lake.html (accessed 20 November 2018).

24 AFN Special Chiefs Assembly, *Support for an Algonquin of Barriere Lake – Canada Reconciliation Process* (Gatineau, QC, 8–10 December 2015), https://www.afn.ca/uploads/files/draft_resolutions_to_2015_afn_sca.pdf.

25 David Gidmark, personal communication with Jonathan Goldner, 29 July 2015.

PART THREE

Telling Histories

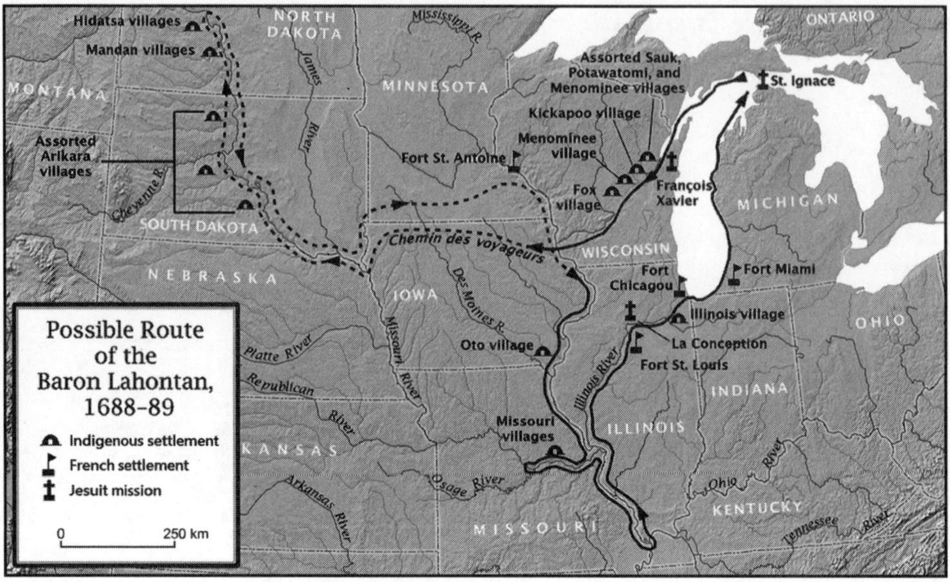
Possible Route of the Baron Lahontan, 1688–89
Indigenous settlement
French settlement
Jesuit mission
0
250 km
Hidatsa villages
Mandan villages
NORTH DAKOTA
MONTANA
Assorted Arikara villages
Cheyenne R.
SOUTH DAKOTA
NEBRASKA
James River
Mississippi R.
MINNESOTA
Fort St. Antoine
Chemin des voyageurs
IOWA
Des Moines R.
Missouri River
Platte River
Republican River
KANSAS
Arkansas River
Osage River
MISSOURI
Oto village
Missouri villages
Assorted Sauk, Potawatomi, and Menominee villages
Kickapoo village
Menominee village
Fox village
François Xavier
St. Ignace
ONTARIO
MICHIGAN
WISCONSIN
Fort Chicagou
Fort Miami
Illinois village
La Conception
Fort St. Louis
Illinois River
ILLINOIS
INDIANA
OHIO
Ohio River
KENTUCKY
Tennessee River

CHAPTER 7

Beyond Birchbark: How Lahontan's Images of Unfamiliar Canoes Confirm His Remarkable Western Expedition of 1688

PETER H. WOOD

By the year 1688, Europeans had been seeking a direct passage through North America to China and Japan for more than a century, beginning with their earliest searches for the imagined Sea of Verrazzano and the equally fictitious Strait of Anian. It would be another 100 years before the ventures of James Cook, George Vancouver, and Alexander Mackenzie ended speculation about any subpolar Northwest Passage through the continent. Coming at a midpoint in this protracted search, one extraordinary but little-known French and Indian expedition, conducted mostly by canoe, sought explicitly to learn prospects for a viable pathway to the West Coast. This objective had eluded earlier French explorers from Jean Nicolet to René-Robert Cavelier, Sieur de La Salle. But by 1688 rumours of La Salle's death the previous year were spreading through French Canada, and younger explorers, including an intrepid Basque adventurer from Gascony named Lahontan, were eager to claim the respect and rewards that would come with finally solving the riddle of a viable route through North America.[1]

Louis-Armand de Lom d'Arce de Lahontan, Baron de Lahontan, was born in southwest France in 1666. He trained as a marine and then sailed to

Canada in 1683, at age seventeen. The young nobleman spent three winters living among Algonquian Indians, learning their language and their admirable skills at cold-weather survival and the management of birchbark canoes. His later descriptions of Indigenous life earned immediate respect, but shifting politics in the court of King Louis XIV at Versailles foiled his aspirations of rising to an important colonial position in Canada. After a decade abroad, Lahontan returned to Europe and prepared an engaging account of his experiences, written in the familiar form of a series of lengthy letters, or reports.

First published in the Netherlands in 1703, *Nouveaux Voyages* became an immediate success. An English-language version appeared in London the same year, with maps reproduced by the distinguished European cartographer Herman Moll. *New Voyages* was promptly translated into several other languages, and it went through numerous editions. But this product of the early Radical Enlightenment had an anti-Jesuit tone, so the pope banned the book, declaring it untrustworthy.[2] Efforts to discredit the man and his memoir focused primarily on a forty-eight-page chapter in *New Voyages* (Letter XVI, dated 28 May 1689), in which the Frenchman claimed to have made an unprecedented trip west of the Upper Mississippi River the previous winter, probing for a passageway to the Pacific, the so-called South Sea. Denied re-entry into French society, Lahontan travelled around Europe in exile for more than a decade. He never returned to North America, and he died in obscurity prior to 1716.

One short essay cannot plumb Lahontan's elusive character and mercurial career, or the fluid international worlds of cartographic discovery, religious controversy, and political intrigue in which his life unfolded. Instead, this essay addresses the way Lahontan's engagement with canoes, so vital to his entire North American experience, may finally help to solve the central riddle of his controversial career. Interpreters, I argue, need to pay less attention to the faulty geography of the unusual schematic map that the Frenchman provided and instead give more regard to the chart's marginal illustrations of canoes. For Lahontan, accustomed to the birch canoes of eastern Canada, clearly depicted on his original map two contrasting and distinctive boats: a midwestern dugout canoe of the sort he learned to use on his journey, and a Northwest Coast war canoe that informants told him about and sketched for him with impressive accuracy.

In the following pages, I first review how historians of exploration have dismissed or misconstrued Lahontan's claim to have spent more than three months visiting Native American groups residing on a major stream far west of the Mississippi. I then suggest that the Frenchman's little-known images of two distinctive canoes, combined with other evidence, demonstrate convincingly for the first time that what Lahontan and his guides called the Long River was in fact the Middle and Upper Missouri, a region he actually managed to visit.

The Problem: "Studied Deceit" or Actual Journey?

Lahontan's book still commands respect in several disciplines.[3] But the effective Catholic campaign to discredit the author left a lasting mark, so historians have long regarded his narrative with scepticism. The French monarchy and the Catholic papacy each had good reasons to oppose Lahontan's popular book. It had been published in The Hague, a hotbed of dissent and free thought, and its frontispiece depicted a proud Native American, standing with one foot crushing a royal crown and the other trampling a Bible. Looking back, later detractors contended that Lahontan's *Voyages* anticipated Jonathan Swift's fanciful *Gulliver's Travels*, clever as literature but utterly untrustworthy as a non-fiction account.[4]

For generations of critics, the key to their argument was Letter XVI, which they attacked with gusto. They debunked the author's claim that, along with his party of French Canadians and First Peoples, he had ascended an impressive stream called "the Long River," searching for a viable course to the Pacific. After all, the chapter's problematic composite map suggesting a presumed route (Figure 7.1) offered no obvious fit with subsequent charts. Besides, the names Lahontan gave for Indigenous groups did not seem to match later terms. Therefore, his critics argued, this entire tale must be a fantastic invention, part of the genre of imaginary travel narratives blossoming in Europe at the time.[5]

Some shortcomings in Letter XVI can be explained by the fact that Lahontan faced striking hardships in a totally unfamiliar realm. Besides, he apparently lost most of his travel notes in a canoe accident before his return to Quebec. Also, European editors and illustrators preparing editions of his text occasionally compounded the confusion.[6] Then too, some of the gaps

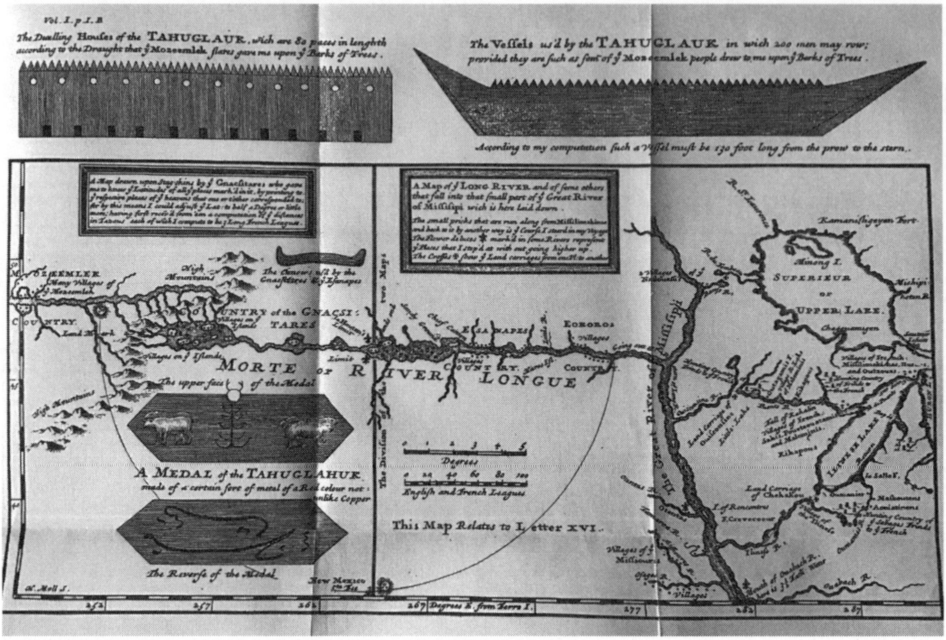

FIGURE 7.1. Lahontan's "Map of the Long River" from the initial English-language edition of *New Voyages*, published in 1703. Copy owned by author.

in his narrative and errors in his map may actually have been intended, if he was trying to lay claim to a significant discovery while still disguising his exact route from competitors.[7] Lahontan understood that some things should be obscured or left unstated in the risky world of long-distance correspondence, especially regarding the secretive and intense European competition to unlock the most pressing major mysteries of North American geography.

At a time when the location and direction of major rivers in the North American West remained unclear to Europeans, new and revealing maps became tightly guarded state secrets. Several years earlier, the ex-governor of Spanish New Mexico, Count Peñalosa, created an international incident by defecting to Paris and revealing to the French for the first time that the Rio Grande did not flow into the Gulf of California but into the Gulf of Mexico instead.[8] Lahontan himself, exiled from France and disillusioned, later attempted to pass geographical information about the North American interior to the English. In a secret memo to the English secretary of state, the Frenchman wrote: "If one could control Acadia it would result in great advantages for New England, and if one could establish the trade in beaver and other furs with the Indians of the French, New York would flourish greatly."[9]

By the nineteenth century, historians had come to accept a dismissive view of Letter XVI, casting a shadow over the remaining 700 pages of Lahontan's narrative. In 1879 Francis Parkman, an early narrator of French exploration, proclaimed that Lahontan's "account of his pretended voyage up the 'Long River' is a sheer fabrication . . . and the populous nations whom he found on it—the Eokoros, the Esanapes, and the Gnacsitares, no less than their neighbors the Mozeemlek and the Tahuglauk—are as real as the nations visited by Captain Gulliver."[10] By the time Justin Winsor reproduced the French-language version of Lahontan's map in 1898, the consensus on the seventeenth-century traveller was clear. "This story-teller," Winsor wrote, "claimed . . . he had found a stream entering the Mississippi . . . which came from the setting sun. By following its sluggish current" upstream, he heard word from Indians of a great range of mountains, "and beyond these highlands there were the sources of another river, which could be followed to the Pacific. The statement gained credence," Winsor conceded, but he proclaimed categorically that this western trip "is now known to have been a studied deceit."[11]

But what if Lahontan, far from creating a studied deceit and an illusion, had actually made an extensive journey with his party of French marines, Ottawa (Odawa, or for Lahontan, "Outaoua") Indians, and Fox (Meskwaki, or as Lahontan called them, "Outagami") interpreters? Beyond the outright dismissals, occasional speculations emerged to explain the extended narrative in Letter XVI where Lahontan claimed to have explored the so-called Long River between October 1688 and March 1689. Far up the river, according to the letter, he encountered three distinctive Native American societies that inhabited separate clusters of very large villages, some of which contained several thousand people, including enslaved captives. One chief, knowing the Frenchman's interests, introduced him to four such slaves, taken from villages far to the west. They said they had lived beyond a mountain range, on a large west-flowing river that entered a great salt lake, or sea, that stretched "a great way to the Southward." These river-dwelling "Mozeemlek Slaves" told of other groups that lived along the coastline farther west. They called these neighbours "the Tahuglauk," perhaps a generic term for an array of coastal peoples, and reported that they were "as numerous as the Leaves of Trees" (194).[12]

In the mid-nineteenth century, a northern interpretation of this tale suggested that the Long River, rather than being fictional, was the St. Peter's, or St. Pierre. That river, now known as the Minnesota, enters the Mississippi near modern-day Minneapolis. Even before Minnesota joined the United States in 1858, newcomers to that region began to wonder, after looking at Lahontan's published map, whether he might have visited this territory.[13] When James H. Perkins published his *Annals of the West* in 1846, he reasoned that Lahontan apparently entered the St. Peter's, and then, at his farthest point on that river, "heard from Indians of the connection by it and the Red River with Lake Winnipeg," and eventually with "Hudson's Bay by Nelson River." Aware that this north-facing interpretation rotated Lahontan's river nearly ninety degrees, Perkins added sardonically that the Frenchman must have been "looking Westward all the while" in his vivid imagination, wishfully "turning Hudson's Bay into the South Sea."[14]

Later this Minnesota River theory, with its orientation toward Lake Winnipeg and Hudson's Bay, found its true champion in the Canadian political scientist and humorist Stephen Leacock (1869–1944), an enthusiastic chronicler of his country's early heroes.[15] Leacock took a liking to Lahontan and resented the Frenchman's harsh treatment at the hands of scholars. In 1932, he edited an updated English version of *Lahontan's Voyages*, praising the explorer and pressing the Canada-friendly Minnesota River interpretation of Letter XVI in his introduction.[16] Speaking to the Minnesota Historical Society the following year, Leacock bemoaned the fact that Lahontan's "voyage of discovery . . . was laughed at as a fabrication," explaining that over time the "legend of Lahontan as a liar grew and solidified," finally becoming "accepted as a fact without further examination. Even the honest and industrious Francis Parkman compares the story to Gulliver."[17]

Unfortunately for Leacock, the book's publishing house went under during the Great Depression, shortly after creating an initial run of several hundred volumes; today the edition remains a rare collector's item. However, Leacock's north-leaning view of Letter XVI resurfaced nearly six decades later. It is not surprising that when Canadian literary scholars published the modern critical edition of Lahontan's *Oeuvres Complètes* in 1990, they offered an elaborate but unconvincing northern interpretation similar to Leacock's.[18] In contrast, two experienced midwestern archaeologists suggested that Lahontan may have travelled up the South Platte River, which flows east through Colorado and Nebraska. Could Lahontan's "salt sea" be Utah's Great Salt Lake?[19]

What we do know is that Lahontan, without ever reaching the distant Pacific, still managed to bring back to the Atlantic world the first sketchy but accurate indications of Indigenous societies along the Northwest Coast. By far the most likely means for obtaining such information was by visiting the large Native American settlements that overlooked a vital portion of the extremely long Missouri River. It seems almost certain, therefore, that he actually made this excursion to the centre of the continent rather than fabricating it as many sceptics have charged. The best indication that, as claimed, he spent more than three months in the region archaeologists now refer to as the Middle and Upper Missouri Region comes from objects that he described in his narrative and illustrated on the margins of his map, including a midwestern dugout canoe and a Northwest Coast war canoe. Though long hidden in plain sight, they help to confirm the underlying truth of his narrative and argue for a journey that took the Frenchman all the way to what is now the state of North Dakota.

Walking across Iowa, and the Shift from Birchbark to Dugout Canoes

According to Letter XVI, Lahontan set out from Michilimackinac, at the strait connecting Lake Huron and Lake Michigan, on 22 September 1688. He was accompanied by his "own Detachment" of at least twenty men, and four or five seasoned Ottawa hunters who "did me a great deal of Service" (167, 185). Crossing northern Lake Michigan to Green Bay in familiar birchbark canoes, they ascended the Fox River to the new Grand Village of the "Outagami." These Fox Indians, or Meskwaki, had occupied this site in the middle portion of the Fox River valley for less than a decade, giving them significant new power in the region. From this strategic location, writes anthropologist Jeffery Behm, "the Meskwaki were able to control the flow of both European and Native American goods in the fur trade."[20]

Once settled, "the Meskwaki did not always conform to French wishes, and often worked at cross purposes to French goals," and after 1700, this led to

FIGURE 7.2. Looking southeast across the Mississippi River from the bluffs in northeast Iowa, one sees the mouth of the Wisconsin River, where it enters the Mississippi just below Prairie du Chien, Wisconsin, 19 June 2010. Photo: Peter Wood.

increased competition, strained relations, and a generation of violent conflict (1712–31).[21] But Lahontan was an early arrival who spoke an Algonquian dialect that they could understand, so he received careful scrutiny and then "a very kind Reception" (175). After the chief received assurances that the Frenchman was not headed northwest to trade arms to his enemies, the Sioux (in what is now Minnesota), the two leaders smoked ceremonial pipes and exchanged gifts. At that point Lahontan inquired, diplomatically, whether his host could "send six Warriours to accompany me to the long River, which I design'd to trace up to its Source" (176).

According to Lahontan, the Fox leader responded warmly to the visitor's request. Indeed, "instead of the six Warriours that I desir'd, he gave me ten, who understood the Lingua, and knew the Country of the *Eokoros*, with whom his Nation had maintain'd a Peace of twenty years standing."[22] The "Eokoros," for phonetic and other reasons, were evidently the Arikaras, located along the Middle Missouri River. It also appears clear that Indians from east of the Mississippi who went overland regularly to trade with them referred to the Middle Missouri as the Long River. Significantly, Lahontan's Ottawa companions were delighted by word of "this little Reinforcement, and were then so incouraged, that they told me above four times, that we might venture safely so far as the Plantation of the Sun" (177). The expanded party then portaged from the headwaters of the Fox River to the Wisconsin and descended that stream, reaching the Mississippi on 22 October (Figure 7.3). Two days later they had crossed and made camp on the west bank, in what is now eastern Iowa.

Then comes a mysterious nine-day gap in Lahontan's narrative, for the next sentence (still in the same paragraph) states: "The 2*d* of *November* we made the Mouth of the *Long River*" (178). The map, drawn up in Europe, suggests that Lahontan paddled north up the Mississippi during those days before entering directly into his Long River. But in fact the French appear to have moved swiftly across Iowa in those days, led by their experienced Fox guides and using a familiar east-west Indian trail that already existed.[23] The distance was long—roughly 300 miles—but several points make this journey conceivable. Autumn offered ideal hiking weather, and the men were extremely fit. Their packs contained minimal food supplies, since game was plentiful. Nor were extra trade goods necessary beyond appropriate gifts, since this was a journey of exploration, not trade. The land was open and relatively flat, with few streams to cross, and they could follow a well-travelled trail. Within a generation, that ancient trading path stretching across northern Iowa, from the mouth of the Wisconsin to the vicinity of Sioux City, would appear on French maps labelled as Chemin des Voyageurs (Road of the Voyageurs) (Figure 7.3).

Lahontan's Fox guides had travelled this path on prior occasions to trade with Indians living along the Missouri, and bits of archaeological evidence seem to confirm the connection.[24] So this direct land crossing between two major rivers appears quite plausible. But did the expedition manage an extended cross-country portage with their birchbark canoes or acquire other boats when they reached the Long River? Large birch canoes were sometimes shouldered, pulled with ropes, or moved overland using rude carriages with wheels, but such a long trek would be demanding. Besides, we now know that seventeenth-century Indians on both the Mississippi and the Missouri had an abundance of large dugout canoes, shaped from massive bottomland trees. These leafy giants disappeared during the 1800s, split into firewood for steamboats or cleared away by settlers in search of building material and rich farmland. But in prior centuries, Native American dugouts, usually made from poplar, were present in abundance and were constantly being created, borrowed, and exchanged.[25]

The natural habitat of white birch trees, with their pliable bark, did not extend south of Wisconsin, and portages demanding light canoes were infrequent throughout the vast Mississippi-Missouri watershed. Traditional dugouts, though heavy, gave ample protection against floating tree trunks and the submerged "deadheads" created by annual flooding, not to mention the huge sturgeon that inhabited the river system.[26] Lahontan's guides may have convinced him that such boats could be obtained readily when they reached the area where the Big Sioux River joins the Missouri, as that river turns south. (For the guides, this juncture may well have seemed the lower end of their "Long River," since above that point the Missouri flows from a northwesterly direction for hundreds of miles.) On the other hand, if the men somehow trundled their canoes across Iowa, they may have launched them again upon reaching the Missouri. When they transitioned to dugouts remains unclear, but there is no question that the shift occurred.

Lahontan's men moved rapidly up this Long River, which I shall call the Missouri. Soon his party reached the first of the three major Indian tribes that inhabited separate clusters of large villages along the river. On 8 November, they spotted a hunting party of Arikaras (Lahontan's "Eokoros"), who recognized the speech of his Fox Indian guides and welcomed them.[27] After a visit of several days, they proceeded upstream to the territory of the Mandans (Lahontan's "Essanapes").[28] But the Fox guides were now entering unfamiliar territory, and the Arikara chief, at odds with the Mandans in recent years, was reluctant to provide a "convoy" upriver. Instead, Lahontan writes, he offered to release half a dozen Mandan slaves "which I might carry home, and make use of as I saw occasion" (182). So with "six Slaves of that Country" serving as their guides, they arrived at the Mandans' "principle [*sic*] Village" or "Capital Canton" on 3 December "and there met with a very honourable Reception" (182, 186, 187).[29] As with the Arikaras, Lahontan

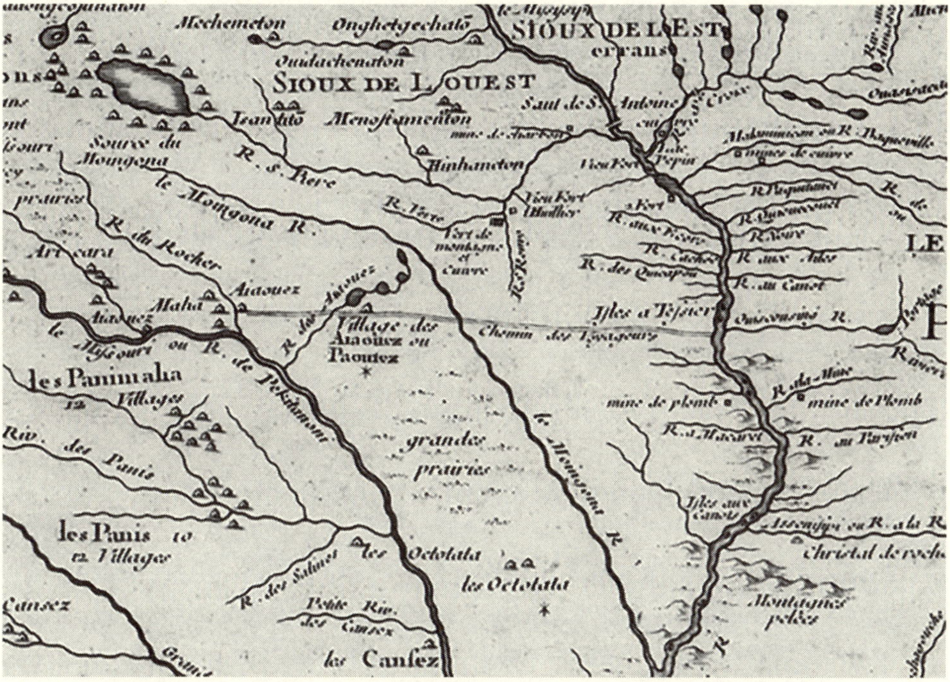

FIGURE 7.3. This detail from a 1718 French map by Guillaume Delisle, "Carte de la Louisiane et du Cours du Mississipi," shows the Mississippi on the right, the Missouri on the left, and the Des Moines (Moingona R.) in the centre. The Chemin des Voyageurs runs east-west from the mouth of the Wisconsin (Ouisconsing R.) to a group of villages, probably the Blood Run complex near the mouth of the Big Sioux. (Delisle labelled that river as "R du Rocher"; the Rock River is actually a tributary of the Big Sioux.) Note the vague location of Arikara (Aricara) villages on the left.

was struck by the huge population.[30] "The large extent of this Village might justly intitle it to the name of a City," he wrote, going on to admire the dozens of circular earth lodge dwellings. "The Houses are built almost like Ovens, but they are large and high; and most of 'em are of reeds cemented with fat earth" (188).

Seeking four rugged local dugout canoes to proceed farther upstream, Lahontan had no trouble obtaining them from his host. "I ask'd four Pirogues of him, which he granted very frankly, allowing me to pick and choose that number out of fifty" (187). "I was resolv'd to lose no time; and with that view order'd my Carpenters to plane the Pirogues; by which they were thinner and lighter by one half."[31] Lahontan's journey took place just as the French were learning to use these unfamiliar boats effectively. So if his men had managed to portage their bark canoes across Iowa, they might have paddled them up until this point, planning to use them again on their return journey.[32] But by the time he reached the Mandans, if not before, his guides may have convinced him a change was in order. The sight of ice chunks on the river in December may also have hastened the transition. Later, when Lahontan drew a log dugout on his map (Figure 7.4), he described it as the sort of canoe used by the "Essanapes" (or Mandans) and by the people he would encounter next, the "Gnacsitares." They appear to be the tribe later known by the similar term Minitaris, or the modern name Hidatsas.

The First European Account of a Northwest Coast War Canoe

Crossing Iowa on foot and proceeding up the Missouri, eventually in dugout canoes, might seem problematical, even a fabrication, if not for what happened next. As fierce winter weather set in, the explorers proceeded upriver, guided by "four *Essanapes* Slaves" (189), until they reached the settlements of the "Gnacsitares." These Hidatsa people lived in three villages near the mouth of the Knife River, roughly fifty miles northwest of modern Bismarck, North Dakota.[33] The party would remain here more than five weeks before turning homeward in late January. Once the Indians determined that the newcomers were not unwelcome Spaniards, relations warmed; the chief treated the guests hospitably, and he worked to answer their questions. Here, Lahontan gained the most striking information of his entire expedition, provided to him by four "slaves," or hostages, captured from a nation much farther west called the "Mozeemleks."[34] Most "unluckily," he lacked "a good Interpreter" and had to make do "with several Persons that did not well understand" (196). The picture that emerged seems clear even though, amazingly, it has been overlooked or misconstrued for three centuries.

Despite difficult translations involving several languages, Lahontan still managed to obtain a tantalizing, but clearly recognizable, description of Northwest Coast Indian cultures. His informants assured him "that the *Tahuglauk* wear their Beards two Fingers breadth long," and "that they cover their Heads with a sharp-pointed Cap." These people, he learned, were

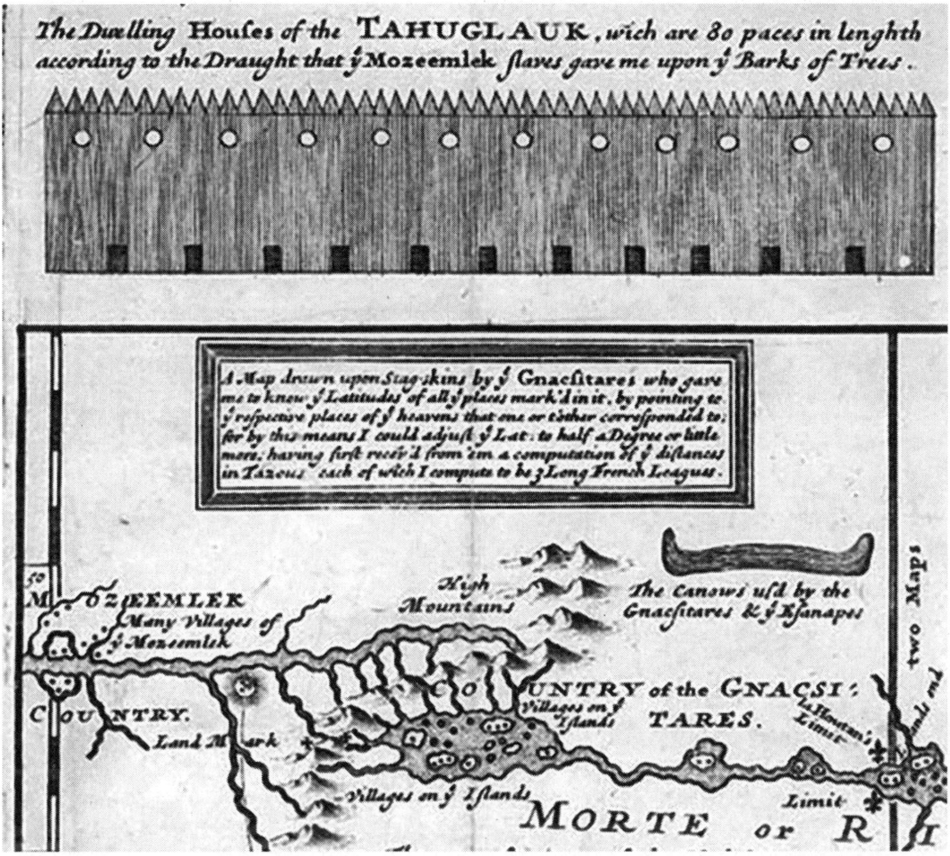

FIGURE 7.4. This detail from the English version of Lahontan's Long River map shows a dugout canoe of the sort used by inhabitants of the Upper Missouri.

avid traders and skilled artisans, with warlike dispositions and a hierarchical government—all recognizable traits of the region. Aware that he had a rare opportunity, the Frenchman "pumped" the westerners, as best he could, about the "Tahuglauk" and any further details they recalled "with relation to the Country, Commerce and Customs of that remote Nation," living beside salt water. "I would fain have satisfied my Curiosity in being an eye-witness of the Manners and Customs of the *Tahuglauk*," he lamented; "but that being impracticable, I was forc'd to be instructed at second hand by these *Mozeemlek* Slaves" (195–96).[35]

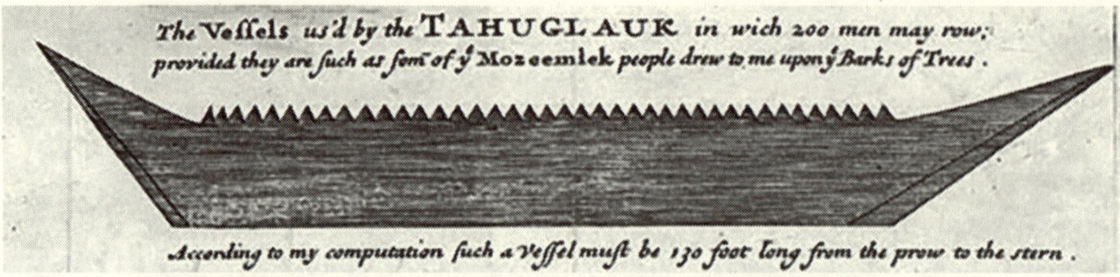

FIGURE 7.6 AND 7.7. When aligned bow to bow, the distinctive canoe likeness drawn on bark for Lahontan (left) conforms impressively with a "Diagram illustrating the Making of a Canoe," prepared by pioneer anthropologist Franz Boas more than two centuries later. Franz Boas, "The Kwakiutl of Vancouver Island," in *The Jesup North Pacific Expedition*, ed. Franz Boas, 10 vols. (New York: American Museum of Natural History, 1905–9), V, 349, Figure 63 (detail).

Several of Lahontan's questions drew revealing answers, augmented by simple illustrations that were originally sketched upon a deerskin or a strip of tree bark. For example, the Frenchman was told that the "Tahuglauk" lived in large distinctive houses with platform roofs "as you see 'em drawn in the Map" (194). The rough drawing his informants provided resembles the rectangular facade of a "plank house," with its characteristic row of cedar logs—massive, protruding, and evenly spaced—holding up the roof (Figure 7.4). In addition, one of the "*Mozeemlek* slaves had a reddish sort of Copper Medal hanging upon his Neck, the figure of which is represented in the Map" (Figure 7.1). Lahontan bargained for the object and asked the slaves for "a circumstantial Account of these Medals." In reply, "they gave me to understand, that they are made by the *Tahuglauk*, who are excellent Artisans, and put a great value upon such Medals" (195). As with the accounts of pointed hats and the short beards, both these drawings—the plank house and the copper gorget—capture prevalent and unmistakable characteristics of Northwest Coast traditional cultures from what is now southeast Alaska to northern Oregon.

That observation holds true as well for the map's largest image, the one that concerns us the most. The simple but thoroughly recognizable sketch portrays "The Vessels us'd by the TAHUGLAUK ... as som of ye *Mozeemlek* people drew to me upon ye Barks of Trees" (Figures 7.5 and 7.6). Lahontan relayed with confidence that when travelling by water along the "Sea" coast,

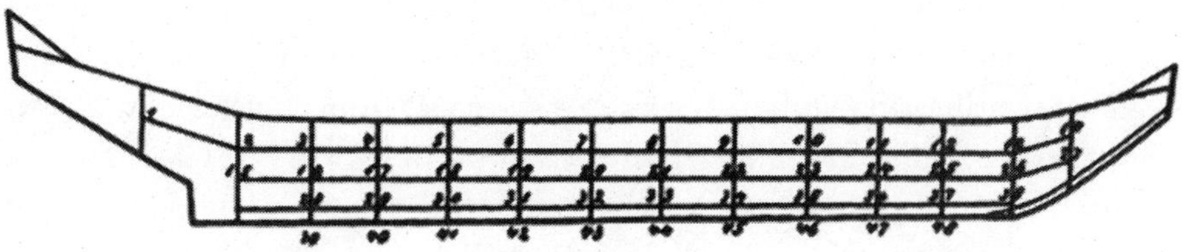

"they navigate with such Boats as you see drawn in the Map" (194). In conveying that these boats were enormous, larger than any they had ever seen on interior rivers, Lahontan's informants clearly embellished, leading him to state in his caption that some boats could hold "200 men" and to calculate that therefore "such a Vessel must be 130 foot long from the prow to the stern." Even at half that size, the boats were huge.[36] And if the speakers exaggerated the dimensions, they captured the distinctive design impressively. Their sketch, even after being transcribed several times by different hands, still shows clearly the long raised prow and the shorter stern protruding upward at a sharper angle that are central characteristics of what has become the most iconic of all Northwest Coast canoes.

European newcomers to the Caribbean and the Atlantic coast had marvelled at the size and variety of Indigenous canoes for nearly two centuries.[37] But no one, as yet, had taken back to Europe any likeness of North America's largest boat, the cedar war canoe of the Northwest Coast. Over centuries, Northwest Coast dugout canoes had evolved into at least half a dozen basic types, each varying in size and shape, with recognizable local characteristics. "Each of the types," as two experts explained a century ago, "has its own particular uses." Some are suited for the rough seas and rolling "combers" of the Pacific itself, while others are "designed for use on rivers and lakes." By far the largest, most wide-ranging, and most highly regarded of these types was called *tsaba ́xad* by the Salish and later became known to early anthropologists as the great "Alaska" canoe. This impressive war canoe was specifically "built for going to sea, and . . . designed with the idea of enabling the craft to ride waves without shipping water."[38]

Modern experts agree that "Chinookans west of the Cascade Mountains shared plankhouses, dugout canoes, dependence on fishing, and beliefs about social stratification with peoples along the coast from southeast Alaska to northwest California, all of whom are part of the Northwest Coast culture area."[39] Moreover, specialists on the Northwest Coast's canoe culture have long understood that "great Alaska canoes," created and "manned usually by Haida from the Queen Charlotte islands, or by Nootka from the west coast of Vancouver island; occasionally by people of other tribes." They often "came down from the north" at least as far as Puget Sound, creating a significant spectacle. Log boats of this striking size and design "were not used by the Puget Sound people, and were looked on with some curiosity." Through trade networks and other contacts stretching farther south, a rough sense of this "ultimate" Northwest Coast canoe and its awe-inspiring reputation would have been familiar to generations of inhabitants of the lower Columbia, even if they had never seen such a vessel first-hand.[40]

Lahontan's marginal depiction of such a huge and recognizable canoe is therefore significant for several reasons. It helps to broaden our understanding of how widely people and information travelled in the North American West, well before the relentless European intrusion into that region got under way. And, as with the dugouts that Lahontan had used on the Long River and then depicted, the unmistakable image of a Northwest Coast canoe helps to confirm that his journey was no fabrication. His explorations had taken him far up the Missouri River to winter among peoples who had long possessed captives from beyond the Continental Divide and used them as informants and guides. Only the large Native villages of the Upper Missouri, with their perpetual presence of such hostages from much farther west, could have provided him with striking, if frustratingly thin, evidence about lifeways on the Northwest Coast. No comparable path for transmitting such information existed, by land or sea, in 1689.

More than a century later a young Shoshone prisoner, taken east to serve as a slave among the Mandan, would share her valuable knowledge about the distant Northwest with the Lewis and Clark expedition. But Sacagawea is only the best known of hundreds of captives over many generations taken from beyond the Rocky Mountains to the valley of the Upper Missouri. Some of these sojourners brought with them striking first-, second-, or third-hand information about societies located still farther west, beyond their homeland. As North American scholars venture beyond their traditional fascination with northeastern birchbark canoes, learning more about Missouri river dugouts and the largest canoes of the Pacific coast, it becomes clearer that Lahontan actually visited the Upper Missouri in the winter of 1688–89 and became the first person to provide information to Europe about these remarkable boats and their distant makers.

Notes

1 On Nicolet, see Patrick J. Jung, *The Misunderstood Mission of Jean Nicolet: Uncovering the Story of the 1634 Journey* (Madison: Wisconsin Historical Society Press, 2018). On La Salle, see Peter H. Wood, "La Salle: Discovery of a Lost Explorer," *American Historical Review* 89 (April 1984): 294–323; Robert S. Weddle, *The Wreck of the* Belle, *the Ruin of La Salle* (College Station: Texas A&M University Press, 2005); and James E. Bruseth and Toni S. Turner, *From a Watery Grave: The Discovery and Excavation of La Salle's Shipwreck*, La Belle (College Station: Texas A&M University Press, 2005).

2 See the numerous references to Lahontan in Jonathan I. Israel, *Radical Enlightenment: Philosophy and the Making of Modernity, 1650–1750* (New York: Oxford University Press, 2001), 13, 67, 72, 74, 77, 89, 102, 134, 180, 272, 371, 580–82, 593, 597, 633, 685.

3 Lahontan's respectful treatment of Native Americans helped to inspire Jean-Jacques Rousseau's "noble savage," so scholars in cultural studies and literature have long been fascinated by *New Voyages*. Likewise, anthropologists have found that the book's early first-hand ethnographic observations regarding Indigenous life in North America hold up surprisingly well under scrutiny.

4 Jonathan Swift, *Gulliver's Travels* (London: Benjamin Motte, 1726). Lemuel Gulliver, Swift's convincing narrator, recounted his fictional 1699 voyage to Lilliput in the Indian Ocean. Gulliver went on to claim that in 1703, blown off course in the North Pacific, he had discovered Brobdingnab, a huge (and non-existent) peninsula extending west into the ocean. Playing on European ignorance of and interest in the geography of America's Northwest Coast, Swift even included a rough map of Gulliver's supposed "discovery."

5 At the time Lahontan published *New Voyages*, Europeans were devouring travel literature, real and imaginary, with equal relish. See Geoffroy Atkinson, *The Extraordinary Voyage in French Literature from 1700 to 1720* (Paris: É. Champion, 1922); Percy G. Adams, *Travelers and Travel Liars, 1660–1800* (Berkeley: University of California Press, 1962).

6 Lahontan wrote in a preface to the first English edition of *New Voyages* (London, 1703) that he had "corrected almost all the Cuts [drawings] of the Holland Impression, for the Dutch Gravers had murder'd 'em, by not understanding their Explications, which were all in French" (9–10). This and subsequent quotations of Lahontan are taken from volume 1 of Baron de Lahontan, *New Voyages to North America*, ed. Reuben Gold Thwaites, reprinted from the English edition of 1703, 2 vols. (Chicago: A.C. McClurg and Co., 1905). Letter XVI spans pages 167–215 in volume 1.

7 In Letter XV (18 September 1688) the young baron, afraid to commit a bit of New World political gossip to paper, remarked to his unnamed patron in Paris: "I must go no farther upon this matter, lest my Letter should be intercepted.... If it pleases God to allow me a safe

Return to France, I shall tell you the Story by word of mouth." Lahontan, *New Voyages to North America*, 165.

8 Wood, "La Salle," 296, 313–14.

9 The Clements Library, University of Michigan in Ann Arbor, contains this "Brief Discourse" in French, which the library describes as "An important plan offered by Lahontan to the British for Control of North America." The thirteen-page manuscript was given to William Blathwayt, the English Secretary for Trade and Plantations, who forwarded it "to My Lord Nottingham" (Daniel Finch, Second Earl of Nottingham, Secretary of State under Queen Anne, 1702–4).

10 Francis Parkman, *La Salle and the Discovery of the Great West* (New York: Random House, 1985 [1879]), 349–50. Such comparisons with Swift became commonplace. A generation later, Louise Phelps Kellogg, a scholar of the early French presence in the Great Lakes region, wrote, "After reaching the Mississippi, Lahontan indulged in pages of description of a voyage to an imaginary river which he calls 'Long,' with unknown tribes thereon. Whether this journey was intended as a satire like Gulliver's voyage to Lilliput, or was a deliberate fabrication, has never been determined." Kellogg, *The French Régime in Wisconsin and the Northwest* (Madison: State Historical Society of Wisconsin, 1925), 240.

11 Justin Winsor, *The Mississippi Basin: The Struggle in America between England and France, 1697–1763* (Boston: Houghton Mifflin, 1898), 80–82. Commenting on the fresh edition of *New Voyages* prepared by Reuben G. Thwaites after the turn of the century, an anonymous reviewer in the *Bulletin of the American Geographical Society* 37, no. 9 (1905): 576 observed: "It is not surprising that Lahontan's volumes had great vogue in Europe and were published in its five leading languages. . . . But all the really good material he presented came, in time, to be neglected by writers on the New World because his story of Long River and its discovery was false."

12 Page numbers in parentheses refer to volume 1 of Baron de Lahontan, *New Voyages to North America*, ed. Reuben Gold Thwaites.

13 The mapping of the upper Mississippi river basin had been completed in 1843 (Joseph N. Nicollet, *The Hydrographical Basin of the Upper Mississippi River, 1843* [St. Paul: Minnesota Historical Society, 1976]), and new settlers were beginning to explore and promote their regional history. Searching for early European arrivals, they turned to Lahontan and his map. In January 1850, a local minister discussed Lahontan before an early gathering of the Minnesota Historical Society. Rev. Edward D. Neill, "French Voyageurs to Minnesota during the Seventeenth Century," *Collections of the Minnesota Historical Society* (St. Paul: Minnesota Historical Society, 1872), 1:13.

14 James H. Perkins, *Annals of the West* (Cincinnati, 1846), 20. Expanded editions were published in St. Louis in 1850 and Pittsburgh in 1857.

15 Born in England and raised on a farm in Ontario as the third of eleven children, Leacock's numerous interests included early Canadian history. He wrote three contributions to the Chronicles of Canada series, all published in 1914. Leacock's academic education bridged the United States and Canada, so he was well positioned to argue for an explorer who had travelled on the Mississippi and roamed somewhere across the upper Midwest of the United States.

16 Baron de Lahontan, *Lahontan's Voyages*, ed. Stephen Leacock, reprinted from the English edition of 1703 (Ottawa: Graphic Publishers, 1932).

17 "Finally," Leacock concluded, "Mr. J.E. Roy, in a paper—admirable but erroneous—presented to the Royal Society of Canada in 1894, covers the whole career of Lahontan and rules him out of court as an infidel and a liar. Since then oblivion has fallen on the baron. In the latest edition of the *Encyclopaedia Britannica* there is no article on Lahontan and no reference to his name appears in the index." Stephen Leacock, "Lahontan in Minnesota," *Minnesota History* 14, no. 4 (December

1933): 367–77 (abstract of an address delivered to the Minnesota Historical Society on 18 October 1933).

18 Lahontan, *Oeuvres Complètes*, ed. Réal Ouellet and Alaine Beaulieu, 2 vols. (Montréal: Les Presses de l'Université de Montréal, 1990), 1:383ff., and editors' map of "Voyage à la Rivière Longue" following 1:199.

19 W. Raymond Wood, "A Review of Past Criticisms and the Baron Lahontan's Mapping of His Long River"; Steven G. Baker, "Spanish Documentary Confirmation of Lahontan's Observations Regarding the Great Salt Lake and the Atypical Bearded 'Ainu-Like' Indians of Utah's Grand Teguayo" (papers given at the 64th Plains Anthropological Conference, Topeka, Kansas, 2006).

20 Jeffery A. Behm, "The Meskwaki in Eastern Wisconsin: Ethnohistory and Archaeology," *Wisconsin Archaeologist* 89, nos. 1–2 (January–December 2008): 7–85. Grand Village sat on the south shore of a big lake that the French associated with an ancient burial mound, or "Butte des Morts." The large town, surrounded by "extensive areas of garden beds used to cultivate maize, squash, beans, and tobacco," and known to archaeologists as the Bell Site in Winnebago County (47WN9), was occupied for half a century between 1680 and 1730. Quotations from pp. 12–13.

21 Behm, "The Meskwaki," 13: "After 1730, following two disastrous wars with the French and their Native American allies, the Meskwaki began to relocate westward, first to the lower Wisconsin River in western Wisconsin and eventually west of the Mississippi River." Also see R. David Edmunds and Joseph L. Peyser, *The Fox Wars: The Mesquakie Challenge to New France* (Norman: University of Oklahoma Press, 1993).

22 "Two of the ten Warriours that he gave me, could speak the Language of the *Outaouas*, which I was well pleas'd with; not that I was a stranger to their own Language, for between that and the *Algonkin* there is no great difference, but . . . there were several words that puzzled me" (176).

23 Peter H. Wood, "'A Venture to the Plantation of the Sun': Lahontan's 1688 Journey across Iowa and Beyond," *Journal of the Iowa Archaeological Society* 62 (2015): 1–12.

24 Jeffery Behm, who has led excavations in Wisconsin, reports a rim sherd suggesting that "at least one pottery vessel" from Lot 1615 at the Bell site "is nearly identical to protohistoric vessels from the Middle Missouri Region." Behm, correspondence with Peter Wood, 4 June 2018.

25 Peter H. Wood, "Missing the Boat: Ancient Dugout Canoes in the Mississippi-Missouri Watershed," *Early American Studies* 16, no. 2 (Spring 2018): 197–254. When Marquette and Jolliet explored the Mississippi in 1673, they encountered "great wooden canoes." Reuben Gold Thwaites, ed., *The Jesuit Relations and Allied Documents*, vol. 59: *Lower Canada, Illinois, Ottawas, 1673–1677* (Cleveland: Burrows Brothers, 1899), 151. Later, Jolliet drew a map of their explorations: *Nouvelle decouverte de plusieurs nations dans la Nouvelle France en l'année 1673 et 1674*. It shows Indian villages at the mouth of the Des Moines River (below modern Keokuk, Iowa). His French inscription beside a Peoria town there reads: "300 Cabanes 180 canots de bois de 50 pieds de long" (300 cabins, 180 wooden canoes of 50 feet in length).

26 See Wood, "Missing the Boat," 231–37: "Indeed, the very word *Missouri* comes from *Missouria*, an Algonquian (and Siouan) term meaning 'wooden canoe people' or 'people of the big canoe,' used to name the Indians who lived along the Lower Missouri" (236–37).

27 "As soon as the Huntsmen heard the voice of the *Outagamis*, they threw down their Arms, and presented the Company with some Deer that they had just kill'd, which they likewise help'd to carry to my Canows. The Benefactors were . . . *Eokoros*, who had . . . come thither to hunt" (180).

28 An authority on Mandan history discusses Lahontan's use of names as follows: "What about the Essanapes, the Eokoros' upstream neighbors? Were they the Mandans, upstream neighbors of the Arikaras? The evidence is circumstantial. There is little similarity between the name 'Essanape'

and any of the known names of the Mandans. (Numakaki and Matátana come closest.) But the Essanapes and Eokoros were confirmed enemies, as were the Mandans and Arikaras. The Mandans in turn had friendly relations with their own upstream neighbors, the Hidatsas or Minetares." Elizabeth A. Fenn, *Encounters at the Heart of the World: A History of the Mandan People* (New York: Hill and Wang, 2014), 46.

29 By mistake, Lahontan gives the date as 3 November 1688, instead of 3 December.

30 The extensive populations that Lahontan reported along the Long River have often been used to discredit his account. But recent scholarship underscores the large size of these groups on the Upper Missouri before they were overtaken and decimated by smallpox. As Elizabeth Fenn notes, "the enormous number of Eokoros Lahontan reported on the Long River, rather than proving his story false, may support its truthfulness." Fenn, *Encounters at the Heart of the World*, 46.

31 According to Lahontan, the handiwork of voyageurs, using sharp metal axes and adzes, left the Native American onlookers awestruck. "The poor innocent People of this Country," he recalled, "could not conceive how we work'd with an Axe; every stroke we gave they cry'd out, as if they had seen some new Prodigy; nay, the firing of Pistols could not divert' em from that Amazement, though they were equally strangers both to the Pistol and the Axe" (188). Native Americans west of the Mississippi were getting their first close look at the amazing efficiency of metal axes. For their part, the early French explorers were learning about the effectiveness of the large native dugouts that had been in use in the American heartland for centuries.

32 "As soon as my Pirogues were got ready, I left my Canows with the Governour or Prince, and beg'd of him that they might remain untouch'd by any body; in which point he was very faithful to me" (188). When Lahontan called these boats *pirogues*, in contrast to the *canoes* he left behind, was he signalling a transition? Elsewhere he seems to use both terms interchangeably.

33 By the early nineteenth century, both the Mandans and Hidatsas, greatly diminished in numbers, would be living in the Knife River area. In 1804–5, the Lewis and Clark expedition spent the winter in the vicinity, at Fort Mandan on the eastern bank of the Missouri River.

34 It remains unclear which western groups these four represented. They may have been from the vicinity of the major Indigenous trading centre on the Columbia River called the Dalles, or, like Sacagawea in the early 1800s, they might have been Shoshone. Through translators, the slaves told Lahontan that it was "their Misfortune to be took Prisoners by the *Gnacsitares* in the War which had lasted for eighteen Years; but, that they hoped a Peace would be speedily concluded, upon which the Prisoners would be exchang'd, pursuant to the usual Custom" (194–95).

35 Significantly, the Chinookan word along the lower Columbia for "Downstreamers" (peoples living farther west near the mouth of the river, and associated groups beyond) was *itgígʷalatkš*. This term, when passed to Lahontan through a series of Native informants, might well have yielded the label that he transcribed as "Tahuglauk." David V. Ellis, "Cultural Geography of the Lower Columbia," in *Chinookan Peoples of the Lower Columbia*, ed. Robert T. Boyd, Kenneth M. Ames, and Tony A. Johnson (Seattle: University of Washington Press, 2013), 47.

36 The Great Canoe in the American Museum of Natural History in New York City was constructed on the Northwest Coast in the late 1870s, perhaps by Haida carvers. This massive dugout canoe was made from a single trunk of western red cedar, and it measures 63 feet long. Experts in 1920 reported the existence of another canoe specimen "which has a length of 80 ft." T.T. Waterman and Geraldine Coffin, *Types of Canoes on Puget Sound*, Indian Notes and Monographs series (New York: Museum of the American Indian, Heye Foundation, 1920), 12–13. This source is available at http://www.gutenberg.org/files/49144/49144-h/49144-h.htm.

37 On 13 October 1492, the day after Columbus reached the Bahamas, he described in his log the impressive dugout canoes in use among the islanders. "After sunrise people from San Salvador again began to come to our ships in boats fashioned in one piece from the trunks of trees. These boats are wonderfully made, considering the country we are in, and every bit as fine as those I have seen in Guinea. . . . Some can carry 40 or 50 men." Robert H. Fuson, trans., *The Log of Christopher Columbus* (Camden, ME: International Marine Publishing, 1987), 77.

38 "Its most characteristic features are a prominent and lofty bow and stern." These "elevated additions to the hull are designed to throw aside the seas. The naked hull without these bow and stern pieces would soon fill in rough water. . . . In the course of generations they have been reduced to the most slender proportions which will give the necessary protection, and they are wonderfully effective in aiding the actual navigation of the canoe. Many Indians and whites who have followed the sea tell us that this type of canoe ships less water in a storm than any craft in the world." Waterman and Coffin, *Types of Canoes*, 11–15.

39 "Through the mid-20th century, some anthropologists tried to distinguish divisions and subdivisions of culture areas by defining clusters of culture traits. This method placed many adjacent peoples into different culture areas and subareas, ignoring intimate social ties among them. Chinookans—as well as most of their neighbors—participated in a much larger social network, known as the Greater Lower Columbia." Robert T. Boyd, preface to *Chinookan Peoples of the Lower Columbia*, xi.

40 Waterman and Coffin, *Types of Canoes*, 11–14. "No better craft for rough water," these authors concluded a century ago, "has ever been devised."

CANADA
WINNIPEG
Red River
Bois de Sioux River
Minnesota River
UNITED STATES
Mississippi River
ATLANTIC OCEAN
New Orleans
South Padre Island
Gulf Of Mexico
La Pesca
Tropic of Cancer
MEXICO
Cancún
Cozumel Channel
Veracruz
BELIZE
HONDURAS
Caribbean Sea
NICARAGUA
COSTA RICA
PANAMA
Punta Peñas
Port of Spain
Pedernales
VENEZUELA
Orinoco River
PACIFIC OCEAN
Puerto Ayacucho
COLOMBIA
Casiquiare Canal
Equator
Rio Negro
Santarém
BELÉM
Manaus
Amazon River
N
0
100 km
BRAZIL

CHAPTER 8

Monumental Trip: Don Starkell's Canoe Voyage from Winnipeg to the Mouth of the Amazon

ALBERT BRAZ

But now
That the forests are cut down, the rivers charted,
Where can you turn, where can you travel?
—Douglas LePan

At the beginning of his 1987 book *Paddle to the Amazon: The Ultimate 12,000-Mile Canoe Adventure,* Don Starkell reflects on the significance of the fact that there was no one waiting for him and his son Dana after they completed their epic trip from Winnipeg to Belém, Brazil, and remarks that "perhaps we deserve such a fate. We have come too far."[1] However, I would argue that Starkell had not just travelled too far but in the wrong direction. He did not journey either east or west—or north, as he would do in his subsequent kayak trip to the Arctic—but south. His Latin American destination likely explains the astonishing lack of scholarship on his record-breaking accomplishments as a canoeist.[2] For most Canadians, the portion of the continent below the United States–Mexico border remains largely what Starkell would call uncharted territory and outside the national sphere of interest. But I suspect that two other interrelated factors account for his neglect by literary scholars and social scientists who study the social significance of the canoe: his lack of a wilderness ideology, and his working-class identity. The literature on canoeing, unlike canoeing itself, tends to be rather genteel, focusing extensively on affluent and environmentally conscious individuals who try to attain oneness with their world and themselves by navigating rivers and lakes in self-propelled watercraft. Starkell, though, is very much a working-class figure—his limited cultural capital being most conspicuously illustrated by the fact he could not even claim full authorship of his book about the trip. While proudly flying the Maple Leaf everywhere he travelled, he used the canoe not only to test himself but also to prove that he was worthy of the respect of his better networked co-citizens.[3] He is thus a reminder that there are other critical divides in Canada beyond the one between humans and nature, which may indicate why he has not attained the iconic standing he merits.

Donald George Starkell was born in 1932 in the North End of Winnipeg, the city where he would spend almost his whole life until his death, of cancer, in 2012. He came from a troubled family, as reflected in his being unable to "recall a [single] conversation with his mother or father."[4] In *Paddle to the Amazon*, Starkell identifies 1939 as the defining year in his life, when his "household dissolved."[5] He relates that both he and his sister were often left on their own by their father and stepmother. In particular, he recalls the harrowing memories of "shivering for hours at night by the outside door, sometimes in 30-below temperatures, as I waited for my father or stepmother to come home and let me in."[6] When the Children's Aid Society was apprised of their father's negligence, the whole family was hauled to court. There, the judge offered Starkell and his sister "the choice of returning home or going to live in the Children's Home, an enormous yellow-brick institution on Academy Road. [They] chose the Children's Home."[7] Starkell would spend the next five years in that "awful place," an ordeal that would leave him full of "poisons,"[8] poisons that he would battle for decades. In 1944, to his utter bewilderment, he was dispatched to the foster home of an elderly widow named Mrs. Bale. But just as he was starting to adjust to his new environs, Mrs. Bale died and he was returned to the Children's Home. Soon afterward he was sent to live with another foster family, that of Eric Roberts, who saved him, not the least by introducing him to canoeing on a creek that bordered their property in the Winnipeg neighbourhood of North Kildonan.

Starkell confides that he was so scarred by his five years at the Children's Home that by the time he left it, he had no sense of self. With "no love that mattered, no real friends or family, no home," he came to see himself as "a thoroughly insignificant human being."[9] Yet the experience had another indelible impact, which was to impress upon him the determination not to allow it to shape his destiny. As a child, he "developed a consuming need to overcome that insignificance, to *be* somebody."[10] Moreover, he could envisage such a possibility only thanks to his discovery of the canoe, which afforded him "the first freedom in [his] life," enabling him to "paddle miles in any direction."[11] He states that the canoe was "the most reliable antidote" to the many toxins that assailed him and that when he was paddling, he "felt free, independent, self-sufficient." Most significantly, he felt "in control."[12]

The power of the canoe was dramatically demonstrated to Starkell in the spring of 1950. When Winnipeg was inundated by a historic flood, he "spent a good deal of time paddling up and down our street, delivering bread and milk to stranded neighbours."[13] Later that year he joined the Kildonan Canoe Club and gradually transformed himself into a highly successful competitor in both canoe and kayak races. In the 1950s and '60s, Starkell entered "hundreds of races, including 12 professional races, of which I won 10."[14] The most celebrated of these contests was the 1967 Centennial Trans-Canada Canoe Pageant, in which ten six-paddler teams representing either a Canadian province or territory[15] journeyed from Rocky Mountain House in Alberta to the Expo 67 site in Montreal. The 5,283-kilometre race, sponsored by the federal government as part of a suite of centennial year events, was judged by the minister in charge as "the most difficult and personally hazardous of all the national celebrations."[16] Each canoe was named after an explorer associated with Canada. Starkell was part of the Manitoba team and its "canoe bore the name of one of his heroes, Pierre-Esprit Radisson."[17] Interestingly, he deduced that he was the target of anti-Winnipeg feeling from the rest of the crew, notably its leader, Norm Crerar. "The captain," alleges Starkell, "wanted an all Flin Flon team and he did everything possible for 104 days to get me off the team and I wouldn't break."[18] Manitoba led most of the way and would reach Montreal in "531 hours and 6 minutes" (just over an hour ahead of British Columbia),[19] nearly four months after departing the headwaters of the North Saskatchewan River.

The Centennial Pageant would appear to be directly linked to the Amazon trip, although Starkell does not make that connection. Besides the purported animosity of his Flin Flon–based teammates, Starkell faced another major obstacle in 1967, which was the length of the race. He had been working as a sales representative for the Canadian Pacific Railway (CPR) but when he "asked for a leave of absence . . . , it was flatly denied."[20] Starkell, who felt that as an adult he "had seldom broken form," took the rejection personally and one day "walked into my supervisor's office and quit my job"[21]— or was fired. By then he had three children, two boys and a girl. There are indications that his wife, Ann, was not overly enthusiastic about his decision. Three years later, in the summer of 1970, Ann not only handed him "a letter saying that she was leaving, immediately," but also informed him that she was taking the children. Considering that Starkell describes the breakup of his marriage as "swift and painful—and thoroughly unexpected"—one cannot help but surmise that his obsession with canoeing was not shared by all his intimates, a view that would have been only reinforced when he soon started planning a singular trip to South America with his sons, Dana and Jeff.[22]

Starkell was not the first Canadian to head for Latin America in the wake of the dissolution of a long-term romantic relationship.[23] What is unusual about him is that instead of flying, driving, or riding either a motorcycle or a bicycle, he elected to make his journey by canoe. Not only that, he would take his young sons along on the great adventure. Within a year of his wife leaving Starkell, Dana and Jeff had gone back to live with him, with only his daughter Sherri remaining with Ann. Haunted by the spectre of coming from "a broken home," Don deduced that what he and the boys needed was "a new focus, a long-range plan of some sort that would carry the three of [them] purposefully into the future."[24] This would be "a monumental canoe-trip—not just of a few hundred miles or a few weeks but of many thousand miles and many months—possibly even years," the kind of feat that would give his sons both "a challenge and an education."[25] Starkell remarks that Dana had long talked about walking to the Amazonian jungle, so one day he asked his oldest child, "How about we canoe from Winnipeg to the Amazon?"[26] Or as Dana recollects the exchange, "Dana, how would you like to get in a canoe one day, and we'll paddle so far south, we'll paddle right outta winter?"[27] Given the magnitude of the enterprise, as well as the fact that at the time

Dana and Jeff were respectively nine and eight years old, it would be a full decade before they could try to carry out their audacious plan.

The canoe is often perceived not only as "a symbol unique to Canada" but as "perhaps the greatest gift of the Native Peoples to later cultures,"[28] a vision of the country that some have argued has been used to "justify a history of colonialism."[29] Part of the appeal of the long canoe trip for Canadians is that it enables "paddlers to take up the subject positions of the explorer or voyageur (or even the 'Indian')," evincing the popular "belief that by paddling a canoe we make ourselves Canadian."[30] As Misao Dean says of the celebrated Winnipeg canoeist Bill Mason, Mason was convinced that the canoe would help "to overcome the alienation of white Canadians from the land."[31] But this is not quite the case with Starkell, as one might deduce from his trajectory. Starkell, in fact, does not seem to be driven by the need to prove his Canadianness, but rather his self-worth. That said, he does not escape the shadow of the giants of the waterways, albeit not northern ones.

Starkell states that soon after the "fantasy plan" to take a marathon canoe trip with his sons entered his head, he began wondering if it would be possible "to paddle all the way from Canada to South America."[32] While aware that such an expedition had never been attempted, he also knew that this was no reason for not trying. Those sorts of challenges had certainly never stopped the famed navigators of the past. He acknowledges that he had "always been fascinated by the great travels of Columbus and Cortés, of Orellana and von Humboldt, and, in more recent years, of Papillon. I had read about them since childhood, and had never been more intrigued by their achievements than I was now."[33] Starkell was particularly inspired by Francisco de Orellana (1511–64), the Spanish conquistador and explorer who made the first recorded navigation of the Amazon River, promptly named the Orellana River.[34] So influenced was Starkell by "the first white man to navigate the Amazon River in 1541" that he and his sons decided to name their custom-built fibreglass canoe after the Renaissance explorer, calling it the *Orellana*.[35]

After ten years of planning, Dana, Jeff, and Don Starkell departed Winnipeg on 1 June 1980, for what they expected to be a two-year trip that would take them through thirteen countries and culminate in the symbolically named Brazilian city of Belém, or Bethlehem. Dana was then nineteen and Jeff eighteen, but Don had reasons to be concerned about his companions besides their youth. Dana, an aspiring classical guitarist, "had been severely asthmatic and heavily addicted to medications" for a dozen years.[36] The would-be electronics technician Jeff, in turn, showed "something less than total" commitment to the voyage, an attitude Don attributed to the influence of "his relatives on his mother's side."[37] Jeff himself later admitted that his maternal aunts and uncles told him he was "crazy" to be joining his father and that he was "gonna die."[38] The trip was relatively uneventful along the Red River and its tributaries, except for the portages across the north-south Continental Divide, in which they twice had to pull the *Orellana* on a trailer "like horses."[39] The journey remained undramatic down the Mississippi all the way to New Orleans, and then along the Intracoastal Waterway of Louisiana and Texas, even if the Canadian "*long-haired hippies*" were publicly admonished in the latter state for "*going around smoking pot and sinning—Repent!*"[40] But it was a different story once they reached the Gulf of Mexico. Partly because of their lack of experience with open-sea canoeing, the Starkells kept getting "licked" by the Gulf,[41] which would overturn their canoe and leave them so dispirited that even Don feared he was "developing a near-psychosis about quitting the trip."[42] Then after they finally reached Laguna Madre in October, they discovered that the waters were too shallow for paddling, requiring them to drag the canoe for kilometres and resulting in painful cuts and bruises. Don professed to be "proud of our accomplishment," being the first individuals to have "ever paddled from Canada to Mexico," something he doubted anyone else would try to replicate.[43] But the three of them were so physically and mentally battered that they were unable to contemplate going back on the Gulf and were "forced to accept [their] fate," their "defeat,"[44] and abandoned the trip.

Their intention was to spend the winter in the port city of Veracruz, approximately 800 kilometres south of Laguna Madre, and then determine what to do in the spring. Jeff, though, complicated matters by deciding to return home. He not only felt that he was "wasting his time" in Mexico but, more disconcerting, that canoeing in the Gulf was "just too crazy . . . , suicide!"[45] While disappointed that his "sensible" son[46] was bailing out on their odyssey, Don agreed that the Gulf was "no place for a canoe."[47] Serendipitously, almost as soon as they arrived in Veracruz, they were approached by a Mexican engineering student named Gabriel Delgado, who wanted to practise his English. Hailing from the interior city of Aguascalientes, Delgado had "never been in a canoe."[48] But as he got to know Don and Dana, he became captivated by their voyage and before long was persuaded to join them as far as Veracruz. So in February 1981, the three of them travelled north to Laguna Madre to resume the trip where the Starkells had left off. The Gulf was not nearly as calm as Don had been led to believe, but then he did not wait until June, as advised. After experiencing "a comedy of both errors and terrors," as they confronted "bank upon bank of deafening 8-foot breakers," Don, Dana, and their new Mexican crewmate at last were on their way.[49] Don, who had long prided himself on being able to dictate the distance he would paddle on any given day of a canoe trip, had to concede that this was no longer the case. "The Gulf," he states, "tells us what *it* wants us to do—what it will allow us to do."[50] Working in concert with Delgado, Don and Dana were able to significantly improve their "launching and landing techniques"[51] and started making excellent time. By 5 March, they were back in Veracruz.

Don and Dana formed a close bond with Delgado,[52] who among other things introduced them to the guava fruit and showed them "how to peel cactus leaves and retrieve the thin layer of core pulp, which is full of moisture and can be used as a source of water in an emergency."[53] They would have loved for Delgado to accompany them all the way to Belém, but after Veracruz they were on their own. Don and Dana spent little time in town, since they were in a hurry to round the Yucatán Peninsula and enter the ostensibly more placid waters of the Caribbean Sea. But a mere few days out of Veracruz they were "picked up" by a rogue wave and "flung . . . through the air, upside down, into the sea," and then watched helplessly as a "deadly current" carried them "steadily further from shore."[54] Luckily, a group of fishermen spotted them and towed them back to land, where they were able to repair the serious damage inflicted on the *Orellana*. Don and Dana eventually made it out of Mexico and into their "fourth country," Belize.[55] They were warned by local fishermen to pay special attention to their safety because of the high levels of crime, but instead of being targeted by humans, they were pounded by nature. The small island where they spent the night was hit by a thunder and lightning storm, with gale-strong winds so potent that they became convinced only "a miracle"[56] prevented their canoe from becoming untethered.

If anything, things only got more ominous in the other Central American countries and then in South America—but usually because of the human factor. Despite their best efforts to avoid Guatemala's high-risk coast, they were intercepted by a military gunboat whose taciturn crew dragged them into deep water and ordered them to unload the canoe. Don became so exasperated with the Guatemalan soldiers that he "let loose with a tirade in Spanish: We're Canadians! We're a father and son! We're peaceful people! You have no right to keep us here!" He further warned the soldiers that they were "reporting . . . regularly" to the Canadian government and its embassies in the region,[57] at which point the captain allowed them continue.[58] After Don and Dana entered Honduras, as they got set for dinner on a windy beach, they were confronted by two drunken men, one of whom was armed. Suspecting that Don and Dana were working for the Sandinistas, the two men took the Canadians captive and three times forced them to kneel, as if ready to execute them, leading Don to ask himself: "Why, why did I ever drag my son into this?"[59] Don and Dana were then taken to a small military station, and they realized that part of their dilemma was that people were not able to accept their story, since "*nobody* paddles the ocean in a canoe!"[60] Thanks to the intervention of the local storekeeper, who spoke English and believed them, Don and Dana were reprieved, but without many of their most prized possessions, notably their machete, survival rifle, and handgun. As Don lamented soon after reaching South America, "If it's not the thieves, it's the seas; or the rain; or the bugs; or the sun; or the police or the army."[61] Indeed, there must have been many times when he and Dana could not have but felt that both the natural and human world, particularly the latter, had conspired to ensure that they would not complete their journey.

The most striking aspect of the Starkells' Amazon trip is of course its sheer length, both in terms of distance and time. Don has been labelled "an extreme canoeist,"[62] an assessment that is hard to dispute, and has been roundly condemned for exposing his teenaged sons to such extraordinary dangers, including by his former wife.[63] One of his most strident critics has been the religion scholar William C. James, who disapproves of the voyage's goal orientation. James is caustic in his condemnation of the trip's focus on the distance travelled, which he claims renders it "a classic instance of the ultimate male canoe adventure."[64] He goes as far as to contend that mothers and daughters do not have relationships like the one between Don and Dana, and that "it would be difficult to imagine two women even wanting to attempt the kind of trip the Starkells made."[65] Notwithstanding the fact Don never seems to have contemplated taking his daughter Sherri on the

Amazon expedition, it is not self-evident that such ventures are exclusively male pursuits. Grey Owl's most famous paramour, Anahareo, for example, is well-known for taking extended canoe trips for the simple pleasure of prospecting for silver and gold.[66] Even more germane, kayaker Victoria Jason did not consider Don's plan to paddle from Churchill, Manitoba, to Tuktoyaktuk, Northwest Territories, a male travesty but "grand and remarkable," the reason she pestered him until he agreed to let her join him.[67]

Admittedly, there is no way of avoiding the conflict between Don and Dana during their trip, which could degenerate into physical confrontation at times and prolonged silences at others. Commentators have placed Don "on the spectrum between heroic and certifiable,"[68] and I myself wonder if his almost pathological obsession with always "being the first and strongest to the finish"[69] was not a manifestation of his traumatic experiences as a ward of the child welfare system. Still, it seems reductive to characterize Don and Dana's relationship, as James does, as "fundamentally adversarial."[70] While underscoring the class divide that infuses the discourse on the canoe, James is oblivious to the fact that working-class individuals with little formal education do not have many avenues to enter history, except through their physical prowess. The Amazon voyage was never merely a canoe trip, it was a race. The Starkells had to paddle farther than anyone else in order to make a name for themselves, which they accomplished. This was definitely the position of Don, who maintained that "you can't lose" if you do something exceptional. "Even my own kids will say, 'My dad was sort of weird, but at least he did something.'"[71] No less crucial, given his familial background, was that Don had other reasons for taking his sons along.

Don was quite aware that he was "the true motor behind the trip" and that Dana and Jeff did not "necessarily share [his] conviction,"[72] but he hoped that the trip would provide them with "a sense of discipline and self-confidence that they would never lose."[73] Not the least of Don's objectives was to inculcate in his sons a sense of togetherness that would survive him, the sort of ethos that permeates so much of wilderness mythology, with its multi-generational family gatherings at the cottage. Besides, not everybody has denounced his decision. The journalist Andrea Bellemare finds "the audacity of the Starkells' journey . . . inspiring" and avers that Don and "Dana wouldn't have made it if hadn't been for Don's mental strength and obstinacy, pushing them onwards."[74] The adventurer Colin Angus is even more effusive, envying what Don and Dana experienced. Angus, who rafted the entire length of the Amazon River and who considers *Paddle to the Amazon* "one of the most original adventure books" he has read, has nothing but admiration for the Starkells. Angus grew up without his biological father, a mysterious sea captain, and can only fantasize what it might have been like for the two of them "to have shared a trip" such as the one undertaken by the Winnipeggers.[75]

Moreover, James overlooks the extent to which Don and Dana did collaborate. This is never more evident than when it comes to mapping. Throughout their trip, Don and Dana rely faithfully on maps and a crisis usually ensues whenever the information they contain is faulty. Part of the reason the Starkells have to halt their voyage on Laguna Madre is that they are using "pathetic [maps]—50 or 60 miles to the inch—and we have no real idea where we are on this enormous water system."[76] Also, Dana is much more adept at reading maps than his father, something that Don proudly admits, noting that Dana spends "hours poring over our maps."[77] When they are unable to buy maps, as happens when they enter Brazil, it is Dana who borrows "tissue paper" at a military base so that he can copy its maps.[78] Early in Jason's and Starkell's Arctic expedition, Jason actually quotes him to the effect that he "never was good with maps.... Dana did the navigating on our South American trip."[79] That is, if Don is the pilot, Dana is the navigator; they play different but equally pivotal roles.

The centrality of mapping during the Amazon voyage is not politically unproblematic, highlighting the cultural and ideological affinities between Don and European explorers like Orellana. From the moment he begins contemplating canoeing to South America, Don is transparent about his historical models. Thus when he and Dana paddle along the coast of Honduras, and he reads that both Columbus and Cortés had sailed those waters in the early 1500s, he confesses that he often does "a little time-travelling and can easily imagine myself arriving with those daring explorers of the sixteenth century. In a small way we are fellow travellers."[80] Similarly, when they reach Venezuela and he realizes that their travels along the Orinoco and Rio Negro "overlap" with those of Alexander von Humboldt, he remarks that "even though we're 182 years behind him we'll be using his writings to guide us."[81] Ironically, one factor that sets the Starkells apart from the earlier navigators is their access to maps. Don states that as he and Dana paddle, he often thinks of "Orellana, who in 1541 made his incredible Amazon voyage, all of it uncharted, from the Andes in the west to the river's mouth at present-day Belém."[82] These feelings are echoed by Angus, who discloses that he "spent a lot of time thinking about the Spanish conquistadors, the first Europeans to cross South America.... How tough and ruthless they must have been—no maps, no inkling of what lay ahead."[83] "Without a map," he adds, "we were at the mercy of the river gods,"[84] like Don, underlining his admiration for his predecessors.

While potentially troubling from a contemporary perspective, Don's identification with European figures is not unusual. In fact, it is paradigmatically Canadian. As I have argued elsewhere, "Canada has always been extremely ambivalent about its spatial location," perceiving itself as part of the "Northern Hemisphere" rather than "the Western one."[85] If anything, Don is uncharacteristically open to Latin Americans, not the least in his dogged determination to learn Spanish.[86] It is true that he complains about a cross-section of the humanity he and Dana come across during their southern travels, as in this encapsulation of the trip in *Paddle to the Amazon*:

> We have encountered hundreds of species of creatures: snakes, crocodiles, piranhas, morays, sharks, whales, bees, and scorpions. Strangely enough, the only animal that has given us any trouble was man; we have been arrested, shot at, robbed, jailed, and set upon by pirates. At one point we were led off at gunpoint to be executed. We have been taken for spies and saboteurs, have capsized 15 times at sea and spent terrifying nights in pitch blackness riding the ocean breakers without navigation. We have had brushes with the drug trade, suffered food poisoning, blood poisoning, and dehydration. Forty-five times our canoe has been broken on rocks or reefs. Our skin has been baked to scab by the sun. We have been close to starvation.[87]

Yet both Don and Dana repeatedly stress how struck they are by the graciousness shown to them by most of the people they encounter, especially the economically deprived, which is the overwhelming majority. Time and again they seem perplexed that people who have almost nothing welcome them into their homes and are willing to share whatever little they possess with two strangers they will likely never see again.

In the dominant Canadian story, canoeing expeditions are supposed not only to cleanse your body and spirit but, as Pierre Trudeau famously phrased it, to turn you into "a child of nature."[88] Typically, Mason contends that modernity "has put a lot distance between ourselves and the natural world" and that a vigorous canoe trip is "a pretty good way to re-establish that relationship."[89] But there is no evidence that any such metamorphosis occurs to Don, or Dana for that matter. Although father and son are often tested by nature, this leads to neither communion nor animosity. It is as if they anticipated being challenged by the elements, in both expected and unexpected ways. What they were not quite prepared for was their encounters with other cultures. Despite participating in what Don describes as "the longest legitimate canoe voyage in history,"[90] they are seldom able to evade other people. This is remarkably dissimilar from a national tradition in which one canoes north, as Mason has it, to explore "what is left of the natural world"[91] and therefore not to seek oneness with other humans but to flee human contact. One's co-citizens are not required in such a pilgrimage because the "Canadian Face" is not human but natural, being the "rock of those rocks, bush of those bushes."[92] Again, while inconceivable without the canoe, the Starkells' Amazon trip is not just about canoeing. It is also very much about entering continental contact zones, cultural areas that they inevitably have to approach as outsiders.[93]

The Starkells appear to commit a series of heresies against the written (and unwritten) Canadian canoeing code, especially the cottage-country version. To begin with, by heading to South America, they seem to accept Douglas LePan's sentiment that it is no longer possible to replicate the experiences of the explorers and voyageurs, for Canada's forests have been "cut down" and "the rivers charted."[94] No less impudent, they journey in a fibreglass canoe, a twenty-one-foot vessel with a thirty-four-inch beam built for them by Don's "long-time friend and canoeing partner, Bill Brigden."[95] Such a modern watercraft hardly approximates the mythical birchbark canoe, which, as Mason eulogizes it, is "made entirely from materials found in the forest: birchbark, cedar, spruce roots, ash, and pine gum." Also, not only can it "be repaired easily from the materials at hand" but after "it has served its purpose, it returns to the land, part of a never-ending cycle."[96] In short, it is a "natural" watercraft, an integral part of the land itself. In a discussion of his concept of the habitus, the physical embodiment of cultural capital, the

French sociologist Pierre Bourdieu maintains that taste is a choice, "but a forced choice, produced by conditions of existence which rule out alternatives as mere daydreams and leave no choice but the taste for the necessary."[97] Don's selection of a fibreglass canoe for his trip would seem to be informed by his conditions of existence, revealing that he is either ignorant of Canadian wilderness mythology or resists it. Given his hyper-individualism, I suspect the latter. In any case, his choice befits someone who fell in love with canoeing not at some pristine northern lake or river but in the heart of one of Canada's largest cities.

Yet in many ways, the Starkells' Amazon trip remains profoundly Canadian, since it compels them to confront their national particularity. Dana, for one, claims that "it's impossible to have a perspective of what you've got" without leaving home. He elaborates that there was "a gift" hidden in their seemingly reckless voyage, one of which his father may not have been fully conscious, which is the family's relative privilege. "It's not until you live in the Third World," asserts Dana, "actually live in people's homes with them, day after day after day, and you're hungry yourself, and you go through all these things, that you can truly kind of look at what you've got and really appreciate it."[98] Don, too, comes to recognize that the misery he endured as a youngster does not quite compare to that experienced by most people they encounter in Latin America. Although before departing Don had copiously researched the places through which they would be travelling, he is shocked by the "parade of poverty" that they find along the coast of countries like Belize, with "shack after hovel after tumbledown hut,"[99] or in cities like Panama's Colón, where human misery is "superficially masked by the enormous volume of international retailing that goes on here."[100] As he witnesses the absence of food in the homes of the people with whom he and Dana stay as they approach the Amazon delta, he divulges that when "I lie at night trying to sleep, my mind often wanders back to all the thin and hungry people we've met over the months."[101] Even Don, with his impecunious origins, cannot deny that most of the people with whom he interacts are considerably less privileged than he is. They almost certainly cannot fathom an odyssey such as his and Dana's.

Another way in which Don and Dana exhibit their Canadianness is in their passionate identification with the Maple Leaf. They not only fly the flag on the *Orellana* whenever possible but also have it painted on the side of the canoe and on their paddles, wear T-shirts bearing the Maple Leaf, and even carry "a pile of souvenir maple-leaf badges to hand out"[102] to people who help them along the way. Curiously, it is not clear that either the Maple Leaf or Canada itself means much to most of the people they meet. From the Mexican Mayans who are shocked when told that "our rivers turn to ice three feet thick in winter"[103] to the Venezuelan soldiers who appear to think that Don and Dana are "making fun of them" when they insist that they came from Canada,[104] they find little evidence of knowledge about their homeland. The two are particularly "surprised" when told by a Brazilian schoolteacher they meet near the mouth of the Amazon that "he'd never heard of Canada. We hear the same thing from almost everyone around here. 'Ca-na-da,' they say with puzzled looks when we try to tell them our story. '*Dos años*—Ca-na-da.' Some of them pretend to understand, but we know they're confused." The fact that Don (inadvertently) addresses Brazilians in Spanish[105] is not conducive to communication, but the reader can easily discern that Canada is not exactly a point of reference in the region.

Perhaps even more disheartening, when Don and Dana finally arrive in Belém, "freshly bathed and shampooed" and smartly dressed in their "Canadian flag T-shirts,"[106] they discover that there is no representative of the Canadian government awaiting them. The only official welcome they get is a letter from the chargé d'affaires in Brasília informing them that their "feat, the first of its kind, is a landmark in the realms of anthropology and human endurance" and that their "achievement has brought credit to Canada and the profound respect of the staff of this embassy."[107] Needless to say, whatever admiration the Canadian civil servants stationed in Brazil had for the Starkells, it did not warrant travelling to Belém to meet them. Much less did it entail helping them transport the *Orellana* back to Canada, as Don and Dana hoped—instead, they had to depend on the generosity of the captain of the Dutch freighter *Saba*, who gave them and the *Orellana* a ride to Gulfport, Mississippi, from where they then made their way home.[108] Considering that Canada's relations with Latin America have always been first and foremost commercial,[109] one suspects that had the Starkells been selling canoes in South America, as opposed to sailing them, the federal government would have been much more supportive. Similarly, had they been better networked and moved in the same circles as diplomats, entrepreneurs, journalists, or academics, they would have been much more difficult to ignore.

The tepid responses by Canadian elites to Don and Dana's trip demonstrate that neither patriotism nor athletic achievement is enough to enable an event to enter a country's imaginary. In 2016, upon coming across a copy of *Paddle to the Amazon* in a second-hand bookstore in Manitoba, Bellemare asks: "How did I never hear of Don Starkell before? He should be a *Canadian Heritage Minute*, seriously." Her conclusion is that perhaps "it's because so much of the trip took place away from cameras, away from heavily populated areas where people could join in for short sections."[110] But that explanation is not very persuasive, since most of the long-distance canoeing trips so panegyrized in Canadian discourse occur in even less populated places. Rather it seems more likely that the relative obscurity of Don and Dana's voyage has much more to do with its Latin American location and the lack of cultural capital of its two main protagonists, once more highlighting the divides in Canadian society.

The marginality of the Starkells was exposed even by their own bodies, as if they had overextended themselves by undertaking such a journey. The *Winnipeg Free Press* journalist Ritchie Gage, who visited Don and Dana during their stopover in Trinidad, thought it was "a miracle" that they reached South America, given that "they existed only on canned goods. They had no special clothing and they were both deeply tanned when I met them and had no sun protection products."[111] However, this was merely the most tangible proof of their lack of cultural (and economic) capital. Gage, who had "exclusive access" to the Starkells during their odyssey, writes that he "had a hard time convincing the Free Press that this was a story [t]hat should be covered."[112] Then when Don attempted to fashion a book from his painstakingly written journals, which eventually added up to some "1,400 pages, densely typed,"[113] he learned that he was not capable of doing it on his own. Bellemare states that the reason she thinks so highly of "Don's book" is that she was "riveted by his account of the astounding journey."[114] Yet to this day, it remains unclear how much of *Paddle to the Amazon* was authored by Don, who had to turn to the writer Charles Wilkins for assistance. According to Wilkins, he spent "ten months" on the project, reducing Don's "diaries . . . to about an eighth of their original length—a million words would have produced a book of some 2,000 pages."[115] Thus, while Wilkins is listed as the book's editor, he would appear to be its co-author, [116] which would explain why he shares the copyright.

Still, regardless of its negligible place in Canadian scholarly discourse, or the authorship of the book that resulted from it, Don and Dana's historic canoe trip from Winnipeg to the mouth of the Amazon reveals much about not only the physical and mental fortitude of the two men but also Canada's place in the world. As the Starkells approached Belém, they noticed a group of Indigenous people on the shore, who engaged in "an odd pantomime" and "pretended to shoot rifles at us: '*Malvinas!*' they shouted. '*Malvinas! Inglaterra! Boom! Boom!*'" Don and Dana deduced that the Brazilians were attempting to convey something to them, but since they had no idea what it was, they "laughed and carried on."[117] It was only a few days later, after they reached the city and Don read the local newspapers, that they learned about the war raging in the Falklands, or Malvinas, and at last understood "what the Indians were shouting about as we paddled into Belém. They must have taken us for Englishmen, with our Canadian flag."[118] So, when Don and Dana arrived in Belém, not only were they met by no other official welcome than a form letter from the Canadian Embassy, but they even had to go to the British consulate to retrieve it, since their own government does not deem one of the largest cities in the second most populous country in the Americas worthy of a legation. Consequently, its citizens must depend on the goodwill of their former colonial master. Such a state of affairs perhaps also underscores the wisdom of Canadians heading north, instead of south, when contemplating a canoe expedition. After all, in that direction, one is less likely to have one's collective delusions of sovereignty tested, unless it is by the First Nations.

Notes

1 Don Starkell, *Paddle to the Amazon: The Ultimate 12,000 Mile Canoe Adventure*, ed. Charles Wilkins (Toronto: McClelland and Stewart, 1994), 14. In the version of the passage that appears at the end of the book, Starkell does not even qualify his statement: "We deserve our fate; we've come too far" (308).

2 For example, two of the most widely discussed recent books on the canoe's place in Canadian culture—Misao Dean's *Inheriting a Canoe Paddle: The Canoe in Discourses of English-Canadian Nationalism* (Toronto: University of Toronto Press, 2013) and Bruce Erickson's *Canoe Nation: Nature, Race, and the Making of a Canadian Icon* (Vancouver: UBC Press, 2013)—have nothing to say about Starkell's Amazon trip. Jamie Benedickson does call Don and Dana's trip both "extraordinary" and "formidable," but even he treats it only cursorily in *Idleness, Water, and a Canoe: Reflections on Paddling for Pleasure* (University of Toronto Press, 1997), 39, 179.

3 The Starkells' Amazon canoe, the *Orellana,* is now housed in the Canadian Canoe Museum in Peterborough, Ontario.

4 Bartley Kives, "A Lifetime of Paddling Adventures: Winnipeg Senior Says He's Set New World Record," *Winnipeg Free Press,* 25 August 2009, https://www.winnipegfreepress.com/local/-A-lifetime-of-paddling-adventures--54736402.html (accessed 29 March 2018).

5 Starkell, *Paddle to the Amazon,* 18.

6 Ibid.

7 Ibid.

8 Ibid., 18, 19.

9 Ibid., 19.

10 Ibid.; emphasis in the original.

11 Don Starkell and Conor Mihell, "Don Starkell: Expedition Paddler," *Canoe and Kayak* 38, no. 5 (2010): 72; Starkell, *Paddle to the Amazon,* 19.

12 Starkell, *Paddle to the Amazon,* 19.

13 Ibid., 20.

14 Ibid.

15 The teams represented the Northwest Territories and Yukon and every province except Newfoundland and Prince Edward Island. See Judy LaMarsh, "Centennial Summer," in *Memoirs of a Bird in a Gilded Cage* (Toronto: McClelland and Stewart, 1969), 191.

16 Ibid., 191.

17 Pierre Berton, "Paddling through History," in *1967: The Last Good Year* (Toronto: Doubleday Canada, 1997), 50.

18 "Interview with Don Starkell: The Arctic to Amazon Man," *Che-Mun* (n.d.), http://cgi.canoe.ca/che-mun/interview.html (accessed 29 March 2018).

19 Berton, "Paddling through History," 56. See also LaMarsh, "Centennial Summer," 192.

20 Starkell, *Paddle to the Amazon,* 20.

21 Ibid. Ironically, the CPR not only "granted paid leave" to his Flin Flon teammate Roger Carrière, who was "a CPR sub-foreman," but went as far as "declaring their pride in his career as a paddler." Dean, *Inheriting a Canoe Paddle,* 98.

22 Starkell, *Paddle to the Amazon,* 15. This interpretation is supported by the *Winnipeg Free Press* reporter Ritchie Gage, who states that Don's "wife divorced him over his getting fired for going on a canoe trip [and] taking time of[f] work." Gage, email to Albert Braz, 11 July 2018.

23 See Dennis Gruending, *Gringo: Poems and Journals from Latin America* (Moose Jaw, SK: Coteau Books, 1983), 7; and Jeremy Kroeker, *Motorcycle Therapy: A Canadian Adventure in Central America* (Canmore, AB: Oscillator Press, 2006), 1–2.

24 Starkell, *Paddle to the Amazon,* 16.

25 Ibid.

26 Starkell and Mihell, "Don Starkell: Expedition Paddler," 72. See also Starkell, *Paddle to the Amazon,* 33.

27 Quoted in Gary Waleik, "A Canadian Family's Dangerous 12K-Mile 'Paddle to the Amazon,'" *WBUR Marathon,* 6 October 2017, http://www.wbur.org/onlyagame/2017/10/06/starkell-paddle-to-the-amazon (accessed 6 April 2018).

28 John Jennings, "The Canadian Canoe Museum and Canada's National Symbol," in *The Canoe in Canadian Cultures*, ed. John Jennings, Bruce W. Hodgins, and Doreen Small (Toronto: Natural Heritage/Natural History, 1999), 1, 3.

29 Erickson, *Canoe Nation*, xiii.

30 Dean, *Inheriting a Canoe Paddle*, 63.

31 Ibid., 124.

32 Starkell, *Paddle to the Amazon*, 16.

33 Ibid.

34 Gaspar de Carvajal, "Discovery of the Orellana River," in *The Discovery of the Amazon, According to the Account of Friar Gaspar de Carvajal and Other Documents*, by José Toribio Medina, trans. Bertram T. Lee, ed. H.C. Heaton (New York: American Geographical Society, 1934), 167.

35 Starkell, *Paddle to the Amazon*, 17.

36 Ibid., 20. Don devotes considerable attention to Dana's condition. Soon after they reach Veracruz, he states that "the Mexican climate is perfect for [Dana's] asthma; in fact, it's been a good two months since he had any trouble." Later, in Venezuela, he adds that Dana is "celebrating a full year of freedom from his asthma medications." Finally, in the epilogue, we are informed that while "Dana's asthma still affects him, he has not taken medication for it since 1980" (88, 196, 313).

37 Ibid., 21.

38 Quoted in Waleik, "A Canadian Family's Dangerous 12K-Mile 'Paddle to the Amazon.'"

39 Starkell, *Paddle to the Amazon*, 33.

40 Ibid., 65; emphasis in the original.

41 Ibid., 71.

42 Ibid, 84. In an interview, Dana asserted: "I don't think my dad was ever supremely confident that we would be able to do the Gulf portion of the trip .... My sense was that he was quite worried. That he was sort of trying to put up a brave face to us, saying, everything will be fine' [sic] kind of thing." Quoted in Waleik, "A Canadian Family's Dangerous 12K-Mile 'Paddle to the Amazon.'"

43 Starkell, *Paddle to the Amazon*, 85.

44 Ibid., 84, 85.

45 Ibid., 88.

46 Douglas Gibson, *Stories about Storytellers: Publishing Alice Munro, Robertson Davies, Alistair MacLeod, Pierre Trudeau, and Others* (Toronto: ECW Press, 2011), 269.

47 Starkell, *Paddle to the Amazon*, 88.

48 Ibid., 89.

49 Ibid., 95.

50 Ibid., 98; emphasis in the original.

51 Ibid. During their trip to the Arctic, Jason quotes Don: "I'm paranoid of launching and landing from my South American trip." Victoria Jason, *Kabloona in the Yellow Kayak: One Woman's Journey through the Northwest Passage* (Winnipeg: Turnstone Press, 1995), 24. See also p. 12.

52 Dana and Delgado remain friends. In 2017, they were part of a group of paddlers who canoed 1600 kilometres down the Mississippi River from Bettendorf, IA, to New Orleans, partly to celebrate the fact Delgado's "cancer was in remission." Hannah Rodriguez, "Mississippi Canoe Trip Launches from Bettendorf," *QCOnline.com*, 1 June 2017, http://qconline.com/news/

local/mississippi-canoe-trip-launches-from-bettendorf/article_27db908e-f0c9-5e11-8977-63db83626cf2.html (accessed 18 April 2018).

53 Starkell, *Paddle to the Amazon*, 97.

54 Ibid., 101.

55 Ibid., 113.

56 Ibid., 127.

57 Dana, who describes the soldiers as Honduran rather than Guatemalan, maintains that he and his father told them, not about being in contact with the Canadian government, but that "the United States Army knew exactly where we were, they're following us, they had helicopters, if anything happened to us they'd come in there and blow everything up." Quoted in Waleik, "A Canadian Family's Dangerous 12K-Mile 'Paddle to the Amazon.'"

58 Starkell, *Paddle to the Amazon*, 129.

59 Ibid., 134–35.

60 Ibid., 140; emphasis in the original.

61 Ibid., 158.

62 M.T. Kelly, "Paddle with the Ego, under the Sky." *Books in Canada* (n.d.), http://www.booksincanada.com/article_view.asp?id=331 (accessed 15 April 2018).

63 Gage writes that Don "actually risked the lives of his two sons . . . , whose mother was against this." Gage, email to Albert Braz, 11 July 2018.

64 William C. James, "Canoeing and Gender Roles," in *Canexus: The Canoe in Canadian Culture*, ed. James Raffan and Bert Horwood, illustrations by Bill Mason (Toronto: Betelgeuse Books, 1988), 33.

65 Ibid., 34.

66 Albert Braz, *Apostate Englishman: Grey Owl the Writer and the Myths* (Winnipeg: University of Manitoba Press, 2015), 57–58.

67 Jason, *Kabloona in the Yellow Kayak*, 4. See also Don Grierson, "Iron Don," *Saturday Night* 112, no. 19 (1997): 90.

68 Grierson, "Iron Don," 88.

69 Starkell, *Paddle to the Amazon*, 19.

70 James, "Canoeing and Gender Roles," 33.

71 Quoted in Kives, "A Lifetime of Paddling Adventures."

72 Starkell, *Paddle to the Amazon*, 62.

73 Ibid., 16.

74 Andrea Bellemare, "They Canoed All the Way from Winnipeg to the Mouth of the Amazon!" *Medium*, 16 October 2016, https://medium.com/@dreabells/they-canoed-all-the-way-from-winnipeg-to-the-mouth-of-the-amazon-e74ae0fad3cf (accessed 14 April 2017).

75 Colin Angus and Ian Mulgrew, *Amazon Extreme: Three Ordinary Guys, One Rubber Raft, and the Most Dangerous River on Earth* (Toronto: Anchor Canada, 2004), 90.

76 Starkell, *Paddle to the Amazon*, 79.

77 Ibid., 198.

78 Ibid., 281; see also 288.

79 Quoted in Jason, *Kabloona in the Yellow Kayak*, 70.

80 Starkell, *Paddle to the Amazon*, 132.

81 Ibid., 218; see also 247, 250.

82 Ibid., 291.

83 Angus and Mulgrew, *Amazon Extreme*, 41.

84 Ibid., 203.

85 Albert Braz, "Canada's Hemisphere: Canadian Culture and the Question of Continental Identity," *American Review of Canadian Studies* 46, no. 3 (2016): 349, 352.

86 Starkell is not nearly as successful with Portuguese, perhaps because he expected the two languages to be more similar than they are. As he observes after reaching Brazil, "Portuguese is often so close to Spanish that we understand it without difficulty. At other times, there seems to be little similarity between the languages." Starkell, *Paddle to the Amazon*, 298.

87 Ibid., 13–14.

88 Pierre Elliott Trudeau, "Exhaustion and Fulfilment: The Ascetic in a Canoe," in *Wilderness Canada*, ed. Borden Spears (Vancouver: Clarke, Irwin, 1970), 4.

89 Quoted in Dean, *Inheriting a Canoe Paddle*, 128.

90 Don Starkell, *Paddle to the Arctic: The Incredible Story of a Kayak Quest across the Roof of the World* (Toronto: McClelland and Stewart, 2000), 13.

91 Bill Mason, *Path of the Paddle* (Toronto: Key Porter Books, 1995), 3.

92 Hugh Kenner, "The Case of the Missing Face," in *Our Sense of Identity: A Book of Canadian Essays*, ed. Malcolm Ross (Toronto: Ryerson Press, 1954), 206.

93 Tellingly, before leaving Winnipeg, the Starkells "even agreed to give up all but the most casual involvement with women for the duration of the venture. To do otherwise," argued Don, "would compromise our sense of purpose, and would also risk alienating communities in 13 countries, each with different ideas of proper romantic behaviour." Starkell, *Paddle to the Amazon*, 21.

94 Douglas LePan, "*Coureurs de Bois*," in *Weathering It: Complete Poems 1948–1987* (Toronto: McClelland and Stewart, 1987), 63.

95 Starkell, *Paddle to the Amazon*, 17.

96 Mason, *Path of the Paddle*, 3.

97 Pierre Bourdieu, *Distinction: A Social Critique of the Judgement of Taste*, trans. Richard Nice (Cambridge, MA: Harvard University Press, 1984), 178.

98 Quoted in Waleik, "A Canadian Family's Dangerous 12K-Mile 'Paddle to the Amazon.'"

99 Starkell, *Paddle to the Amazon*, 123.

100 Ibid., 163.

101 Ibid., 300.

102 Ibid., 54.

103 Ibid., 108.

104 Ibid., 194.

105 Ibid., 302. In Portuguese, two years is *dois anos*, not *dos años*.

106 Ibid., 306.

107 Quoted in ibid., 309.

108 Ibid., 306–8, 311.

109 J.C.M. Ogelsby, *Gringos from the Far North: Essays in the History of Canadian-Latin American Relations, 1866–1968* (Toronto: Macmillan, 1976), 32; Braz, "Canada's Hemisphere," 354.

110 Bellemare, "They Canoed All the Way from Winnipeg."

111 Gage, email to Albert Braz, 11 July 2018. Don echoes this impression, saying that Gage "obviously saw things that shocked him: our exhausted bodies, parched skin, scrapes and scars and scabs, most of which we've grown inured to. He was especially impressed by the thick scab on Dana's lower lip." Starkell, *Paddle to the Amazon*, 227; see also 156, 287.

112 Gage, email to Albert Braz, 11 July 2018.

113 Charles Wilkins, "Editor's Preface," in *Paddle to the Amazon: The Ultimate 12,000 Mile Canoe Adventure*, by Don Starkell, ed. Charles Wilkins (Toronto: McClelland and Stewart, 1994), 9.

114 Bellemare, "They Canoed All the Way from Winnipeg."

115 Wilkins, "Editor's Preface," 10, 9.

116 According to Grierson, "Starkell claims never to have finished reading the book because, 'I get so mad I want to throw it across the room.' The narrative voice and diction belong not to Starkell but to Wilkins." Grierson, "Iron Don," 92.

117 Starkell, *Paddle to the Amazon*, 306; emphasis in the original.

118 Ibid., 308.

QUEBEC
Noire
River
Ottawa River
River
Petawawa
Brent
McManus Lake
Lake Travers
CFB Petawawa
Big Eddy Rapids
Black Bay
Petawawa Centennial Park
ALGONQUIN
PROVINCIAL PARK
Bonnechere
River
Algonquins of Pikwakanagan
Madawaska
River
ONTARIO
ONTARIO
Map Area
N
0
50 km

CHAPTER 9

The Dam That Wasn't: How the Canoe Became Political on the Petawawa River

CAMERON BALDASSARRA

On a cold, wet day in November 2017, I found myself standing on the banks of the Petawawa, watching it flow freely to its nearby confluence with the Ottawa River. I was joined in my admiration for the churning power of the "Pet" by Dr. Alan Hepbourne, a retired AECL (Atomic Energy of Canada Limited) engineer-turned-conservationist. Having just been interviewed about his activism against a hydro project on that same river, Hepbourne wanted to show me the proposed site. We made our way down the Petawawa's slushy shoreline to a popular paddling, swimming, and fishing spot known locally as Railroad Rapids. Hepbourne pointed out a few favourite features along the way: a large chute called Lovers, popular with paddlers; a gravel shoal important for spawning sturgeon; and old rebar spikes in the bedrock—lingering remnants of the river's long pre-war history of log drives. He was careful to explain how each point of interest would have been impacted by the dam: the spawning grounds below would have dried up, the logging relics above would have been flooded, and the chute reduced to an unnavigable trickle.[1]

Hepbourne's concern for the river was sparked in 2009 when Xeneca Power, an Ontario-based developer of "sustainable, clean and renewable energy,"[2] proposed the construction of a hydroelectric dam upriver from his home on Black Bay, just outside the centre of the town of Petawawa. The proposal was intended to take advantage of the introduction of financial incentives offered by the Green Energy and Green Economy Act,[3] a piece of provincial legislation passed in the same year that was intended to promote the development of emission-free energy. It offered guaranteed electricity rates for "green energy" producers, a category that Xeneca's hydroelectric proposal fell under. The proposal in fact involved two small dams on the section of river running downstream from Canadian Forces Base (CFB) Petawawa to the Ottawa River. Xeneca had all the required components: promises of environmental assessments, processes for consultation with Indigenous communities in the area, and plans to consult with local ratepayers. The company had, however, largely overlooked the canoeists and paddlers who frequented the rapids and "play spots" along the threatened sections of river. A few brief mentions of maintaining navigable flows for canoeists occur throughout the proposal, but a 2010 draft of the plan inaccurately deemed the two most popular rapids to be non-navigable,[4] and suggested building portage routes around parts of the river already in regular use by canoeists, kayakers, and raft guides.[5] Xeneca did not have a clear sense of the interests, activities, or vibrancy of the paddling community on the Pet. The subsequent actions of resistance from within the paddling community centred on demonstrating the navigability of the river, the financial benefits of whitewater paddlers to the local community, and the long history and continuing cultural relevance of recreational paddling within the broader Petawawa watershed—all issues largely overlooked in Xeneca's planning process.

Working in tandem with the paddlers who resisted the dam were Petawawa locals such as Hepbourne. His background in electrical engineering and his staunch opposition to the proposal led him to become the de facto technical expert and spokesperson for a dedicated group of activists made up of the recreational paddlers, professional raft guides, concerned hunters and anglers, local residents, and Indigenous community members who opposed the dam.[6] The interests of the aforementioned communities and activists were reflected in their reasons for opposing the dam. These ranged from Indigenous concerns over the disruption of sacred sites to environmental concerns for fish populations.[7] It was the creation of a whitewater canoeing, kayaking, and rafting festival known as Hell or High Water (HOHW) in 2009 that helped unify the diverse array of community stakeholders and encouraged a strong, lasting connection to the river through fostering and growing the popularity of paddle sports.

A testament to the organizational efficacy and unifying force of the paddler activism of the HOHW festival was the level of engagement from military service members posted at the nearby CFB Petawawa. By 2011, so many teams of military personnel were signing up for the HOHW races that civilian paddlers were being edged out. The organizers responded by adding an additional day of races solely for the Canadian Forces, a clear acknowledgement and embrace of the military's importance in the local community.[8] The river's official standing in the eyes of the Canadian Forces is less clear than its popularity as a paddling destination among enlisted personnel. Beyond the recreational interests of individual service members, there is no publicly available documentation of the military's stance on the dam. Alan Hepbourne and Jim Coffey, a local business owner, both state that the military effectively forced Xeneca to shelve the dam proposal by refusing to allow it to flood base property. The singular political and economic power of the Canadian Armed Forces, not the efforts of the protesters, is seen by grassroots organizers like Hepbourne as the ultimate reason the dam was prevented from being built. However, the ongoing popularity of the HOHW festival and heightened engagement with the river across user groups indicates that canoeing and kayaking played a central role in a unifying political action that left a legacy of community engagement and greater connection to a cherished river.

Though HOHW may not have been the direct reason for the shelving of Xeneca's plans, the festival helped popularize and reinforce the recreational value of the town section of the Petawawa in the local community. Members of the broader paddling community who were unable to participate in local protest and resistance to the dam engaged as best they could through the use of popular online forums such as the Boater Board and Wilderness Canoe Association message board. The objections to the dam project that came from beyond the local community often focused on the perceived potential destruction of a pristine recreational environment, based largely on the widely held view of the Petawawa River as one of Ontario's pre-eminent destinations for wilderness canoeists. The Boater Board was alive with discussions of the pros and cons of the project and the importance of getting out on the river to prove its value as a recreational waterway.[9]

Contrary to the paddling community's perceptions of the Petawawa as a majestic wilderness river, it had long been the site of industry and colonial presence, countering any notion of the river as unspoiled. The rapids and consistent current enjoyed by the canoeists and kayakers at HOHW once facilitated the expansion of the lumber industry into the depths of Algonquin Provincial Park. Since 1905, the Pet had played host to the aforementioned CFB Petawawa, which became one of the largest and most active military bases in Canada. In effect, the Petawawa River had already been completely impacted: the majority of its course is located within the government-regulated boundaries of Algonquin Park and CFB Petawawa, with the remaining lower section running through the settler community town of Petawawa.

The earliest settlers depended on the canoe to facilitate their attempts to survey and explore the watershed. It is perhaps ironic that the act of paddling that was so central to the anti-dam efforts of HOHW was also the preferred mode of conveyance for those seeking to expand the colonial and industrial grasp on the area. The difficult whitewater and rocky terrain of the Canadian Shield, now so industrially attractive to Xeneca and aesthetically pleasing to the canoeists on the Boater Board, was noted as a significant hindrance to travel in military surveys conducted between 1827 and 1853. The river was deemed too treacherous for a strategic canal between the Ottawa River and Lake Huron and the terrain unsuited for agriculture. In 1893, the newly established Algonquin Park further limited potential for the river to develop as a site of colonial settlement. Paired with the aforementioned railroads, the new park was central to the increase in recreational canoeing in the region and helped establish the Petawawa as a highly desirable paddling destination. Present-day canoeists, raised on romantic views of Algonquin Park, reference the pristine natural condition[10] of the river and are highly concerned with maintaining its navigability. There is also a commonly expressed desire among canoeists that the Petawawa's "rich and storied history as a paddler's river" and "relatively pristine" condition remain protected.[11]

Protecting the river's history and ensuring it remained unobstructed were of utmost concern to local Indigenous communities. The cultural and historical significance of the canoe as a symbol of the Petawawa was most clearly and strongly presented by Skip Ross, a Petawawa resident and Algonquin Elder whose activism was central to the anti-dam protests. Ross stated that the Algonquin oral tradition identified the Petawawa as a difficult river to navigate, and that it was not safe to use the Algonquins' light birchbark canoes when moving down river through the challenging whitewater now preferred by recreational canoeists. He noted that the calmer sections were places of exceptional seasonal fishing, especially near the Petawawa's confluence with the Ottawa River, and that the manoeuvrability and utility of the birchbark craft was important for fishing, particularly for eels. Ross pointed out that the sturgeon and American eels that once teemed in the river were culturally significant foods for Algonquins, and that the lower sections of the river, up to the first serious rapids, were annually visited eel fishing grounds. He also indicated that the significant whitewater, as observed by the colonial surveyors, discouraged permanent settlements or regular use of the river by the Algonquins as a travel corridor. The canoe was central to the harvest of the eel, and Ross's childhood memories of the Petawawa revolve around time spent exploring the river in his birchbark canoe or using it to help harvest eel with his mother.[12]

Ross objected to the dam primarily on the grounds that it would impede the recovery of the American eel population, and negatively affect navigation of the river by canoe. His concerns perfectly wed the recreationally based objections of the paddling community, as represented by the HOHW organizers, with the objections of Indigenous organizations such as the Algonquins of Ontario, who actively opposed the dam because of its threat to fisheries and to the implementation of the province's American eel recovery strategy.[13] Ross challenged the Xeneca project in three primary ways: by emphasizing the Algonquin people's stewardship of the land; by highlighting the broader watershed's importance for traditional land-based activities such as the moose hunt; and by speaking to the negative impact the dam would have on the restoration of the traditionally significant fish populations of sturgeon and American eel. Similar concerns were voiced by Chief Kirby Whiteduck of Pikwakanagan First Nation, who emphasized the negative impacts a proposed dam would have on the American eel recovery strategy.[14]

Paddlers and town residents supported Indigenous objections to the dam but focused on promoting the river as a valuable recreational destination, arguing that the dam would not generate enough revenue to benefit the community.[15] They attempted to prove the river's cultural and economic value by enhancing opportunities for canoe-based recreation and tourism through the establishment of the HOHW. Mr. Ross and Chief Whiteduck's approach focused on the intertwined issues of environmental stewardship, traditional land use, and the protection of culturally significant food sources. The canoe-based recreational approach of the local non-Indigenous community worked in concert with the cultural and land-use approach adopted by Indigenous stakeholders to highlight a broad range of issues important to the community as a whole.

The threat of damming clearly stirred the passions of many residents and paddlers. The natural aesthetic of the river matches the romanticized Canadian version of wilderness idealized by the art of Tom Thomson and the Group of Seven. In that sense, the Petawawa River has much in common with a wide variety of canoe-tripping destinations across the province, and to a casual observer, it may not appear significantly different from other famous canoe-tripping rivers such as the French or the Magnetawan. Yet if we consider the impassioned activism that erupted both from within the local area and from the broader paddling community, it is clear that the Petawawa has a unique status. Few other dam projects that proliferated in the era of the Green Energy Act were so vehemently opposed.

What differentiates the Petawawa, especially in the eyes of wilderness canoe trippers, from comparable watersheds is the absence of postwar industrialization. The Pet's neighbouring rivers, the Bonnechere and Madawaska, were dammed, and their shorelines continue to play host to lumber mills (though no longer water powered), cottages, and towns. The Petawawa, once the site of log drives and lumber camps, saw a precipitous decline in industrial use following the end of the Second World War. The dilapidated remnants of log chutes, wooden weirs, and the now trackless bed of a former branch of the CN railroad are all that remain of the once-common presence of the forestry industry. All of the Petawawa's neighbouring rivers have settlements and significant human activity along their lengths, as do comparable well-known canoe-tripping rivers like the French River, the shores of which are lined with cottages, fishing lodges, and marinas, especially along the sections running below the Trans-Canada Highway. The Petawawa has only the single town of the same name, located at its confluence with the Ottawa. The most significant activity along the Petawawa occurs within the confines of the Canadian Forces Base, an area closed to paddlers. The travel restrictions placed on the base incidentally prevent paddlers from witnessing the most significant ongoing human activity along the river. When Algonquin

Park is included, well over two-thirds of the river is protected from development. Each of these massive government-instituted reserves has effectively conserved the Petawawa in a relatively unsettled state. In the case of the park, this aligns with the recreational and environmental management ethos of that organization. The presence of the army base has largely preserved the river by accident: it is not advisable to build a dam or a lumber mill in the middle of a live fire range.

Both institutions limit access to the river. A canoeist interested in paddling the river's park sections needs to be willing to take on a multi-day trip, pay for permits and the cost of transportation into and out of Algonquin. A canoeist interested in paddling the base section of the river is likely out of luck unless they are an active member of the Canadian Army. In comparison, canoeists can freely access the Madawaska via numerous boat launches, public parks, and private put-ins, allowing for shorter trips and less expense. The accessibility of the Madawaska reduces the sense of wilderness sought after by canoe trippers, making it a less desirable venue for multi-day canoe trips; however, the consistent dam-controlled levels make it desirable as a venue for park-and-play paddlers. In contrast, two of the most accessible park-and-play sections of the Petawawa would be lost if a dam were built, due to the upstream flooding and downstream reduction in flow rate. The dams on the Madawaska benefit the paddling community, whereas a dam on the Petawawa, based on the projections provided by Xeneca, would have reduced the flow rate on the most popular park-and-play rapids in town. The remainder of the Petawawa is located in the confines of Algonquin Park or CFB Petawawa, making the town run the only easily accessible portion. The possibility of losing the only easy access to a recreational resource heightened the importance of the town section threatened by the Xeneca project.

The historical context of the hydro developments on the Petawawa's neighbours is also significant in explaining the paddling community's seeming lack of concern over the presence of dams on the Pet's neighbouring watersheds. The Bark Lake Dam on the Madawaska was constructed in 1942, in the midst of the industrial boom brought on by the Second World War,[16] a time when limited thought was given to environmental issues, Indigenous rights, and the protection of recreational wilderness spaces. The entire region was in the throes of war production: the army base was training soldiers and housing POWs, while logging operations like the Canadian Splint and

Lumber Corporation were improving their booms, chutes, and weirs along the region's rivers in response to the increased need for wood products.[17] The threat to the Petawawa in 2009 was of the moment, whereas the damming of the Madawaska is long forgotten and taken as a simple reality of that river. Paddlers enjoy the park-and-play style possible on a dam-controlled river, but as evidenced by the online backlash against the Xeneca project on paddling forums like the Boater Board, canoeists and kayakers actively oppose attempts to dam free-running rivers. The desire to maintain wild spaces is independent of the paddlers' interest in park-and-play paddling at dam-controlled sites. A simple comparison could be made to skiing: skiers enjoy the consistency and availability of groomed trails and artificial snow at large resorts, but also pursue opportunities to explore backcountry runs and natural conditions. This is not unlike the paddling community, whose members enjoy the consistency provided by dam-controlled rivers but also seek out the unregulated conditions of a naturally flowing river.

Canoeists, kayakers, and the paddling community more broadly played a central role in the anti-dam strategy adopted by the Petawawa activists and HOHW. The founders of HOHW, Phil Kompass and Mike Crouzat, used the local popularity of canoeing, kayaking, and rafting as a means to garner publicity for the anti-dam campaign. In order to bring paddlers together and generate support for canoeing on the river, the two founded what would become the annual paddling festival and race that would so effectively build community and connection to the river in the town of Petawawa.[18]

Launched in 2009 to demonstrate the recreational and cultural importance of the Petawawa River, the HOHW River Race took advantage of elevated river levels during the spring melt, pitting racers against a challenging whitewater descent right through the middle of town. To generate a broad appeal and as much attention for their cause as possible, the race was open to multiple categories of canoeists, kayakers, and rafts (solo and tandem canoeists, solo kayakers, and many variations of raft teams). Kompass and Crouzat's aim was to demonstrate the recreational value of the river and to highlight the importance of paddle sports in the community. With the philosophy that you won't defend what you don't love, the two set out to build a sense of attachment to and ownership of the river, both locally and among the broader whitewater community.[19] By the fifth year of the race, HOHW was attracting upwards of 1,000 competitors, including leading international canoeists, kayakers, and raft teams.[20] Over the years, the race has become an annual celebration of the river and has expanded to include flatwater events, paddle boarding, vendors, and a larger festival-style community gathering. The festival grew to such a degree that the army base opened its campgrounds, usually reserved for off-duty military families, to the public in order to relieve a shortage of local hotel rooms.

Kompass and Crouzat's efforts clearly had a positive impact on community engagement and river use. The popularity of the race and the attention it garnered for the conservation movement clearly extended beyond the local community. Of particular importance was the attention HOHW attracted from professional paddlers and guides from the numerous raft companies, outfitters, and outdoor education organizations located in the broader Ottawa Valley and throughout eastern Ontario. The inaugural race in the team raft category was won by a crew from Esprit Rafting, an award-winning paddle sports and eco-tourism company based on the Quebec side of the Ottawa River.

Esprit's founder and owner, Jim Coffey, has a long history as a river advocate. He had previously worked with the James Bay Cree communities of Nemaska and Waskaganish to implement whitewater and canoe safety courses on the Rupert River to help re-establish canoe-based cultural practices such as traditional skill-building trips for youth under the guidance of community elders.[21] The Rupert, located in the James Bay region of northern Quebec, was dammed by Hydro-Québec in 2009. The use of the canoe as both a symbol and tool of resistance on that watershed significantly influenced Hydro-Québec's approach to its dam and diversion project and ensured that the river remained navigable, despite the completion of the hydro project.[22] Coffey had also been involved in consultations to evaluate the viability of running commercial raft trips down the Rupert as an economic alternative to the hydro project, not unlike the strategy adopted by the HOHW organizers.[23] Just two years prior to the first HOHW event, Jim led Esprit's leadership program on what was one of the final pre-diversion, commercially operated canoe trips down a free-running Rupert.

The Cree community was successful in gaining concessions and guarantees of flow enhancements from Hydro-Québec, but Coffey and other non-resident canoeists familiar with the Rupert expressed a sense of loss following the damming. While the river still exists and has navigable flows,

FIGURE 9.1. The cliffs at the Natch. One of the most famous sites on the Petawawa. Photo: Cameron Baldassarra.

the presence of a new dam on what was perceived to have been an unspoiled wilderness river negatively influenced paddlers' desires to canoe in that area.[24] This outcome stands in stark contrast to the park-and-play preferences of paddlers who don't seem to mind the dams on the Petawawa's neighbouring watersheds. The sense of loss felt by Coffey and others is largely linked to a perceived destruction of wilderness rather than to the actual navigability or flow rate of the river. The preservation of navigable water levels on the Rupert did little to allay their concerns that an aesthetically pleasing wilderness destination had been lost. The experience with the Rupert River suggests that the perception of the Petawawa as a relatively unspoiled, free-running river heightens its perceived value among recreational canoeists as a wilderness destination. Indeed, Coffey has said as much in his discussion with me, suggesting that the sense of loss he felt following the damming of the Rupert added a sense of urgency to his engagement with the movement to protect the Petawawa River. In Coffey's opinion, the Petawawa is the best canoeable whitewater river in Ontario, both for its technical challenges and for its aesthetic beauty that culminates in the Natch Rapids, made famous by Tom Thomson's artwork.

The efforts of the HOHW organizers, local community members, and the broader paddling communities were rarely framed in a manner that suggested there was a significant economic alternative to hydro development on the Petawawa. Kompass, Coffey, and especially Hepburn and Ross instead argued that any dams or impediments to the natural flow of the river would negatively impact the cultural and recreational importance of the watershed. Hepburn, based on his professional experience at AECL and as an electrical engineer, was convinced that the generating capacity of the relatively small-scale run of the river project was not significant enough to present a substantial economic opportunity to the town of Petawawa. The loss of recreational and cultural opportunities would not, in Dr. Hepburn's assessment, be justified by the minimal economic benefits being promised by Xeneca.[25] The focus of the resistance to Xeneca's project, then, could centre on highlighting the cultural and recreational benefits of preserving the river rather than trying to prove that canoeing was an economic alternative to the dam. Community building, as evidenced through the deeper connections built between military members, Indigenous communities, local paddlers, and the broader canoeing community attracted by the popularity of HOHW, was the most successful aspect of the political activism centred on the canoe, canoeing, and the Petawawa's paddling culture.

The canoe as a symbol of the river's long history was mobilized to great effect in the personal testimony of Skip Ross. Ross's personal involvement in resisting Xeneca most strongly represented the cultural, emotional, and traditional importance of the river to the residents of the town of Petawawa, and the symbolic link between the river and the canoe. Ross was born on the banks of the river,[26] and grew up near the confluence of the Petawawa and the Ottawa Rivers. As a child he would paddle the lower reaches of the Petawawa while fishing for catfish for dinner with his mother. As a young adult he worked with his father as a canoe guide in Temagami, and as a current resident he believes strongly in canoeing as a means of engaging youth with the local environment.

A handmade birchbark canoe was central to Ross's memories of the river, a narrative he has shared with the media.[27] Throughout his oral history, he recounted many memories of fishing, hunting, swimming, and paddling the river, but the following most clearly highlights his long relationship with the canoe and the Petawawa:

> I was swimming at the bay with my father. I think I was eight or so. As I was swimming an empty birchbark canoe came floating down the river. Now I was a good swimmer, spent a lot of time in the river, so I swam out and got it, even in the current I could get there! I brought it back to shore. I asked my dad if I could keep it. He said that it was somebody else's, but if no one came to claim it, it was mine. I remember asking all over town, but no one knew where it was from. So we kept it in our yard, by the river for a number of months to see if anyone would come looking for it. No one ever claimed it, and I kept it. It was a beautiful canoe, handmade, and made by one of our people [Algonquin] I'm sure of it.[28]

Skip Ross's willingness to share his childhood on the river, along with his knowledge of Algonquin oral history, has been important as an illustration of the cultural value of the river and its tangible link with the canoe. He presented his arguments, memories, and oral histories at a number of public consultations and hearings throughout Xeneca's proposal process. The connections he drew between the canoe and his life on the river generated a strong emotional connection to the Petawawa. His activism was widely embraced and lauded by other members of the community. Alan Hepburn, Frank Knappen, and Jim Coffey all speak highly of Skip Ross and emphasize the importance of his role in directing public opinion toward opposing the dam.

The canoe's symbolic connection to the river might sway some, but often it is economics that wins the day. The Xeneca proposal was a response to the provincial government's introduction of subsidies to encourage green energy development. And yet, in comparison to mega projects such as the dam on the Rupert, where proponents offered job creation in the thousands and years of economic boosts to local communities, the benefits offered to the town of Petawawa were minimal. Additionally, Petawawa was and still is a relatively stable, if perhaps economically stagnant, town. Its economy is largely dominated by services supporting CFB Petawawa, AECL in nearby Chalk River, and the forestry industry. But even though Petawawa couldn't boast of a burgeoning economy, a minor dam project, offering few if any permanent jobs, likely carried little weight when trying to win over community members who were more concerned about maintaining the water levels and accessibility at their local park and wilderness playground than they were with the financial arguments of hydro investors.

Ultimately, the Xeneca dam complex on the Petawawa was never built. Ross, Coffey, and Hepbourne all agree that the military's refusal to allow flooding on base property was the final nail in the project's coffin. Still, if the canoe was ultimately not the reason the dam was not built, it cannot be denied that the paddler-centred activism of HOHW drew broad attention to the importance of maintaining and using recreational spaces, and helped heighten the popularity of whitewater canoeing, kayaking, and rafting on the lower Petawawa. The attention drawn to the Petawawa by a broad range of interests and communities also helped unite the town of Petawawa, encouraged positive discourse between divergent groups of paddlers (kayakers, canoeists, and rafters don't always see eye to eye), and reframed the river, the canoe, and the natural environment as an integral part of the cultural fabric of the community.

Notes

1 Dr. Alan Hepbourne, discussion with Cameron Baldassarra, December 2017.

2 Xeneca Power Development, "About Us," 2015, http://www.xeneca.com/about/index.html.

3 Green Energy and Green Economy Act, 2009, S.O. 2009, c. 12 - Bill 150.

4 Xeneca Power Development, "Draft Aboriginal Issues Tracking Table: Issue 3, Response on Record," 29 May 2013, http://www.xeneca.com/files/Big%20Eddy%20Draft%20ER/Appendix%20E.pdf.

5 Jim Coffey, discussion with Cameron Baldassarra, December 2017.

6 *Protecting the Ottawa and Its Tributaries*, Ottawa Riverkeeper—Annual Report 2010, https://www.ottawariverkeeper.ca/wp-content/uploads/2014/09/Ottawa-Riverkeeper-Annual-Report-2010.pdf.

7 Algonquins of Ontario, *Returning Kichisippi Pimisi—The American Eel—to the Ottawa River Basin: Bridging the Gap between Scientific and Aboriginal Traditional Knowledge*, Traditional Knowledge Report, vol. 1 (Pembroke, ON: Algonquins of Ontario, 2014), 4.

8 Patricia LeBouef, "Paddlers Descend on Petawawa for Annual Hell or High Water," *Post* (Canadian Forces Base Petawawa), 26 May 2016.

9 Phitty, "Update: Damns on the Petawawa," comment on Boater Board (online forum), 13 March 2009, http://boatwerks.com/boater-board/topic/update-damns-on-the-petawawa/.

10 Rob Monti, "Personal Letter to Xeneca Power," Boater Board (online forum), 22 June 2009, http://boatwerks.com/boater-board/users/rrmonti/replies/.

11 Ibid.

12 Algonquins of Ontario, *Returning Kichisippi Pimisi* (2014), 4.

13 Algonquins of Ontario, *Returning Kichisippi Pimisi—The American Eel—to the Ottawa River Basin* (Pembroke, ON: Algonquins of Ontario, December 2012), 6.

14 Linda Heron, "Draft American Eel Recovery Strategy—Skip Ross to Bree Walpole," *Ontario Rivers Alliance* (blog), 10 February 2011, http://www.ontarioriversalliance.ca/draft-american-eel-recovery-strategy-skip-ross-to-bree-walpole-10-february-2011/.

15 Dr. Alan Hepbourne, discussion with Cameron Baldassarra, December 2017.

16 Richard M. Clouthier, "Madawaska: A Community Live and Well. 1867 to 2014 and Onward?," Township of South Algonquin, 13 November 2014, www.southalgonquin.ca/deptdocs/MADAWASKA.dot.

17 Library and Archives Canada, Upper Ottawa Improvement Company Fonds, R2347, Letterbooks, vol. 92, file 3, "Letter from the Hydro-Electric Power Commission of Ontario to Mr. D.A. Gillies concerning construction on the Petawawa River, 1941," 488.

18 LeBouef, "Paddlers Descend on Petawawa."

19 Stephen Uhler, "Petawawa River Race Highlights Its Importance," *Daily Observer* (Pembroke, ON), 10 May 2009.

20 Linda Heron, "The Key to River Protection Lies in River Usage," *Ontario Rivers Alliance* (blog), 26 July 2014, http://www.ontarioriversalliance.ca/key-river-protection-lies-river-usage/#more-4778.

21 Jim Coffey, discussion with Cameron Baldassarra, October 2013.

22 Cameron Baldassarra, "The Lost River: Dams, Diversions and the Death of Canoe Tripping on Quebec's Rupert River", Major Research Paper at York University, 2014.

23 Jim Coffey, discussion with Cameron Baldassarra, October 2013.

24 Baldassarra, "The Lost River."

25 Dr. Alan Hepbourne, discussion with Cameron Baldassarra, December 2017.

26 Ibid.

27 Ned Morgan, "Eternal Sunshine of the Spotless River," *Mountain Life*, 27 June 2016, https://www.mountainlifemedia.ca/2016/06/eternal-sunshine-spotless-river/.

28 Skip Ross, discussion with Cameron Baldassarra, December 2017.

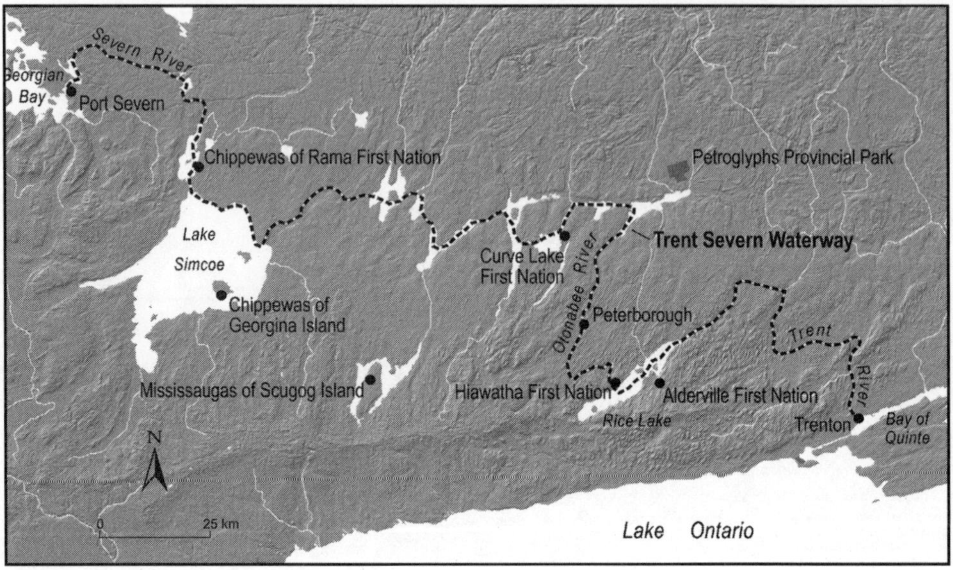

Severn River
Georgian Bay
Port Severn
Chippewas of Rama First Nation
Petroglyphs Provincial Park
Lake Simcoe
Curve Lake First Nation
Otonabee River
Trent Severn Waterway
Chippewas of Georgina Island
Peterborough
Trent River
Mississaugas of Scugog Island
Hiawatha First Nation
Alderville First Nation
Rice Lake
Trenton
Bay of Quinte
N
0
25 km
Lake Ontario

CHAPTER 10

Unpacking and Repacking the Canoe: Canoe as Research Vessel

DANIELLE GENDRON

Some of my fondest childhood memories involve paddling a canoe with my brother. Together we'd push ourselves away from the dock and into another world. We'd focus more on how our paddles sent tiny tornadoes dancing through reflections of trees and clouds rather than where to direct the canoe. Our imaginations would transport us to another reality where cottages and homes that lined the shore disappeared; where we were alone out on the lake, in what we saw as an untouched landscape. We'd point out ideal places to land and set up camp for the night and live in this wild fantasy world until we stepped back onto the dock to run up to our grandparents' camp and grab snacks from the refrigerator. Now that we are adults, the canoe and its imagery continue to hold a prominent place in each of our lives: my brother pays it homage through naming his Saskatoon-based catering and seafood-importing business "Canoe Oysters"; as an anthropologist, I locate the canoe at the centre of my engagement with and study of Indigenous landscapes.

Uncovering bits of knowledge about the life of one of my ancestors guides my own engagement with the canoe.[1] Hipolyte Brissette, my fourth great-grandfather, was born about 1792 in Varennes—now a suburb of Montreal, Quebec. He began employment with the Hudson's Bay Company

(HBC) in 1818. His HBC employment record states that he worked as a middleman in a canoe, a carpenter, and a miller.[2] During his thirty years working for the HBC he was posted as far north as Great Slave Lake and as far west as Fort Colvile (in present-day Washington State); he paddled a canoe, following waterways across the continent. Hipolyte met his wife, my fourth great-grandmother, Archange L'hirondelle, at Lesser Slave Lake. Together, they moved throughout the prairies and Great Lakes region. They raised several children and eventually settled in Penetanguishene on Georgian Bay, where they lived out the rest of their days. My father is the fifth generation of his family born and raised alongside Georgian Bay.

As it has been the case for many other scholars, knowing and connecting with my ancestry has seeped into my academic inquiry.[3] Now I contemplate the ways in which the canoe figures in the colonization of Indigenous lands that today are commonly known as Canada. More specifically, the fragments of knowledge I have about my family history became an invitation to inquire into the complexities of how my own ancestry is interwoven in the origin story of the founding of Canada and processes of colonization.[4] Additionally, these fragments reveal unique historic realities that, for the most part, are absent in our national heritage narratives. These fragments also inspired a journey my father and I took in August 2018, canoeing a waterway where my family history is emplaced. Through this experience, I am still coming to understand the place and meaning of my own Métis ancestry in Canada.

The Trent-Severn Waterway (TSW) is the most direct route via water that connects Hipolyte's place of birth and the site of his and Archange's resting places. Although there is no indication in HBC records of his use of this waterway for work,[5] they likely used the TSW, or parts of it, to travel through. For generations my family lived along the westernmost edge of the waterway, where the TSW meets Georgian Bay. A 386-kilometre chain of rivers and lakes that connects Georgian Bay (Lake Huron) to the Bay of Quinte (Lake Ontario), the TSW cuts through a culturally and geologically significant landscape known as the "land between,"[6] where the rocky Canadian Shield meets the lowlands of the Great Lakes. The Anishinaabe, Wendat (also known as Huron), and Haudenosaunee (also known as Iroquois) have lived with these lands and waters since time immemorial. Historical records point to the TSW as the route through which the Wendat led Samuel de Champlain to attack the Haudenosaunee. The British and later Canadian

FIGURE 10.1. Undated photo of Hipolyte and Archange Brissette that has been copied and recopied and passed through family.

governments built a series of locks, dams, and canals to replace the arduous portage routes, necessary to travel these waters. The patchwork construction of the TSW was completed for changing reasons including tourism and shipping access.[7] However, by the time this infrastructure was completed in 1920, nearly ninety years after its commencement, it was deemed obsolete for its original purposes—tourism and shipping now relied on more direct roadways. Today the TSW is a designated historic site of Canada and a popular cruising destination for recreational motorboats. As a heritage site, it invites visitors to "salute human ingenuity navigating the heritage canals and locks along the 386 km Trent-Severn Waterway, connecting the playgrounds of Lake Ontario and Lake Huron. Cruise Canada's renowned inland passageway through historic lockstations. Travel into cottage country by water or by car and watch the Big Chute Marine Railway in action. Stare up at the towering Peterborough Lift Lock and learn about its history at the Visitor Centre. Explore lumber towns, farm villages and the spectacular pre-Cambrian landscape of the Canadian Shield."[8] The historic site invites visitors to pay homage to a whitewashed colonial history, ignoring the deep layers of a much more extensive Indigenous history also present in this area.

In this chapter I grapple with the challenges that come with paddling through a landscape that at first glance seems thoroughly shaped by colonialism, the types of complicities that are involved in embarking on such a trip, and the possible opportunities for resistance. I begin by looking to the work of many scholars and canoe enthusiasts who have unpacked the role of the canoe in perpetuating and upholding colonial imaginings of Canada.[9] Canoeing involves an imaginative experience, existing beyond childhood, wherein ideas of the canoe itself, where it takes us, and the sensory experience involved each build upon and support one another to reinforce conceptualizations of what Canada is as a place, and what it means to be Canadian. I reflect on my packing list and consider how objects hold history and connection to a reality beyond what we think of as simply a canoe. I invite you, the reader, to use these thoughts and considerations as a guide in preparing your own canoe.

Unpacking the Canoe and the Canadian Imagination

As I set out on this 386-kilometre trip with my father, I asked myself how our choice of vessel might inform my own experience of the landscape, as well as the way that I understand my ancestors' interactions with the landscape. I recognize the way that I understand, use, and relate to the canoe would likely be unrecognizable to my ancestors. I imagine that the ways that I interact with and view the landscapes I encounter are also incredibly different. Geographer Bruce Erickson has observed that his pauses to appreciate and photograph the flora and fauna while paddling the French River, a voyageur heritage waterway, mark the disparate experiences of the people who canoe today and the voyageurs who crossed through these same landscapes.[10] I cannot know for certain the exact perspectives of my voyageur ancestors. Instead, I highlight what the canoe means today rather than what it may have meant to people in the past, in order to provide a window into understanding Canada's colonial history. I examine the ways that my own perception has been shaped and how it informs my own interactions and relationships in Indigenous territories.

In school, the canoe consistently made an appearance in lessons on Canadian history. I learned that European explorers, such as Simon Fraser and Samuel de Champlain, were able to penetrate and survey the "wild" and "untamed" landscapes of pre-Confederation Canada thanks to the canoe. I learned that voyageurs used the canoe to trek across the continent, and that their extensive movement through a network of trading posts and settlements interspersed throughout a vast wilderness asserted the presence and authority of the Hudson's Bay Company. I learned that these voyages through this network mark the dawn of Canada as a nation.[11] For the most part, the school lessons systematically erased Indigenous presence and histories across this same landscape.

The imagery of the voyageur traversing vast empty and natural landscapes via canoe followed me from my classroom history lessons to our summers on the lake. However, this type of imaginative experience cannot be simply written off as naïve childish imagination; imagining voyageurs as the forefathers of Canada, those who created the nation out of a wild landscape,[12] and the canoe as a vehicle that permits access to nature is central to the collective, national myth of the canoe in Canada. Former prime minister Pierre Elliott Trudeau stated: "What sets a canoeing expedition apart is that it purifies you more rapidly and inescapably than any other travel. Travel a thousand miles by train and you are a brute; pedal five hundred miles on a bicycle and you remain basically a bourgeois; paddle a hundred in a canoe and you are already a child of nature."[13] He further affirmed the canoe's place in the national imagination by declaring that paddling through "nature" is foundational to achieving an authentic Canadian identity: "I know a man whose school could never teach him patriotism, but who acquired that virtue when he felt in his bones the vastness of his land, and the greatness of those who founded it."[14] These statements have been regularly quoted to uphold the notion that a close connection to nature is central to Canadian identity, and that the canoe trip through nature is the way to experience and attain an authentic Canadianness.[15] When Trudeau speaks of "those who founded it" he evokes the image of Europeans, not Indigenous peoples, criss-crossing the vast landscape and thereby folds the past into a mythology of the canoe that links Canadian identity, whiteness, and nature. That is, nature (and the canoe moving through it) is meant to remind us of the beginnings of Canada and how it came to be. The history lessons we learn in school as well as the imagery in writings about the canoe most certainly proliferate a mythology that links Canadian identity and nature with the past, and in turn influences the way Canadians view the canoe. Paddling a canoe, then, brings this mythology to life.[16]

Before we even dip our paddles into the water, we have already conceived of the places we paddle through, what exists there, and what our experiences will be like. The way we view the places we visit is socially constructed; that is, when we visit places we do not see them with a neutral eye but rather gaze upon our surroundings with particular expectations of and intentions for being in that particular place.[17] Often, paddling a canoe means an encounter with what is conceived as an untouched, preserved nature that will provide an opportunity to experience the landscape as it existed in the past.[18] This image of unspoilt nature is upheld by guidebooks, parks information, and so on, as well as through details relayed by many who have canoed through these same waters before us. The main attraction of the TSW is its nineteenth-century infrastructure of locks and dams; however, Parks Canada promotes the TSW as an ideal site to explore a "pre-Cambrian landscape"[19] while a popular TSW guidebook describes the landscape as "beautiful, historically rich."[20] And yet the kind of history that is being enshrined throughout the TSW on the Parks Canada website largely excludes Indigenous presence. A 200 page PORTS tourist guide to cruising the TSW mentions an Indigenous art gallery at Curve Lake Nation as only an attraction.[21] What we expect to experience, based on what we read and hear, influences what we perceive as we physically move through the canoe route—a natural setting, including geological features, flora, fauna, and weather conditions. On the TSW we expect to experience a picturesque landscape that was tamed by Canada.

We perceive that we are immersed in a natural setting, and that paddling through it is one of the most authentically Canadian ways through which to experience nature and become part of it.[22] The paddle acts as an extension of our bodies; paddling tunes our bodies to the rhythms of the water. The paddle reaches out and dips into the water; the pushes and pulls of the currents and flows are felt as the canoe propels forward with each stroke. Our bodies respond to the changing water through adjusting our physical exertion and movements to overcome its power. Recognition of these variations and shifts is bodily; change is felt before it can even be thought. In this bodily tuning, we come to understand the environment but also perceive ourselves to be a part of it. Thus, canoeing is interpreted as an authentic way to experience an untouched nature, not only because of what we know and what we are told about it but also because of the closeness we perceive through our own sensory experiences when canoeing.

Canoeing forges what is experienced as an intimate relationship with a natural environment into what anthropologist Amanda Concha-Holmes calls a "HumaNature" event, wherein the distinction between humans and the natural world become blurred.[23] Here, paddlers can imagine that they are enduring the landscape in the same way that voyageurs once did,[24] which in turn supports and reinforces how the canoe has already been perceived as facilitating a bond with nature, a marker of Canadian identity.

The most troublesome consequence of this mythology is that it upholds the belief that prior to the arrival of Europeans, what is now known as Canada was wild and untamed. For example, popular contemporary canoe routes and circuits assist in perpetuating a narrative of Canada that excludes significant Indigenous history and presence. Canoeing the French River is promoted as a way to experience a voyageur route and connect with the founding of the nation.[25] Algonquin and Temagami Provincial Parks are widely considered as places to escape city life and experience natural untouched landscapes.[26] These views work to reify the landscape as empty and untouched prior to the arrival of Europeans, thereby limiting the historical realities and contemporary of Indigenous habitation. The nation, according to this view, rose out of the landscape rather than being founded by social and political processes that acted on the landscape and the peoples already present.[27]

Ideas of the canoe itself and how we think of the places that the canoe takes us through create what Kwakwaka'wakw scholar Sarah Hunt refers to as the "colonialscape."[28] Hunt uses this term to describe how typical Canadian understandings of the landscape, including narratives, mapping, and ownership, stamp out Indigenous histories and presence that have continuously existed across the landscape for millennia.[29] Along quintessential canoe routes, Indigenous presence and history is folded into a sense of the landscape as natural, and these routes are thought to be largely devoid of human influence and interaction. The irony here is that many of these were well-travelled routes prior to the arrival of Europeans, used and maintained by Indigenous peoples for millennia.

The setting of the TSW makes it an unusual choice for a typical multi-week canoe trip. Furthermore, the TSW is primarily used by powerboats; we saw only a handful of paddlers during our time on the waterway. Although colonial processes and associated development have affected all canoe routes, this history is inescapable along the TSW. The physical presence of locks, dams, and canals, as well as the multiple towns, cities, farms, and cottages that the route meanders past overtly tell of how European engineering altered the landscape. The colonialscape here is not the replacement of Indigenous presence with the label of nature but consists of an additional layer in which by way of European engineering, "a viable society"[30] was created in a natural setting.

How can we disrupt these colonialscapes that are perpetuated through the practice of canoeing? How can we understand canoe trips as negotiating colonized Indigenous territories rather than a natural wonderland? Anthropologist Dara Culhane asks us to consider the history of the land beneath us as a way to confront these types of myths.[31] To begin to reconceive the history of the land (and/or waters) beneath us, we must learn whose lands we are in fact on. In recent years, online resources have made this information increasingly accessible. For example, we can simply type the location of our canoe route—as we can with the places we live and work—into the search function on the Native Land (https://native-land.ca/) or Whose Land (https://www.whose.land/) websites. The results will display the Indigenous territories, languages, and treaty agreements that exist in that

FIGURE 10.2. Author and her father, Randy Gendron, waiting to pass through Bobcaygeon – Lock 32.

location. Each of these sites provides links to more resources for learning about the place-specific treaties and languages, the nations as well as their traditions and governance structures. Whose Land also includes videos of land acknowledgements.

For instance, by locating the nearly 386-kilometre route of the TSW on the Native Land site, we learn that the route cuts through traditional Anishinaabe and Wendat territories, which overlap one another, and that Anishinaabemowin (the language of Anishinaabe peoples) and Kanien'kéha (a language of Haudenosaunee people) are the traditional languages spoken across this landscape. The overlap in traditional territories as well as where languages are spoken indicate that the boundaries of Indigenous territories are far more nuanced than European cartographic representations can depict. The fact that Kanien'kéha is identified as a traditional language of the landscape but that this same landscape is not identified as traditional Haudenosaunee territory reveals that these kinds of resources are an incomplete and imperfect representation for understanding Indigenous presence. These resources should never be used as authoritative knowledge but simply as a starting point to learn about and acknowledge the presence of Indigenous peoples. The Native Land website also shows Canada's history of treaty making along the TSW, which includes parts of the Robinson-Huron Treaty 61 of 1850, the Williams Treaty of 1923, Treaty 20 of 1818, and the John Collins' Purchase of 1785. Each of these treaties outlines relationships and agreements on the land between Indigenous peoples and settlers. The Dish with One Spoon wampum, which predates all other treaties along the TSW, is an agreement between the Anishinaabe and Haudenosaunee to share the territory and protect the land.[32] This treaty underlines the existence of Indigenous governance structures and how Indigenous nations relate to one another on a nation-to-nation basis.

To populate canoe routes with the rich cultures and histories of Indigenous peoples is merely a starting point in the disruption of the colonialscape. We can locate on a map the reserves within these traditional territories in order to comprehend the massive dispossession of lands. We can ask whether any of the Indigenous nations are mentioned or credited in the information we find about our canoe routes, and in what way. Do Indigenous nations have any federally or provincially recognized role in land/water stewardship or governance in and along our routes? Are there names of the rivers, lakes, and sites along our routes in the language of the traditional territory? What is the historical significance of these waters to Indigenous nations? How were and are these waters used by Indigenous nations? Not all of these questions are easy to answer; many will likely go unanswered for any number of reasons. Asking these questions is a start to recognizing what often goes unnoticed during a canoe trip: that these routes are not devoid of culture, people, or Indigenous governance.

Along the TSW there are several Anishinaabe First Nations reserves (from west to east): Chippewas of Rama First Nation, Chippewas of Georgina Island, Mississaugas of Scugog Island, Curve Lake First Nation, Hiawatha First Nation, and Alderville First Nation. Each of the lock stations along the waterway provides historic information on plaques and/or boards about the significance of the TSW and its surrounding landscape. But Indigenous

FIGURE 10.3. Plaque at Burleigh Falls – Lock 28 describing nearby petroglyphs. Photo: Danielle Gendron.

peoples are mentioned merely three times throughout. One historical information plaque makes reference to the nearby Petroglyphs Provincial Park as a site of cultural significance to the "Algonkian Indians" 500–1000 years ago, when the petroglyphs were carved—the sign goes on to separate the living descendants of the original carvers and caretakers from the petroglyph site by calling them "Ojibway settlers" who are currently experiencing a rebirth of spiritual practices through their study of the site. Another plaque mentions that Paleo-Indians used the landscape for millennia prior to European arrival; a third describes Indigenous displacement as people moving to make way for European settlement. The only mention of contemporary Indigenous presence in a popular cruising guidebook for the TSW is of the Whetung Ojibwa Centre at Curve Lake Nation as a good place to visit and view or buy "Native art" and moccasins.[33] Curve Lake Nation is host and steward of Petroglyphs Provincial Park, which is located alongside the TSW. There is no information about this role on the parks website; however, the visitor centre in the park explains the role of Curve Lake Nation as cultural caretakers of the petroglyphs site.

Settlers gave names to rivers, lakes, and sites that already had Indigenous names and meaning for millennia. This renaming occurred throughout the entire continent. Along what is now known as the TSW, what the Anishinaabe knew as Wanantgitcheang (where the water turns around on a big scale) became known as the Severn River,[34] Zaagaatay Igiwan (shallow) became known as the Trent River, Pimaadashkodeyong (moving across the prairie) became Rice Lake, and Nogojiwananong (the place at the rapids) became Peterborough.[35] The name for the Otonabee River, also part of the TSW, is derived from the Anishinaabe name for the river, Obenabe, meaning "the river that beats like a heart, in reference to the bubbling and boiling of the rapids along the river."[36] Anishinaabe scholar Leanne Simpson writes about the significance of Anishinaabe place names: "When I hear or read the word 'Otonabee,' I think 'Obenabe' and I am immediately connected to both a physical place within my territory and a space where my culture communicates a multi-layered and nuanced meaning that is largely unseen and unrecognized by non-Indigenous peoples."[37] This lack of recognition of Indigenous history and presence on the TSW works to uphold the colonialscape, wherein Indigenous lives are erased from their traditional territories and made to exist elsewhere, limited to the reserve. Having interest and willingness to learn and understand Indigenous presence and use of the TSW (or any other landscape, for that matter) may not reveal all that we are interested in knowing: some knowledge and information may have been lost due to processes of colonization; some knowledge is only made available to people who have particular rights and privileges according to cultural protocols.

All of this is not to suggest that paddlers should strive to acquire expertise on the history of the Indigenous peoples whose traditional territory their proposed routes cross. What I do suggest is that rather than viewing the canoe as iconic of natural landscapes of Canada, we might use the canoe to engage in understanding colonial processes and the colonialscape of Canada. For starters, we need to learn and use the names of the Indigenous peoples and nations whose territories we visit and pass through. And we need to understand that we do not merely paddle through a natural environment but are visitors in Indigenous territories that hold rich knowledge systems that include histories, memories, and languages, many of which have been stripped away from their peoples.

To me, the TSW exists as a palimpsest of colonialism: each historical layer of the colonial encounter obfuscates what came before. The farms, towns, and cities along the TSW have largely overwritten voyageur and Indigenous histories. As I paddled through the TSW I was aware I was also moving through multiple treaty territories that helped erase the Indigenous landscape. Treaties are the bedrock of the colonialscape, outlining the legally binding relationships between Indigenous peoples and settlers on Indigenous lands. Their existence is often disregarded or viewed as relevant only to Indigenous peoples; however, all who live in Canada are treaty people. The Royal Proclamation of 1763 identified that the North American continent belonged to the Indigenous peoples living on it and set out the directive that Europeans needed to create treaty agreements with the Indigenous peoples before they could legally settle the land. Identifying the treaties through which the TSW meanders reveals the messy patchwork of treaty making: the boundaries of treaties do not correspond to traditional territories or Indigenous understandings of the landscape. Nevertheless, they are foundational to the formation of Canada; treaties make the dispossession of lands from Indigenous peoples "legal" under Canadian law.

Anishinaabe scholar Madeline Whetung has detailed how Anishinaabe bodies experience the impacts of the dispossession of lands by describing her own canoe trip through part of the TSW, which is her traditional ancestral territory. Settlement and private property restrict her physical movement between cultural sites. As Whetung paddles to sites of significance and talks to people about what she was doing, she is told that canoeing makes her *truly* Canadian. Here she experiences how Anishinaabe identity is subsumed by Canadian identity—canoeing is not understood as an Anishinaabe cultural practice but as Canadian. Whetung identifies this as "friendly colonialism":

the well-meaning ways that Indigenous activities have become Canadian, thus perpetuating the myth that Canadians created Canada. In this she experiences the colonialscape—how Anishinaabe realities are limited to the reserve and erased throughout the rest of the traditional territory.[38]

As I continue to excavate the layers of history that exist below the current colonialscape and recognize the impacts on Indigenous peoples, I know that my personal understandings of the canoe and canoe trip have been influenced by the very mythology that I critique. Couple this mythology with the connection canoeing has to my own ancestry: I veer toward imagining my experience in the canoe as a way to follow in the footsteps (or paddle strokes) of my ancestors. The danger in this type of imaginative experience lies in how it divorces me from current reality, and how my entanglements with colonialism differ greatly from the colonial entanglements of my Métis ancestors.

Repacking the Canoe

Scholar and anti-racism activist Peggy McIntosh has unpacked the invisibility of white privilege and how it allows people to be ignorant of the operation of racism in their everyday lives.[39] Similarly, the mythology surrounding the canoe is invisible to most Canadians, which contributes to settlers being oblivious to their own complicity within ongoing colonialism. Thus far, I have drawn on the work of others in order to critique how the canoe and canoeing are imagined as authentically *Canadian*. This is not to suggest that settlers should no longer embark on canoe trips. And I certainly do not suggest that the imagination is, in and of itself, the problem; the imagination is a useful tool in the way that it enables a complex engagement with reality rather than a detachment from it.[40] Instead, I argue that we need to break our imaginations free from understanding Canada and Canadian landscapes through the prism of colonialism, and start to imagine realities of the canoe trip that go beyond experiencing a pristine "natural" landscape. I meditate on how settler colonialism has shaped my relationships and engagement with the canoe and the landscapes it takes me through by thoughtfully repacking my canoe with my ancestors in mind.

Hipolyte's use of the canoe was not solely defined by his work with the HBC; he also travelled vast distances across the landscape with his family. With his wife, Archange, he migrated from Lesser Slave Lake to Red River, from Red River to Drummond Island, and from Drummond Island to Penetanguishene. Archange and Hipolyte did not choose their routes based on the type of natural landscape they wanted to pass through; paddling was their means to arrive at certain locations. Their routes took them through what they knew as the territories of specific Indigenous nations. By contrast, my father and I chose to paddle in order to witness how the landscape changes throughout the waterway and to examine the traces of human history and heritage left upon it, not because it would take us where we needed to go. It took us nineteen days of paddling from Lock 45 to Lock 1 of the TSW, and merely three and a half hours to drive from Lock 1 back to Lock 45. Canoeing is no longer a viable mode of transportation and commerce; it has become purely a recreational activity.

In identifying our different experiences, it also becomes clear how social class defines relationships with the canoe. Archange and Hipolyte were part of the labouring class wherein the canoe itself provided the means for Hipolyte's employment as well as the family's relocation to pursue financial opportunities. My social class affords me the ability to choose to go on a canoe trip for three weeks as part of my PhD research and a way to reconnect with my roots. I have the financial resources required to acquire the gear, including the canoe itself; to transport myself and all of my gear to the route I choose to paddle; and to schedule three weeks away from all other obligations in order to canoe with my father. My ancestors needed the canoe to get to specific sites because there was no better option; they moved their entire family, including young children, vast distances by canoe. My children stayed at home with my mother; I cannot fathom spending three weeks in a canoe with children. Mine, who were seven and three years old at the time, would beg to go home after only twenty minutes of sitting in the centre of the canoe while being paddled around a short circuit. The differences in meaning and purpose between my canoe trip and my ancestors' means that I pack my canoe with different intentions. They would have loaded their canoes with mindfulness of what they needed on the other side of their journey; my father and I just packed for needs and comfort along the way.

As I created my packing list I considered anthropologist Joseph Dumit's suggestion to not only examine the use of objects but also consider their history, processes of production, and cultural/symbolic meanings.[41] I use his provocation as a way to tether my imagination to the colonialscape and to how each of these objects reveals settler complicity in the colonialscape. My repacking list starts with maps. I focus attention on maps because all settlers are familiar with and use maps, regardless of whether or not they ever embark on a canoe trip. Interrogating maps helps re-envision Canada and Canadian landscapes, while also providing an excellent illustration of what I intend to think through as I repack my canoe. I continue to scrutinize other objects as I repack my canoe, though I do not delve into each them as deeply.

Maps and Routes

Before even deciding to canoe the TSW, I pored over paper maps and chartbooks detailing its course; I pinned places of interest such as lock locations, heritage sites, and museums onto Google Maps. Unsurprisingly, Hipolyte would have interacted with and understood maps much differently. Maps were literally part of him: routes were tattooed onto his body, along with protective figures for safety on his travels.[42] These tattoos likely did not include detailed information like the maps I consulted but rather worked as mnemonic devices specific to his knowledge, experience, and needs. It is unlikely that I or many other people living today would be able to read or identify the places and routes represented by his tattoos.

The maps we use today are highly detailed documents designed to be easily read by all. They are widely accepted as accurate scientific knowledge; however, the way that they articulate and structure particular beliefs and politics, such as their role in colonization, is often overlooked.[43] Maps play a foundational role in the deep-seated complicities of being in Indigenous landscapes. In her reading of *Roughing It in the Bush*, the autobiographical sketches of nineteenth-century settler Susanna Moodie, Florence Stratton examines how maps legitimized the colonialscape along the TSW and highlights the complex interplay of Indigenous and European knowledge of maps. Moodie wrote about how her Misssissauga neighbours interacted with the paper map that hung on the wall of her home; they traced the land features and routes, including what we now know as the TSW, with their fingers, recognizing every detail and uttering in amazement the place names in their own language.[44] Moodie's observations of these people's first encounter with a paper map details the capacity to intimately know and visualize wide landscapes without possession of a map. Her account calls attention to the fact that no special skill is required to understand maps, especially of landscapes with which people are already familiar, but it also prompts a consideration of how Moodie and the Mississauga people she wrote about may have interpreted the significance and utility of the map very differently.[45]

Maps of North America, such as the one hanging in Moodie's home, were not produced merely for navigational purposes but were also documents of power; they articulate and structure particular perceptions and politics.[46] Western cartography mapped North America with a series of arbitrary borders and boundaries that reflect the rivalries between European nations in asserting power and control over the land, while the presence of Indigenous peoples was, as it continues to be, disregarded and silenced.[47] Maps acted as the language through which European nations documented their claim over Indigenous territories and declared their dominance over other Europeans in the colonization of North America.

The Mississaugas in Moodie's vignette had a fundamentally different view and understanding of the landscape than the European map creators and owners. Instead of viewing the land as something that was owned and controlled, they understood the land through sets of relations. The Dish with One Spoon wampum would have informed their understanding of land (and thus of the map), its purpose and uses. "The 'Dish' or sometimes it is called the 'Bowl' represents what is now southern Ontario (from the Great Lakes to Quebec and from Lake Simcoe into the U.S.). We all eat out of the Dish—all of us that share this territory—with only one spoon. That means we have to share the responsibility of ensuring the dish is never empty; which includes, taking care of the land and the creatures we share it with. Importantly, there are no knives at the table, representing that we must keep the peace."[48] This agreement conveys that the land does not belong to any one person or nation, but rather its resources are to be shared and cared for by all; it also communicates the fluidity of territories and shifting of boundaries, which Western cartography fails to adequately represent. Maps such as ones found on the Native Land website often represent Indigenous territories as having defined yet overlapping boundaries. Rice Lake, on the TSW, provides an excellent example to understand the permeability of Indigenous territories. Although the Anishinaabe called the lake Pimaadashkodeyong, settlers named it Rice Lake on account of the abundant harvest of wild rice by Anishinaabe peoples. A French map from 1742 labelled this same lake as Lac Quentio; geographer-linguist Rebekah Ingram understands *quentio* as a French interpretation of the Kanien'kéha word *kéntsio*, meaning good fishing.[49] Good fishing on the lake occurs in a different season than the wild rice harvest, so the different names are also an indication of how the uses and significance of this same lake varied not only by season but also between people. Recognizing this variance demonstrates who European settlers and cartographers talked to and/or had relationships with, as well as an understanding of the ebbs and flows of traditional territories. What is known as Rice Lake may have been considered Anishinaabe territory during the wild rice harvest, and as Haudenosaunee territory in a different season when the fishing was good. This understanding communicates how land is relational, wherein people have relationships with the land and understand their relations with other nations through the land.

Indigenous relationships with and agreements on land are represented in Western cartography as overlaps in traditional territory. In Western understandings of land, boundaries and borders are normalized as inflexible, and thus traditional territories that are depicted as overlapping are often incorrectly interpreted as sites of struggle or dispute rather than being recognized through an Indigenous lens. Western cartography did more than map North America: it also established European concepts of land ownership. The imposition and naturalization of European names and fixed boundaries on maps stamp out Indigenous presences from the landscape, and as such maps act as vital documents in the creation and perpetuation of the colonialscape.

The Canoe

After looking to the advice of other canoeists, I found that the cost of the ideal canoe for my trip was far beyond my meagre graduate student budget. So I drove over 200 kilometres to buy a sixteen-foot red Mad River Canoe that I found on an online classified ad. After thoroughly inspecting it and cross-checking information from the manufacturer's website, I'm still not positive of the exact model; what I do know is that the young man who sold it to me bought it from an Algonquin Park outfitter the year prior and was told it was ten years old and made of a fibreglass composite. I do not know, nor could I confirm with research, the exact materials it is made of, where and how they were sourced, or where the canoe was actually manufactured. My lack of information about this canoe and the very way that I acquired

FIGURE 10.4. Randy Gendron canoeing at the eastern end of Rice Lake, near the mouth of the Trent River. Photo: Danielle Gendron.

it speaks volumes about the difference between my relationship with the canoe and Hipolyte's. He did not choose which canoe was best for his use and needs; he was an employee of the HBC and paddled York boats and birchbark canoes. Being a carpenter as well as a middleman, he likely had a hand in making, mending, and repairing the canoes.[50] I, like most other paddlers, am completely disconnected from how, where, when, and who created the canoe I paddle.

In contrast, previous chapters have shared how canoes made from land-based materials hold connection and significance to Algonquin, Heiltsuk, Chinook, and Maliseet cultures. Such canoes figure in the practice of cultural identity that is intertwined with the landscape. Chuck Commanda, Larry McDermott, and Sarah Nelson (Chapter 5) describe how the process of building a birchbark canoe embodies the seven sacred teachings of the Algonquin; in building a canoe people not only learn about these teachings but also put them into practice. Rachel Cushman, Jon Daehnke, and Tony Johnson (Chapter 2) illustrate the centrality of the dugout canoe to the revitalization of Chinookan lifeways and cultural practices. In Algonquin and Chinook cultures, as in many other Indigenous cultures, canoes are not merely a symbol of identity with an accompanying mythology but are the tangible outcome of interwoven relationships between people, culture, and landscape.

Upon reading a draft of this chapter a dear friend and colleague pointed out that the word canoe itself has some unexpected colonial roots. She, like I, had always assumed that the word canoe derived from an Indigenous language of Canada, until she followed my logic of questioning the history of objects from her perspective as a linguist anthropologist. A simple search for the etymology of canoe reveals that it came into English through the Spanish word *canoa,* which derived from the Arawakan (a nearly extinct Indigenous language of the Caribbean and South America) word *canaoua.*[51] The history of the word canoe is enmeshed with the most notorious colonizer himself—the first recording of *canoa* is attributed to a letter written by Christopher Columbus in 1493.[52]

Most people who paddle the symbol of Canadian identity are detached from its materials and construction, and even the origins of its name yet mythologize the canoe as something that has been derived directly from the land. They believe the canoe to be authentically Canadian and of Canada, without acknowledging the likelihood of its manufacture outside this country. The staunch belief that the canoe is central to Canadian identity erases Indigenous histories tied to the canoe much in the same way that maps silence Indigenous presence.

Food

Archange and Hipolyte would have packed food that they produced or traded for their journeys, but they would have also fished, hunted, trapped, foraged, and traded food during their travels, forming connections both to the landscapes they passed through and the people within them. I think about the implications of the freeze-dried food packages that I pack: the amount of labour and technology involved in their production, which I am detached from; how this is connected to both local economies and global agribusiness. Packing freeze-dried food emphasizes my inability to identify and prepare local edible plants, as well as the environmental changes and settlement patterns that have impacted the health (and edibility) of the plants and animals, and the wider landscape. For instance, *manoomin* (wild rice) used to grow in abundance throughout many lakes that now make up the TSW. Construction of the TSW altered the landscape by cutting canals through land and flooding out rivers to make lakes, and ultimately created a new watershed. *Manoomin* harvest sites were devastated by the construction of the TSW and the new uses of the waterscape. Anishinaabe people have been revitalizing the *manoomin* harvest throughout their territories, which include the TSW, yet this practice has been a source of contention between cottagers (or vacation homeowners) along the waterway and those reclaiming the *manoomin* harvest. The TSW, through Parks Canada, has asserted control over the water by allocating permits for cottagers to dredge up the *manoomin*, sparking what Al-Jazeera has covered as "Canada's wild rice wars."[53] In addition to thinking about how appropriation of land obstructs access to food, I think about the environmental changes and pollutants that have altered the health of local plants and animal life. Using freeze-dried food at once disconnects us from understanding the bounty of the landscape and the techniques my ancestors would have used to preserve foods for long journeys, makes the impacts to the food basket invisible, and ties us to global food markets.

I continue to question the objects that I pack and consider how each anchors me in, yet renders invisible, the reality of living in the colonialscape. For instance, I have begun to consider how the lifesaving capabilities of life jackets and other personal flotation devices are regularly made useless by paddlers when they are left lying on the bottom of the canoe. The reality here is that the life jacket is often packed in order to avoid being fined rather than because of a genuine concern for safety. What does this tell us about the role of the government in regulating and asserting authority over people, even in the supposed "wild" places we traverse? Additionally, I consider how the history of GPS devices and cellphones is entangled in military history.[54] The technological advances made with the intention of controlling territory, which is part and parcel of the narrative of colonialism, have made way for the personal use of these same technologies. Though we may believe that our use of these technologies is severed from the colonial narrative, it is colonialism that has allowed their existence in our lives. I invite you to continue questioning these objects and to interrogate the different dimensions of the objects you pack. What do the materials they are made of, their histories, and any legislation associated with their use have to tell us about their role in the colonialscape? We could go on to consider bear spray, rope, fishing line and tackle, fishing licences, tents, sleeping bags, paddles, rain gear, biodegradable soap, sunscreen, bug spray—the list continues.

Conclusion

Canadians have much work to do in comprehending how colonialism has shaped and continues to shape the nation. It is not the responsibility of Indigenous peoples to teach Canadians about the implications and perpetuation of colonialism; this work can be started through questioning Canadian symbols of identity, as I have done here with the canoe. Identifying how Canadianness is informed by colonialism and thus creates complicity within the colonialscape is vital to understanding how and why it should be disrupted. Simply recognizing this complicity is not an act of decolonization,[55] but it does help create a context in which Canadians can begin to have meaningful conversations about the reality of living on colonized lands, and identify ways that the colonialscape can be dismantled.

The dominance and authority of Western knowledge and ways of understanding the world have silenced Indigenous histories and presence, in order to naturalize the notion of Canada and Canadian identity as deriving from a natural landscape. Considering the mythology of the canoe trip and the items we pack sheds light onto how this seemingly innocuous practice of Canadian identity works to uphold the colonialscape. Each item we pack plays a part in upholding the colonialscape and helps us to forget that we are entrenched within it. I look to the reality of my voyageur ancestors as they paddled through this same landscape, whether for work for the HBC or as a mode of transportation, to highlight how the mythology of the canoe trip allows Canadians to believe they can experience Canada just as we imagine our voyageur forefathers did. We do not, nor did they, paddle through wide, empty, natural landscapes. The difference is that they recognized that the landscape was filled with Indigenous history and presence; Canadians tend to limit that reality to the reserve. The way that our bodies move in order to propel the canoe through water is perhaps the only thing we experience in the same way that the voyageurs did. Over the three weeks I spent on the TSW, I stopped imagining myself following a route that Hipolyte may have once paddled and began imagining what he would think of my embarking on such a trip. The most salient of these imaginings was him questioning why I would choose to paddle at all, and why I did not mount a motor on the back of my canoe.

Notes

1 Métis scholar David McNab uses the term "spirit memory" for the way in which following ancestors brings about research inquiry. See David McNab, "A Long Journey: Reflections on Spirit Memory and Métis Identities," in *The Long Journey of a Forgotten People: Métis Identities and Family Histories*, ed. Ute Lischke and David McNab (Waterloo: Wilfrid Laurier University Press 2007), 21–37.

2 Hudson's Bay Company Archives, Archives of Manitoba, Biographical Sheets https://www.gov.mb.ca/chc/archives/_docs/hbca/biographical/b/brissette_hypolite.pdf.

3 See Jennifer S.H. Brown, "Cores and Boundaries: Metis Historiography across a Generation," *Native Studies Review* 17, no. 2 (2008): 1–18, for discussion of ancestry and Métis scholarship; Heather Devine, "Being and Becoming Métis: A Personal Reflection," in *Gathering Places: Aboriginal and Fur Trade Histories*, ed. Laura Peers and Carolyn Podruchny (Vancouver: UBC Press 2010), 181–210; Margaret L. Clarke, "Reconstituting the Fur Trade of the Assiniboine Basin, 1793 to 1812" (MA thesis, University of Winnipeg, 1997); and Lischke and McNab, eds., *The Long Journey of a Forgotten People*, for examples of Métis scholarship being guided by ancestry.

4 See Janet Carsten, *Ghosts of Memory: Essays on Remembrance and Relatedness* (Oxford: Blackwell Publishing, 2007); and Avery F. Gordon, *Ghostly Matters: Haunting and the Sociological Imagination* (Minneapolis: University of Minnesota Press, 2008) for how tracing family histories can reveal new ways of understanding historical narratives and reconstituting identities.

5 Hudson's Bay Company Archives, Archives of Manitoba, Biographical Sheets, https://www.gov.mb.ca/chc/archives/_docs/hbca/biographical/b/brissette_hypolite.pdf.

6 See the Land Between Conservation Organization website (https://www.thelandbetween.ca/) for more information on this particular landscape.

7 See James T. Angus, *A Respectable Ditch: A History of the Trent-Severn Waterway, 1833–1920* (Montreal: McGill-Queen's University Press, 1998) for a history of the political project of the TSW infrastructure and its changing uses.

8 Parks Canada, "Trent-Severn Waterway National Historic Site," https://www.pc.gc.ca/en/lhn-nhs/on/trentsevern.

9 See Jamie Benedickson, *Idleness, Water, and a Canoe: Reflections on Paddling for Pleasure* (Toronto: University of Toronto Press, 1997); Misao Dean, *Inheriting a Canoe Paddle: The Canoe in Discourses of English-Canadian Nationalism* (Toronto: University of Toronto Press, 2013); and Bruce Erickson, *Canoe Nation: Nature, Race, and the Making of a Canadian Icon* (Vancouver: UBC Press, 2013).

10 Bruce Erickson, "Embodied Heritage on the French River: Canoe Routes and Colonial History," *Canadian Geographer* 59, no. 3 (2015): 325–26.

11 See Dale Standen, "Canoes and Canots in New France: Small Boats, Material History and Popular Imagination," *Material Culture Review* 68 (2008): 34–47, for a discussion of how Canada is popularly imagined to have been found by fur trade voyageurs.

12 Erickson, "Embodied Heritage on the French River."

13 Pierre Trudeau, "The Ascetic in a Canoe," *Canadian Geographic* 120, no. 7 (2000): 40–42.

14 Ibid., 42.

15 The work of Susan Knabe and Wendy Gay Pearson, as well as Liz Newberry, have used these same quotes in order to underscore how the canoe is iconic to Canadian identity and nationalism. See: Susan Knabe and Wendy Pearson, "Unpacking the Canoe: Alternative Perspectives on the Canoe as a National Symbol," *Kunapipi* 23, no.1 (2001): 114–29; and Liz Newberry, "Paddling the Nation: Canadian Becoming and Becoming Canadian in and through the Canoe," *TOPIA: Canadian Journal of Cultural Studies* 29 (2013): 133–62.

16 See Erickson, "Embodied Heritage on the French River."

17 See John Urry and Jonas Larsen, *The Tourist Gaze 3.0* (London: SAGE Publications, 1990).

18 See Dean, *Inheriting a Canoe Paddle*, chap. 4, for a discussion of pageantry in following the footsteps of voyageurs via paddling.

19 Parks Canada, "Trent-Severn Waterway National Historic Site."

20 Metroland Media Group, *Trent-Severn & Lake Simcoe: PORTS Cruising Guide*, (Oakville: Premier Publications and Shows, 2016): 2.

21 Ibid., 96.

22 Jonas Larsen, "Leisure, Bicycle Mobilities, and Cities" examines how the perceived authenticity of experiencing place is related to how we move through place. In *Tourism and Leisure Mobilities: Politics, Work and Play*, ed. J. Rickly, K. Hannamm, and M. Mostafanezhad (London: Routledge, 2017), 39–54.

23 Amanda Concha-Holmes, "Senses of HumaNature on Florida's Silver River: Evocative Ethnography to Craft Place," *Visual Anthropology Review* 31, no. 1 (2015): 62.

24 Erickson, "Embodied Heritage on the French River," 317, discusses how this operates as what he calls embodied heritage.

25 Ibid., 5–6.

26 See Ian Puppe, "Conduits of Communion: Monstrous Affections in Algonquin Traditional Territory" (PhD diss., University of Western Ontario, 2015); and Jocelyn Thorpe, *Temagami's Tangled Wild: Race, Gender, and the Making of Canadian Nature* (Vancouver: UBC Press, 2012) for a discussion of First Nations land tenure and stewardship within these parks.

27 Erickson, "Embodied Heritage on the French River," 322.

28 Sarah Elizabeth Hunt, "Witnessing the Colonialscape: Lighting the Intimate Fires of Indigenous Legal Pluralism" (PhD diss., Simon Fraser University, 2014), 72.

29 Ibid.

30 See John P. Heisler, *The Canals of Canada* (Ottawa: National Historic Parks Branch, Department of Indian Affairs and Northern Development, 1973). This collection of papers issued under the authority of Jean Chrétien, Minister of Indian Affairs and Northern Development, follows the history of waterways and canals from Egypt, Babylonia, and China to their construction in

Canada as a means for creating civilization out of wilderness. Although this 162-page collection was produced by the Department of Indian Affairs and Northern Development, it contains no mention of Indigenous peoples.

31 Dara Culhane, "Sensing," in *A Different Kind of Ethnography: Imaginative Practices and Creative Methodologies*, ed. Denielle Elliott and Dara Culhane (Toronto: University of Toronto Press, 2017), 59–60.

32 See Victor P. Litwyn, "A Dish with One Spoon: The Shared Hunting Grounds Agreement in the Great Lakes and St. Lawrence Valley Region," *Archives of the Papers of the Algonquian Conference* 28 (1997): 210–27, available at: https://ojs.library.carleton.ca/index.php/ALGQP/article/view/507/409 for discussion of the history and significance of the Dish with One Spoon wampum.

33 *PORTS The Cruising Guides*, 96.

34 William A. Allen, "Wa-nant-git-che-ang: Canoe Route to Lake Huron through Southern Algonquia," *Ontario Archaeology* 73 (2004): 40.

35 Leanne Simpson, "Bubbling Like a Beating Heart: A Society of Presence," in *Dancing on Our Turtle's Back: Stories of Nishnaabeg Re-Creation, Resurgence, and a New Emergence* (Winnipeg: ARP Books, 2011), 107.

36 Ibid., 107.

37 Ibid., 108.

38 Madeline Whetung, "Nishnaabeg Encounters: Living Indigenous Landscapes" (MA thesis, University of Toronto, 2016), 105.

39 Peggy McIntosh, "White Privilege: Unpacking the Invisible Knapsack," *Peace and Freedom Magazine* (July/August 1989): 10–12.

40 See Arjun Appadurai, *Modernity at Large: Cultural Dimensions of Globalization* (Minneapolis: University of Minnesota Press, 1996).

41 See Joseph Dumit, "Writing the Implosion: Teaching the World One Thing at a Time," *Cultural Anthropology* 29, no. 2 (2014): 351–54, for a near-exhaustive list of questions to gain understanding of the social lives of objects.

42 Dylan A.T. Miner, "Radical Migrations through Anishinaabewaki: An Indigenous Re-Mapping of the Great Lakes," in *Deep Routes: The Midwest in All Directions*, ed. Rozalinda Borcila, Bonnie Fortune, and Sarah Ross (Compass Collaborators, 2012), 7.

43 See J.B. Harley, "Maps, Knowledge, and Power," in *The New Nature of Maps: Essays in the History of Cartography*, ed. Paul Laxton (Baltimore: Johns Hopkins University Press), 51–82 for a discussion on how maps are used as a mechanism of state control in the expansion and founding of nations, as well as how they are used to conceptualize the nation.

44 Florence Stratton, "Cartographic Lessons: Susanna Moodie's *Roughing It in the Bush* and Thomas King's *Green Grass, Running Water*," *Canadian Literature* 161–62 (Summer/Autumn 1999): 84.

45 See also Sarah Wylie Krotz, *Mapping with Words: Anglo-Canadian Literary Cartographies, 1789–1916* (Toronto: University of Toronto Press, 2018), 3–5.

46 See Harley, "Maps, Knowledge, and Power," for a discussion of the subjectivity, both intentional and not, of map making and map reading for political purposes.

47 Ibid.

48 Ryerson School of Journalism, "Land Acknowledgement," https://trc.journalism.ryerson.ca/land-acknowledgement/.

49 Rebekah Ingram, "Rice Lake," https://geolinguistics.ca/2018/03/19/rice-lake/.

50 Although many of the canoes used in the fur trade were Indigenous built, French-Canadian and Métis middlemen also learned the trade of canoe building from First Nations communities. See Timothy Kent, "Manufacture of Birchbark Canoes for the Fur Trade in the St. Lawrence," in *The Canoe in Canadian Cultures*, ed. Bruce Hodgins, John Jennings, John, and Doreen Small (Toronto: Natural Heritage Books, 1999), 100–43.

51 Online Etymology Dictionary, "canoe" https://www.etymonline.com/word/canoe#etymonline_v_670. See also Erickson, *Canoe Nation*, 5.

52 See John H. Pollack, "Native American words, early American texts" (PhD diss., University of Pennsylvania, 2014), 4, for a thorough examination of the complicated etymology of the word canoe.

53 Lisa Jackson, "Canada's Wild Rice Wars: How a Conflict over Wild Ricing on Pigeon Lake Is Drawing Attention to Indigenous Rights and Traditional Foods," Al Jazeera.com, 20 February 2016.

54 See Sean Ryan, ""Go West Young Man': using navigational technologies to find oneself," *Leisure/Loisir* 29, no.1 (2005): 95–120 for a discussion of the history of GPS devices.

55 I follow Eve Tuck and Wayne Yang, "Decolonization is not a metaphor," *Decolonization: Indigeneity, Education and Society* 1, no.1 (2012): 1–40, in asserting that decolonization is not a metaphor, but rather decolonization requires action such as the transfer of land back to Indigenous peoples.

Contributors

Cameron Baldassarra took his first trip down the Petawawa River as a fourteen-year-old camper. He has since returned to the river as a guide, researcher, outdoor educator, and recreational canoeist. His early experiences on rivers like the Pet instilled in him a lifelong interest in the history and culture of paddling that eventually led to graduate studies in geography at York University. The research for this chapter was completed while he was a PhD candidate at McMaster University working on an environmental history of recreational canoeing in Algonquin Park. Baldassarra is currently a teacher in Toronto and still manages to guide the occasional canoe trip.

Hillary Beattie is a researcher and filmmaker from Winnipeg. She has a Bachelor of Arts degree in human geography from the University of Winnipeg. She had the opportunity to work on the research in this book as part of her Master of Environment degree from the University of Manitoba. As part of the project, she co-directed the documentary film *Glwa: Resurgence of the Ocean-Going Canoe* with Vina Brown. She is currently studying to be an urban planner.

Albert Braz is a professor in the Department of English and Film Studies at the University of Alberta and the author of *The False Traitor: Louis Riel in Canadian Culture* and *Apostate Englishman: Grey Owl the Writer and the Myths*. As a literary comparatist, he is particularly interested in how members of one culture see other cultures. Thus his initial attraction to *Paddle to the Amazon* was how Don Starkell (and, to a lesser degree, his sons Dana and Jeff) portrayed his encounters with Latin Americans. While in his previous book he examined how Grey Owl used the canoe to fashion a new identity in Canada, his chapter in this book shows how Don Starkell used the canoe to create a space for himself not only in Canada and the world but, most importantly, within his own family.

Frank Brown is one of the original founders of the Tribal Canoe Journeys, with which he has thirty-three years of experience. He has coordinated multiple journeys and gatherings, including the Qatuwas gatherings in Bella Bella in 1993 and 2014. He produced the award-winning films *Voyage of Rediscovery* (1990) and *Qatuwas: People Gathering Together* (1997). Brown is a Yimas hereditary leader within traditional Haíłzaqv governance structures. He works in the Aboriginal forestry, fishing, and ecotourism industry. Frank Brown also holds an Honorary Doctorate of Law from Vancouver Island University, and is an adjunct professor at Simon Fraser University. He serves as the Senior Advisor for the Indigenous Leadership Initiative. He and his wife Kathy are the owner-operators of a marine transportation business called Yuwala Marine Charters.

Vina Brown is Frank Brown's daughter, and is a Haíłzaqv and Nuu-chah-nulth scholar. Her Haíłzaqv name is ƛ̓áqvas gí̓w̓ags, which means Copper Canoe. She is the Executive Director of the Kunsoot Wellness Centre, located in Haíłzaqv territory, and a part time faculty at Northwest Indian College (NWIC). She holds a Bachelor of Arts degree in Native studies and leadership from NWIC and a Masters of Jurisprudence in Indigenous law from the University of Tulsa, and is presently working on a PhD from the University of Alaska in Indigenous studies, with concentrations in knowledge systems, research, and pedagogy. Vina Brown has participated in Tribal Canoe Journeys her whole life and was raised within Haíłzaqv territory, where she witnessed the resurgence and renaissance of her own Haíłzaqv culture.

Chris Ling Chapman's research background is in media and cultural studies; he is a graduate of Simon Fraser University's Master of Communication Program. He became interested in canoe building was sparked by way of the National Film Board film *César's Bark Canoe* (*César et Son Canot d'Écorce, wikwas timanikan César,* Bernard Gosselin, 1971) which depicts late Attikamekw canoe builder César Newashish and his family building a birchbark hunting canoe on reserve in Quebec in the late 1960s. Writing about this film led to further thinking about how archives recording canoe cultures and Indigenous languages are important tools for contemporary decolonization efforts. Other work in carpentry and design both informs and is informed by canoe building as a way of thinking and working.

Chuck Commanda is a master birchbark canoe builder from the Algonquin community of Kitigan Zibi. He has been building canoes since he was a child, learning from his highly respected grandparents, Mary and William Commanda. He has spent more than a decade building canoes in the traditional Algonquin style as well as teaching birchbark basket and miniature canoe-making workshops to Indigenous and non-Indigenous children, youth, and adults. Commanda's work embodies the use of cultural practices to transmit Algonquin teachings among peoples and between generations in the spirit of reconciliation and Indigenous community revitalization. His work included a canoe build at Plenty Canada in 2017, which involved a partnership with Larry McDermott and Sarah Nelson that grew beyond the canoe itself to include arts-based events and workshops promoting Indigenous knowledges associated with the canoe.

Rachel Cushman is a direct descendant of Clatsop Chief Wasilta, a primary negotiator and signer of the 1851 Tansy Point treaties. She is the elected Secretary/Treasurer of the Chinook Indian Nation. The focus of her tenure is restorative justice. Cushman is committed to ensuring that the Chinook Indian Nation exercises sovereignty, practises self-determination, and has autonomous control over its narrative. Cushman is also a dedicated leader of the Chinook Canoe Family. She is a lead puller, singer, and dancer, and in 2019 became a skipper. All her work is grounded in the commitment to preserve and carry on Chinook's cultural protocols. Cushman feels that her most important leadership role is being a mother to sons Kanim (canoe) and Isik (paddle).

Jon Daehnke is an associate professor in the Anthropology Department at the University of California, Santa Cruz. His research, much of which has been conducted in conversation and collaboration with the Chinook Indian Nation, focuses on heritage studies and the anthropology and history of the

Pacific Northwest. At its core, Daehnke's work is driven by two overriding interests: the interplay/connections between the past/present/future, and the power of landscapes (especially the effect of landscapes on bodies as they move through them). The intersection of these two interests are what naturally led him to the fundamental importance of canoe revitalization and the protocols attached to canoe culture.

Jessica Dunkin is a white settler, raised in Anishinaabe and Haudenosaunee territory, and living in Sǫ̀mba K'è, Yellowknives Dene territory, since 2015. Dunkin came to know the canoe first as a recreational vessel under the tutelage of her father and grandfather, and later as a tool and symbol of settler colonialism through a detailed study of the early encampments of the American Canoe Association (*Canoe and Canvas*, University of Toronto Press, 2019). Dunkin and John B. Zoe met through the NWT On The Land Collaborative. Through Zoe's stories about the canoe in Tłı̨chǫ culture, she has come to know the canoe, the land, and the people of her adopted home in new ways.

Bruce Erickson is an assistant professor of geography at the University of Manitoba. He learned to canoe on the lakes of northwestern Ontario, working with kids throughout Treaties 1, 3, 9, and even across to Treaty 10 territory in Saskatchewan. He completed a degree in outdoor recreation, parks, and tourism at Lakehead University, where he developed an interest in canoeing as a way to rethink his place as a settler in Canada. Eventually this resulted in a book on canoeing and settler identity in Canada (*Canoe Nation*, UBC Press, 2013) and a desire to connect those challenging the canoe's role in colonialism. Early on, Sarah Wylie Krotz was a part of that conversation on trips to the Allenwater and English Rivers, among others.

Danielle Gendron canoes as a way to relate to her halfbreed/Métis ancestry and to immerse herself in the same landscapes that her ancestors once moved through. She focuses on how their movements through and uses of the waterways were at once colonizing and colonized, and explores their relationships in/to place in the past, as well as her own obligations in the present. Danielle is currently a PhD candidate in anthropology at the University of British Columbia, where she has the privilege of weaving together a personal exploration of her ancestry with her scholarly interests in settler colonialism as her research. Her dissertation project investigates the creation, understanding, and uses of "Canadian heritage" narratives along the Trent-Severn Waterway.

Jonathan Goldner is currently involved in collaborative research building birchbark canoes with First Nations communities and is working toward a doctorate degree in archaeology at the University of Oxford. He holds a master's degree in anthropology from Concordia University in Montreal. As a member of the Centre for Sensory Studies, Jonathan's research advocates for skilled apprenticeships as enhanced learning models for teaching young adults in Canada. The core of this research highlights the diverse ways of knowing that occur when people endeavour to learn directly through interactions with materials in natural landscapes. He remains highly committed to a socially engaged archaeology that collaborates in research with First Nations to prioritize community outcomes and develop attractive opportunities for youth to increase their practical skills and gain solid personal formations, while remaining in school. The canoes and the valuable skills the young participants learn remain with and benefit the community.

Tony A. Johnson is the elected chair of the Chinook Indian Nation, whose headquarters are in Bay Center, Washington, and includes the five westernmost Chinookan speaking tribes—the Clatsop, Kathlamet, Lower Chinook, Wahkiakum, and Willapa. Johnson was born in South Bend, Washington, and is a direct descendant of oskalawiliksh, a signer of the 1851 Tansy Point treaties. He was educated in art and anthropology and continues to be dedicated to the learning and practice of Chinookan art and language. Johnson was a founding member of the Chinook Canoe Family and serves as the skipper. He and his wife, Mechele, continue to live in their traditional homelands on Willapa Bay, Washington.

Sarah Wylie Krotz is an associate professor of English at the University of Alberta. She learned to canoe on Lake of the Woods with her dad and eventually worked as a canoe tripper for the YM-YWCA's Camp Stephens. Canoe trips through Anishinaabe territory (Ojibway and Oji-Cree, Treaties 3 and 9) profoundly shaped her relationship to the land. In particular, they sparked her interest in the landscape of the Precambrian Shield and the ways that literature maps colonial and ecological relationships within it. Her explorations of this topic can be found in her book *Mapping with Words: Anglo-Canadian Literary Cartographies, 1789–1916* (University of Toronto Press, 2018), as well as in a recent article, "The Affective Geography of Wild Rice: A Literary Study" (2017). Krotz got to know Bruce Erickson while working as a canoe tripper. Their shared love of swamp drags as well as curious, challenging, and contemplative conversations convinced her that co-editing a book on the politics of the canoe was a good idea.

Ian Mauro is an associate professor and the executive director of the Prairie Climate Centre at the University of Winnipeg. He is an environmental scientist, geographer, and filmmaker who uses participatory video to collect, communicate, and conserve local and Indigenous knowledges. He has directed several award-winning films including *Qapirangajuq: Inuit Knowledge and Climate Change* (2010), co-directed with acclaimed Inuk filmmaker Zacharias Kunuk. Mauro met Frank Brown and his daughter Vina while filming the documentary film *Beyond Climate* and they decided to collaborate on a larger documentary about Tribal Canoe Journeys.

Larry McDermott is a culture carrier, knowledge holder, and storyteller recognized as an Elder by his community of Shabot Obaadjiwan, who has worked on behalf of the broader Algonquin community for many years, including as head Elder at the Silver Lake pow wow. He was taught by the respected Algonquin Elder William Commanda, and is the executive director of Plenty Canada, an Indigenous environmental organization based in Lanark, Ontario. McDermott has been an Ontario human rights commissioner and currently sits on the Indigenous Advisory Group and Indigenous Elders Circle for the Law Soceity of Ontario. He holds an honorary doctorate in laws from the Unvierity of Geulph and is part of a seven-year national research project focusing on Indigenous Conserved and Protected Areas. He is currently also coordinating COVID-19 relief efforts with traditional people in Guatemala and Peru through his work with Plenty Canada.

Sarah Nelson is a non-Indigenous assistant professor at the University of Nebraska Omaha whose current research is focused on Indigenous community health related to oral history, memory, and land-based knowledge in what is now known as eastern Ontario. As part of deepening her knowledge of Indigenous realities in eastern Ontario, the unceded Algonquin territory in which she was born. Dr. Nelson has come to know Larry McDermott and Chuck Commanda in a variety of capacities, including through helping to build a birchbark canoe at Plenty Canada. She has been fortunate to be able to contribute her writing skills to this project and in the process developing deeper understandings of Algonquin teachings and natural law.

When **Peter H. Wood** was a small boy in St. Louis, Missouri, close to the Mississippi, he delighted in a children's book by Holling C. Holling called *Paddle-to-the-Sea*. He spent early summers paddling kayaks and canoes in coastal Maine. A lucky teenage job caring for a boat in northern Lake Huron sharpened his interest in contacts between North America's First Peoples and early foreign explorers. Before his recent retirement, he spent decades teaching colonial American history and North American Indigenous history at Duke University. His varied work has involved the beginnings of race slavery in South Carolina, the French explorations of La Salle, and the paintings of American artist Winslow Homer. He has also published essays on Baron de Lahontan's travels and on "Ancient Dugout Canoes in the Mississippi-Missouri Watershed." In 2019, the Archaeological Institute of America named Professor Wood to be their J. Richard Steffy Lecturer in Marine Archaeology.

As a young child, **John B. Zoe** observed Tłı̨chǫ Elders using canoes they made with canvas; traditionally they used birchbark. One summer, he watched the old Chief test a birchbark canoe he had made for leaks. In his preteens, he paddled canoes with his dad and relatives, harvesting muskrats in the spring for food and pelts to trade. Zoe has heard many stories over the years about travel by canoes to the harvesting areas, going back to the beginnings of our own time. His early observations grew into a passion for reviving canoeing as an annual activity and eventually as a storytelling subject, too. The stories are really in the landscape, and the pages turn with dips of the paddle.

Index

C

D

X

Z